Europe Overland

Seeking the Unique

by

Graeme Robert Bell

EUROPE OVERLAND

MORE TITLES BY GRAEME BELL
We Will Be Free
Travel The Planet Overland
Overlanding the Americas "La Lucha"
www.a2aexpedition.com

GRAEME R BELL

Introduction

We knew while overlanding the Americas that we would eventually find ourselves in Europe and the question first and foremost was this: can modern Europe be an overland worthy destination - sure the subcontinent overflows with culture and history but what of opportunities to escape modernity and reconnect with nature? By comparison, the United States and Australia both have modern, democratic societies yet have relatively small populations and incredible wide-open spaces - overland travel in those countries is natural, if not necessary. Would our Land Rover Defender with her large mud-terrain tyres, skull adorned bullbar and self-built habitat be as out of place and inappropriate on the streets of Europe, as a rooftop tent is bolted onto the feminine slope of a Porshe 911? And would Europe be so expensive that we would have to flee for Africa and Asia, desperately? Would we find adventure and un-spoilt nature, would we be able to travel freely and live our outdoor lifestyle?

This book is written to answer those questions, and the best way to do so is to continue the narrative of our continuous intercontinental overland journey as written in our previous books - We Will Be Free and Overlanding the Americas "La Lucha", the story of our family of four giving everything we have to give to achieve our goal of living the explorers lifestyle. And please remember – our goal while travelling the planet overland is to learn and study the countries which we explore. As South Africans who grew to adulthood in isolated Apartheid South Africa, we are burdened with the preconceived notions of a world imagined – we seek to discover through experience and try to dismiss (or sometimes to confirm) stereotypes and have the unique gift of an outsiders perspective. Overlanding the Americas "La Lucha" was somewhat controversial as we documented modern America (as well as northwestern South America and Central America) from that outsider's perspective, witnessing the entire election debacle and observing a fascinating culture. We do not suffer from patriotism or nationalism and are able to see a subject for what it is without the blinkers of emotion and vested interest. So, yes, we are certainly interested in socio-politics and are not afraid to point the weapon of reason at a worthy target. But, this book is about overlanding - the pursuit of freedom, peace of mind and unique experiences. While we observe society, we often prefer to be independent. We seek nature, beauty, tranquillity and adventure. Many Europeans who read this book may ask themselves whether us outsiders might have found what they may have not, in their own backyard. I think we have.

I hope you will enjoy experiencing the continent through our eyes.

And let's not forget about astounding Turkey! Our experiences there would change our lives, and we now have an insight into what must be, one of the most wonderful countries and people on this fair planet.

Here is something to look forward to;

"And this free/ wild/ bush camp was the perfect example of why independent vehicle-based travel has so many advantages over other forms of travel - we were having a unique, life-altering experience at almost no cost, we did not have to share that experience with strangers and we were free to come and go at will. Nothing else comes close!".

But first, let us start at the beginning of this story.

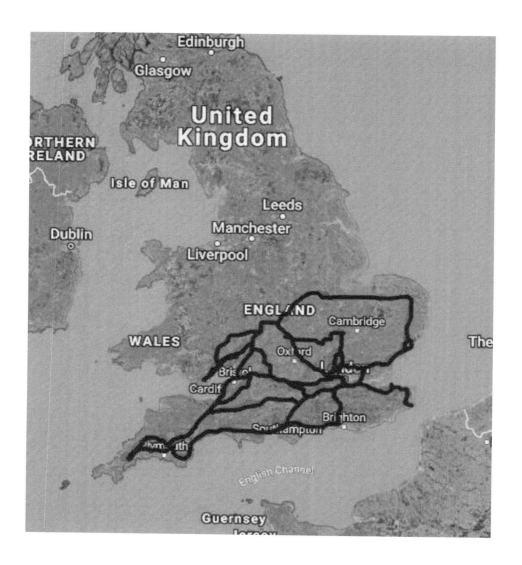

1

The First Weeks. Waiting for the Land Rover, learning Englishness and, urghh, house sitting

A flight from Boston, Massachusetts delivered us to the green island, and we were fortunate to arrive at Gatwick International Airport on a cloudless day, the patchwork of farms and their villages lay before us lush and inviting. In a sense, we were coming home.

You see, my mother had left the UK when she was 12 years old with her two siblings and her parents. South Africa offered a new life, filled with sunshine and large open spaces. My maternal grandfather was quietly courageous and had met and married my German grandmother in France at the end of World War 2. He was a tank commander, and she was serving food in an Allied mess hall on the outskirts of her city, Paderborn. Returning with "the enemy" to Great Britain immediately after the war took immense courage, and I respect my grandfather's nerve, he must have been deeply in love though he never seemed the romantic type. They set about building a home and having their children but were never truly accepted. That, at least, was part of their reasoning to move to South Africa in the mid-Fifties. And, as a former British colony, South Africa had inherited British architecture and infrastructure. Krugersdorp, a large mining town west of Johannesburg, became their new home and they moved into a house identical to those found in England, albeit larger and with a sparkling swimming pool. They felt at home.

And I felt at home on British soil. I had never been to the UK, but everything seemed incredibly familiar. The villages, roads, drizzle, pies, beer, accents, stone walls, green lawns, ancient buildings and modern cities all felt like home. I could not understand why the emotional side of me suggested it had something to do with ancient memories within my DNA, with a timeless connection to my ancestors and their memories. Perhaps, but more likely I had spent too much time watching Benny Hill, Only Fools and Horses, Faulty Towers, Mr Bean and the Carry On movies. Oh dear. When you grow up in a country geographically and politically isolated, you learn about the world through the prism of media and grandpa Norman (his full name was Norman Norkett which translated, essentially means Northman of the North) was British to his last atom, as was his TV set.

My mother, brother and sister had all moved to the UK after ten years of ANC leadership in South Africa had slid the country down a slippery slope, greased by the corruption of the elite. The family live in Bournemouth, and we drove a rental car to the reunion. It had been seven years since we had last seen each other and a fish 'n chips dinner welcomed us to our new temporary home. The family was well, and we fell into their warm embrace. But, not one of them could explain mushy peas and curry sauce on the fish 'n chips. We set ourselves up in my mom's cosy little apartment for a week, tried to braai in the drizzle, learned about cold meat pies from Greggs, the excellence of British television and that pork fuels the entire island.

It was early March when we arrived, and Luisa had been diligently searching for house sitting assignments which would offer us the opportunity to save money and liberate my mom's lounge. House sitting has, like everything in life, it's positives and negatives, and I have a love/ hate relationship with the concept. I love that I get to save money, enjoy the modern conveniences of a lovely home and get to take care of beautiful, pampered pets. I do not like sleeping in someone else's bed, I do not like driving someone else' car and I do not appreciate the opportunity to be forced into a relationship with someone I do not know. Those of you who have been following our journey and reading our books will know that I am not a "peoples' person", I am not particularly social, and I do not go out of my way to meet people. Yes, I am an introvert (like Einstein, Isaac Newton, Bill Gates, Steven Spielberg and my compatriot Elon Musk), nothing wrong with that except we are all expected to be extroverts, it is a measure of confidence and success. And that first night of sharing a meal and house with your new house owner friends can be pure torture for me.

Terry and Tracey's house near Worcester was our first assignment and, thankfully, they were Land Rover owning part-time travellers, and we immediately felt at ease in their beautiful home. The house sat surrounded by green fields, and a tall, ancient church tower stood guard over the home and the neighbouring school whose grounds resemble a botanical garden patrolled by metal rhinoceros and gargoyles. A herd of deer occupied the field below the clock tower, a flock of sheep occupied the area behind the house, and a field of corn occupied the ground between the house and the nearest road, a few other fields were dormant. The two T's bred Labradors and Scottish Terriers, and there were five dogs in total, each competing for our attention and, once the two T's had left for their holiday, we walked the dogs twice a day. We bought wellington boots and ate bacon sarmies. At night we would enjoy a pint and cook a meal on the AGA cooker which had been converted to gas. I finished all words ending in G with guh, i.e. thing-guh, ring-guh, etc.

There was little to be done around the house, other than walking the dogs and pick up poop and mow the lawn, so I settled down to work while Luisa continued the never-ending task of dealing with bureaucracy. As a British citizen, I had the right to live and work in the UK, but my African wife and children had no right to remain or realistic requirements to achieve residence. We had a few choices; I could get a job and send the Land Rover out of the country when it arrived (the vehicle had to be legally and permanently imported to the UK or had to leave the country within six months), we could remain in the UK illegally, or we could leave. We did not have the funds available to qualify for the conventional visa. The Brexit fiasco had taken place a few months earlier and, other than bleeding six thousand dollars from our pockets when the pound plummeted (our Kickstarter campaign was based in the UK, and we had to transfer most of that to the US for book fulfillments) it also gave us the distinct impression that immigration was a hot topic in the UK and we were going to have to give up our dreams if we were to stay on the green island whose government and media seemed hell-bent on transforming the nation to be a model of multiculturalism, which might explain Brexit, to some degree, but does not explain why my children (who have British blood) and my wife of twenty years cannot live in the country. The British government was quite happy to send their people off to bolster their presence in far-flung colonies with promises of wealth and sunshine, but how many people would have gone if they had also been told that their descendants would be forced to jump through elaborate hoops to return. We want nothing for free and have always paid our way, we would never be wards of the state, but we were frustrated by the British red tape and fresh from the USA, we noticed a stark contrast. In the US, for example, I was able to open a bank account after walking into a bank with an address written on a piece of paper, passport in hand. In the UK I needed to make an appointment with the bank and had to wait two weeks to be attended to and had to prove that I was registered for tax, social security, all registered to the same address, ad nauseum. I did not want a credit card or a home loan, I wanted to deposit the $5000 cash I was carrying. Simple, take my money, dammit. It became clear to us, very early that institutional Britain was not welcoming, but the British people were colourful and fascinating, and we were enjoying beautiful weather and all the pies while making plans to leave the country which was to have been our base in Europe.

And then the first of the 2017 terrorist attacks slammed into the island. On 22nd March 2017, a coward who will not be named used a rental car to kill four people on Westminster Bridge before fatally stabbing a policeman. The attack itself did not surprise us quite as much as the British response. In the USA, enticingly violent crime is given wall to wall 24-hour news coverage and the radio talk shows, Facebook and Twitter explode with opinions, condemnation, blames, calls for revenge and general hysteria. In the Uk, the media responded by, essentially, refusing to feed the beast of frenzy and recrimination – the BBC morning show dedicated fifteen minutes to the attack and then ran a story about a farm in Surrey where a rare owl had been discovered nesting in a barn. Virgin Radio dedicated an entire day after the attack to playing songs of love, peace, forgiveness and enlightenment. I had a distinct feeling that I was being managed. I was outraged and, subconsciously, needed fuel to feed that fire – I realised soon that I harboured intense sentiment regarding Islamic extremism and the correct reaction to it. If the majority of Britons had felt how I did, they would inadvertently have given the terrorists what they wanted – a reaction, which would ultimately bolster their numbers and fuel their goal towards a caliphate. But the British, I found, are obstinate. They would not give that which the terrorists were so desperate to elicit – reprisals, fear and discrimination. The British reacted to barbarity with civility, and that famous stiff upper lip, and in doing so diminished my own knee jerk response – an eye for an eye blinds us all. And I am reminded that, unlike the USA, the UK has experience dealing with domestic terrorism, the IRA had waged their war against British occupation for years, an empire must accept certain risks and the population of that empire persuaded to fall in line.

With "All You Need Is Love" ringing in my ears, I took the dogs for their morning walk. The sun shone brightly through the clouds, and the herd of white deer scattered dramatically as we approached their fence. The immaculate greens of the British countryside squelched underfoot as we herded our unleashed pack of fur around two fields and back to the house where Luisa had prepared their breakfast. We had two weeks of rural bliss before we were to move to our next house sitting assignment although we encouraged the two T's to stay on holiday as long as they wanted, we could have lived in their wonderfully comfortable home for the rest of eternity. But, they had to return and we had to leave and when they returned they found a healthy, happy pack of pooches, a cut lawn and tended garden and a house spring cleaned by Luisa, who loved nothing more than vigorously scrubbing a house while listening to Tracy Chapman and fueling her activities with an anger born from frustration - the world refuses to cooperate, things do not happen as they should, the chaos of our independent lives all becomes less so, when she has scrubbed the floors, and the house is gleaming.

With the Land Rover still on the water somewhere near Rotterdam, we drove our stuffed to the gills rental car to Shropshire and a village called Craven Arms where Liz and Ken welcomed us into their recently renovated country home. They had lived in India for many years and had rescued a stubborn St. Bernard and a couple of street dogs who competed for attention with two rescued horses, three rescued pigs, one rescued cat and a fiercely independent cat who had dedicated his life to killing every small creature in Shropshire. The stables and sties required regular cleaning, the horses were skittish, and the pigs always hungry. Walking the dogs in the rolling hills was a highlight of every morning and afternoon, except when the St. Bernard refused to walk another step and had to be seduced with meaty treats to return home. I discovered a power washer and spent two weeks removing every trace of moss from the damp driveway, jungle gym, paving, stables, walls, roof, duck. If it stood still and was green, it got the power wash treatment (which was, apparently, not a great idea. Some people like mossy green, it is how an English country home looks and I managed to eradicate a few years of studiously ignored fungus). We had our bums in the butter, and with no fuel or accommodation costs, we spent our daily budget on Guinness stout, bacon, Italian Prosecco, more pies and delicious loaves of bread. My mom came to visit for a week and declared that this was the type of property I had promised to buy her when I was a foolish kid who loved his mama and thought he was going to be the richest man in Africa one day. When my mom reluctantly left, we were visited by our Kiwi friend Rob, who we had first met in Peru and who rode his Ducati up from London to drink Venezuelan rum with me and have an argument about automation and electric cars. My opinion is that we will have self-drive cars within the next decade and eventually most, if not all, public roads in the developed world would be exclusively designated for the use of self-drive vehicles. I had been doing some reading, and it seems that vehicle manufacturing and ownership is set to be revolutionised. Instead of owning a vehicle, you will have a contract with a service provider (think Uber on a grand scale). When you need to go somewhere, a vehicle will show up on command and whisk you away. Motorways will be high speed "trains" of self-driven cars which will enter the motorway at speed, join the "train" and detach at the appropriate exit. 80-year-old Bob and his polished Ford Cortina will certainly not be allowed to join the train, even if he could drive at 200 kph. Performance, luxury, styling and personality will no longer drive vehicle production and when all vehicles are identical, what will become of the world's largest vehicle manufacturers - Toyota, Volkswagen, etc.? What will become of the millions of truck drivers, bus drivers, cab drivers and delivery men? And what will become of overlanding? (We will rule the secondary roads, the "Freedom Roads" where a man can still drive an internal combustion engine into the wild). Rob disagrees. He believes that self-drive vehicles will never be accepted by the greater population, that these vehicles have proven to be unreliable and that they will never be able to dominate and service an entire road network. Diplomatico (the Venezuelan rum) plays the devil's advocate. Eventually, we are no longer debating self-driven vehicles - we have moved on to robotics, Universal Basic Income, Socialism, unrestricted Capitalism, the death of privacy and personal freedom, climate change, World War Three and the nuclear winter. Diplomatico Reserva, get your hands on a bottle if you can.

2

Mafuta Arrives!

The slippery German who facilitated the shipping of our Defender from Florida to the UK eventually answered Luisa's daily emails. The Land Rover would arrive at the Felixstowe port on the 19th of April. We were nervous about the Defender being allowed into the country, and for good reason; we had converted the vehicle into a camper, but the title documents had not been changed, the car was described as a pick-up. Also, we needed to drive the Landy across the breadth of the UK, and the roof was held on with a climbing rope, and the license plate was duct-taped to the rear window. If there was an inspection of the vehicle for road-worthiness (by British MOT standards) she probably would not pass. On the morning of the 20th we received an email, the Land Rover had passed through customs and was awaiting collection. Luisa and I drove to the port while the kids stayed at the house in Shropshire to tend to the animals and the house.

We arrived at the port and located the warehouse, and there she was looking lonely and pale - Mafuta! She was parked outside the warehouse with a sticker on the windscreen which bore the legend "Non-Starter". Not a good start. A young man in a reflective jacket came out to the vehicle and had us sign a few documents before handing us the keys to the Landy and the original title papers which had been stamped both with ink and perforated with a larger customs logo. Anyone who has ever shipped a vehicle across continents will understand how incredibly stressful the entire process is and, even though we were miffed about the ruined title document, we were relieved how relatively smooth and painless the actual customs procedure had been. And relatively cheap. It had only cost $2000 to ship the Landy from the US to the UK, and that included all the customs procedure. We had paid more than $3000 to ship from South Africa to Uruguay five years earlier, and we had to do much of the customs work ourselves at both ends. I inspected the vehicle. She bore no new scratches or dents, and despite being a "Non-Starter" (which meant they had manhandled her in and out of the shipping container), she was as she was when I handed her over. But the engine refused to turn over. We checked the battery connection and, with the help of our luminous new friend, we tried to push start her. Five times we tried without success with Luisa behind the wheel, ignition on and dropping the clutch in second gear. We tried swopping the batteries (we have two), but that did not work either. For some strange reason, Mafuta consumes electricity when sitting still for longer than a week, maybe she listens to the radio and is afraid of the dark. Our neon friend eventually realised that resuscitating heavy Land Rovers was not in his job description and he quietly escaped, the day was coming to an end, the light fading and he had a pint with his name on it waiting at the pub. He was a cool guy, I wish I could have bought him that pint. Eventually, we connected our rental car to the Defender with a tow strap and after dragging her down the road for two hundred meters, the Landy bouncing in second, the engine coughed to life and a plume of burnt black Floridian fuel belched out of the exhaust and destroyed the O Zone over Great Britain, Northern Ireland and Wales. Driving the Landy, I followed Luisa out onto the motorway for the tortuous three-hour drive back to Shropshire where a shed awaited Mafuta. My mouth was as dry as a camel's unmentionables as we joined the peak hour traffic. I had not finished all the work converting the Defender into a camper in Florida when we had driven to the port without a test drive, which had been the most nerve-wracking drive of my life. Imagine, doing a project that immense and not even having the luxury of driving the vehicle gently down the road to make sure that the whole thing would not fall apart and kill everyone on the highway. No, in the USA, I had barely finished constructing the rear door before filling her with everything we own and driving her at highway speeds to meet the 5 pm deadline at the shipping agent, flights booked and paid for, the point of no return. And, here I was again, driving the Landy, fresh from the shipping container and a month journey across the Atlantic, at highway speeds, my balls constricting my throat. I do it to myself, that is why it really hurts.

Police drove past me a few times and gave me curious looks but, gratefully, did not pull me over to practice their penmanship or confiscate the vehicle. And twenty kilometres into the journey the engine began to shudder and misfire under load, overtaking or driving uphill. The misfire became worse the longer we drove, and we had to stop and put in fuel; hopefully, the battery had charged enough to restart. It had not. For some inexplicable reason, it took ten minutes to half fill the fuel tank, I had to restrict the flow of diesel to a trickle (the diesel must be refined from the urine of a dry and expensive God, $2 a litre as opposed to just over $1 a gallon (3.80 litres) in the good old USA back in 2017) we managed to get the Landy started again and continue our journey across the UK. At midnight we arrived at the house, exhausted, relieved and very, very thirsty. Mafuta was locked safely in the shed, and we hit the sack after a few calming refreshments. Defenders are now a prime target for theft in the UK, and we are simply unable to tour the world and afford comprehensive insurance, if Mafuta is stolen our journey is over, I even considered sleeping inside the vehicle while in the UK.

In the morning, we set about continuing our work on the Landy. We still had plenty to do, including recharging the batteries, securing the roof, building the interior, installing the water tanks, building a roof rack and a million other little jobs, before we could camp comfortably. We needed to find the cause of the misfire and establish why it took so long to fill the fuel tank. And we had no workshop. I know, we were insane to try and attempt such a massive project while travelling, but our ignorance is matched only by our stubborn determination. We do it to ourselves…

Luisa had found another house-sitting gig for us, and this new assignment was in Gloucestershire in an area known as the Cotswolds. Liz and Ken returned from their holiday, and we set off in the Landy, heading south. Their home had been incredibly comfortable, and we had been productive and active, we had made friends with Liz and Ken and had shared a few tasty meals and had interesting conversations. Our next encounter was going to be quite different.

A little square lady in blue welcomed us into her home and introduced us to an amazing tiny animal. His name is Paddy, and he is the hero of this story, everyone else is a villain. Once we were convinced that the neighbour was the devil incarnate (that the neighbour was always watching and listening and would not hesitate to phone our little blue friend no matter where in the world she might be) and that little blue was born of pure blood, and of incredible means, we were given a tour of the house and property. It was suggested that one of our children might want to sleep in a shed with a bed at the end of the garden. We were instructed to walk little Paddy an hour at each end of the day, and we were briefed extensively on the particular do's and don'ts. Not once were we told that her bedroom was off bounds, or that her coffee was grown, ground and sourced from a Colombian messiah, we were also not told that the house was held together with sticky tape and strategically placed little nails which held everything from ornamental plates to shopping bags to towels. The house was so full of wonderful books that the building seemed to be sinking into the ground. One of the shelves, held together with sticky tape and small nails, eventually committed suicide shortly after we left and we were held accountable for murder.

Little Paddy (who suffered a sexual fit the first evening and ejaculated all over the carpet) was walked an hour every day and brushed every night, his teeth were brushed, and we were sure to take care of the inflammation between his toes, caused by all that walking in the meadows. At night he lay next to me where Luisa and I slept, upstairs in a loft made for small, blue people while my son slept in the spare room and my little daughter slept in the main bed. I slept with my hand on Paddy's ribs, and he would not leave the house until I was ready to walk him in the morning, come rain or shine. I, being a villain, first had to have some Colombian Jesus coffee, of which there was plenty. I would fill my favourite Stanley coffee flask and after walking Paddy and having a shower, using our soap, our shampoo and our conditioner, I then brushed my teeth with my toothbrush and, coincidentally, my own toothpaste, before settling down in a small chair made of balsa wood by a tiny Thai girl with arthritis and a tube of paper glue, to work on our third book. An arm of the balsa chair broke, we tried to fix it. For 25 days we ate our own food, using mostly our own pots and pans. We kept the house clean even though cleaners arrived every Monday to push a broom around. We were told not to wash the sheets as our little blue friend has them dry cleaned. The dryer broke, and we were accused of its murder through negligence, a large glass water container cracked when my daughter filled it with hot water and an ornamental plate, regretfully, also broke. Our little blue friend arrived home an hour early on the last day, while we were packing and rushed us out the door, we told her about the broken water bottle and said we would replace it, "don't worry", she said, "breakages happen". We quickly took most our possessions and left the house in the condition we found it, albeit with less but still plenty coffee and a few of our possessions. A day later we read a review on the house sitters website which summed up our family as, "Just no, not with a barge pole, contact me for more information". What on earth did little blue think we were there for? We were house sitters for the love of, not once was it ever discussed that we would be engaging in any activities which required poles, large or small. I immediately phoned little blue who cheerfully asked me how I was. Strange. I asked about the review, and she explained that she was tired and frustrated and that we had used all the coffee. I told her that we had already bought a replacement water container and that it would soon be delivered to her and reminded her that there was coffee in the cupboard. I then asked, calmly and repeatedly, what we could do to rectify the situation with the words, "what do we need to replace or repair?". "No, no, it is fine," she said. "Ok then, will you consider changing your review, it will definitely not help when we apply for future assignments?", "Um, ok, bye-bye". I thought that was that. She changed the review too, "Just no, not with a barge pole". Wonderful. Over a few emails, we were told that our possessions would be posted to us. They never arrived. When we enquired, we were told that we should not go to her house or contact her again. Amicable, civil. We sent two new water containers, the first mysteriously disappeared, and the second she refused to accept.

Among the list of grievous infractions were the following;

"We left food in the food refuse bin". God forbid. When we put the bin out for collection we were told by the waste company that little blue had not paid the collection fee, we told little blue, she said okay. In hindsight perhaps we should have reheated the food and consumed it to spare our new friend inconvenience.

"We left cardboard boxes in the waste area". When we arrived, all of the waste bins were full after what could only have been a convention of little blues. Ugh. The boxes we left were flattened and neatly stored, ready for collection.

"We used all the tea bags, toilet paper and salt and left dirty frying pans in the cupboard". Lies! Fabrication! If only we had spent some time doing a hand over when little blue returned then we could have addressed this litany of charges, but instead I am forced to try and convince you, dear reader, that we are clean and considerate people who have only had excellent reviews and who have always gone above and beyond to ensure that all parties are satisfied (without the need for barge poles or other such phallic devices).

It is all just too bloody frustrating and what kills me is that my favourite Stanley coffee flask is now on the lips of someone who does not deserve it. It was a perfect flask, it had a built-in press so it would not only keep the coffee hot but was also a coffee maker. My only consolation is that the person who now uses it a true coffee connoisseur, someone who loves coffee so much that she would insult an innocent family and concoct a plan of character assassination to keep a very nice coffee flask, bizarre.

In review: The flask was superb, the dog was outstanding, the house a nightmare, the owner a sadist, conniving little troll and the neighbour lovely. Poor Paddy.

Despite Little Blue being all poo in a blue power suit, we had a good time in the Cotswolds. We managed to get some work done on the Landy, the dog was a good buddy and loved our long walks in the country, and the countryside was sublime. Despite all the daily walks, I was as fat as one of Liz's pigs and had to make a serious effort to stop eating all the bloody pork pies, slices of bread, chocolates and pastries and stay away from the lager. Keelan had also put on a lot of weight in the USA. It was time to make some serious changes to our diet and daily habits.

There was to be an Ariana Grande concert in Manchester in May, and when Jessica heard about it, she begged us to take her to the show, as an early birthday present. We considered it, as we could take a train up to Manchester and then return the same evening, but the outing would have cost around 250 GBP, I could buy her a new computer for the same money. We decided not to go and were naturally incredibly relieved that we did not.

On the 22nd May, another terrorist detonated a homemade bomb which killed 22 people, many of whom were teenagers and children. I hope there is a hell for suicide bombers as certainly as there is not a heaven full of virgins. The British press reacted as they had done after the Westminster attack, as if by script. "All You Need Is Love, a squirrel found it's way into a royal palace. Look at the pretty flowers. We need to do more, give more".

The Manchester bombing was a devastating reminder of the shift emerging in the world which, I feel, is on the brink. With access to more information than any other time in history, and the unstoppable march of technological advancement, some might believe that this is the end of the old world, and if they can't stop progress now, they will never be able to. Isis wants exactly that, as does Al Quaeda. They want to plunge us all back into the dark ages where monarchies and clerics ruled absolutely. They will not succeed.

3

Plan B

Lord knows you have to have a Plan B. With the UK base option not working out we had to look at our options (I have tried not to bore you with the details but, believe me, we put many days, weeks and months of research into the immigration process for the UK. As a self-employed author with a dream to travel the world, we hit a stone wall of bureaucracy). We intended to overland Europe and to discover for ourselves whether the continent was indeed a viable overlanding destination. Now, remember, when we are talking about overlanding, we are referring to vehicle dependent travel. Yes, the adventure of touring the developing nations is intoxicating, but we like to discover the world for ourselves, our way. My impression of Europe had always been what others had told me - that it is built up, extremely expensive, politically diverse, very safe, incredibly beautiful, full of ancient and modern history and a bit dull. Europeans love to escape their long winters and head south, east or west seeking sun and adventure and a life less ordinary. My question was, could Europe be an adventure?

We were soon to find out, but first, we had to get there. Now, it might seem a bit crazy to ship to the UK without having already been granted Schengen visas for Europe, but we also had Plan C. Plan C was Ireland. In Ireland, we can live and work visa-free, and after having been in Ireland for a year, we would be able to then live in the UK. It is a loophole which South Africans have been exploiting for a few years. After further researching the Schengen visa we found that no embassy would grant us the visa in the UK. We were told that we had to return to South Africa and apply for the visas there. So, that would be a $10 000 round trip, all expenses considered. Well, that was not going to happen. I realised that our dream of travelling the planet overland was about to go up in a puff of smoke. At least for the next few years. It seemed I would have to start looking for a job as this was the only way that we would be able to stay in the UK or Ireland. Luisa toyed with the idea of starting our immigration firm up again, but the very thought of losing our way of life was too painful to bear. You have dreams, you have goals, and you know what you are willing to sacrifice to achieve those dreams and goals. Some days were tougher than others, and we began to lose hope of finding a solution. But, we jump in the deep end, and we swim, sinking is not an option.

After a month of research, Luisa seemed to have found a solution to our Schengen visa dilemma. By European law, Europeans with foreign families are allowed to apply for Schengen visas within Great Britain. But every European country demands application in country of residence. Our home is a Land Rover, dammit. We are citizens of the planet, of the universe. Our intentions are noble, and we never benefit unjustly from the labour of others, we want to explore the beautiful water covered orb, while we are living and breathing, we certainly can't explore any other planets, but there are walls and fences and laws which keep us from moving freely as we should have the right to. And it is a right which we claim simply because we have proven ourselves to be travellers with dignity and we are not looking to improve our lives by settling in a wealthy nation. If we had that intention, we would have never left the USA or Canada. But, immigration law is not written to accommodate people like us, people like us do not really exist. We will be free, and we will fight!

Determined to succeed, Luisa took to staying up late at night studying European immigration case law. And, eventually, she found a European country which would allow us to apply for the Schengen visa in the UK. Now, I am not going to tell you which country, simply because I believe it is a well-kept secret for a reason and I want to ensure that those who follow us have the same opportunity if they have the same problem. So, if you send me a message one day and I can help, I will. We began the process of accumulating the documents for the visa application. I asked European friends for letters of invitation, and they all complied, some providing not only invitations but also letters of commendation attesting to our good character, dignity and honesty. Within a week we drove to London, and two weeks later the Schengen visas were issued!

Plan B, essentially, was to get residency in Europe, either in Spain or Portugal. Maybe those countries wanted us, and we could set up our base for global exploration there.

Once again, we had achieved the impossible. But there is a price to pay. Your nerves can be on edge, there are periods of massive uncertainty, self-doubt and conflict. You question yourself, your motives and your sanity. But these times of struggle are the layers of sediment which become the rock of our foundation.

4

Don't Wear Yellow in August

All this stress can also make us a bit grumpy. Add to that the fact that we were trying to build a camper interior using basic tools and no workshop. Shortly before leaving Paddy the dog and the cottage of the Little Blue creature, we were offered some workshop space by a friend of mutual friends. His name was Steve, he lived in Lincolnshire and owned a handful of old Defenders. We arrived at Steve's house, preparing for Europe. Since we knew that we could enter Europe, we were able to plan for the journey across to Asia but, we only had a few months of summer left, by now we were in June, and we needed to move quickly, particularly as we had come to the attention of a German overlanding magazine who invited us to the Abenteuer and Allrad show in Germany where we could do a presentation at their stall and sell our books. We did some research, and it made sense to attend the Abenteuer and Allrad show as it was the largest overlanding event in the world (by far), and we would be able to meet overlanders from every corner of the planet, but mostly Europeans. There were a host of UK Land Rover and overlanding events which we wanted to attend but time, seasons, finances, visas, everything it seemed was working against us staying longer in the UK. I realise now that, in many ways, we made a mistake by not attending the UK events. There are many people who follow our journey in the UK and many who wanted to meet us. I tried to explain our decision on social media, but the explanation is complicated, and I fear that many Brits felt slighted that we rushed off to Germany, instead of making an effort to meet our British followers and friends. If we could have, we would have. But, it was simply not possible, and we would have had to sacrifice our opportunity to reach Asia by the end of summer.

In 1995, I was recovering from a break up with a long term girlfriend and a motorcycle accident which had shattered my right leg. It was a tough, formative period in my life, I was emotionally and physically broken and spent almost five winter months, completely alone in my dreary home; a black cat and a black and white television my only companions. My friends and family had lives and jobs, and I discouraged visitors as I wallowed. I lived on painkillers, hardly ate and preoccupied myself with physio and tending to the Hoffmans External Fixator (think of an old fashioned TV aerial) which was bolted into my tibia and required daily cleaning. I could write a book about those five months, adrift. I emerged back into society, eventually able to walk (and eternally grateful to the medical staff who had saved my leg) but mentally completely removed from society. I needed something different in life other than the tedium, which engulfed most of my high school friends and promised a life of routine.

My childhood (and now sadly departed) friend Brian Geyer returned from travelling to Israel and Europe and brought stories of adventure, border crossings, Scandinavian girls, wild parties and freedom. I worked for a year as a barman, saving every spare cent, and in late 1996 boarded an El Al flight bound for Israel. There, eventually and after being scammed of every cent I owned in Tel Aviv, I found myself on a Kibbutz with a swimming pool, nightclub and 17 Scandinavian girls. Now, men, I will let your imaginations wander, those first few weeks were… interesting. I had experiences which were quite unique for a naive young man from a country which had just emerged from decades of conservative Calvinistic rule. But, after a month of constant female companionship, I needed a friend who I could share a beer with without any drama, and Lord, girls are good at drama (*you* try and keep 17 girls happy, impossible!) A bus arrived one Wednesday evening, there was a nightclub on the Kibbutz (I worked maintaining the nightclub and was eventually trusted with the keys) and Wednesday night was club night! Kelly, Steve, Simon and Adam emerged from the bus and were greeted by a large man, dressed in luminous lycra, a giant green afro wig and a tube sock stuffed into his shorts (it was fancy dress night, not my idea and I had been undressed and dressed by the girls). The four young Englishmen, all gifted musicians, became my very close friends. We had many adventures and eventually ended up living in a youth hostel in Tel Aviv where we worked to sustain our Mediterranean lives (dishwasher, construction worker, house painter, gardener) and spent many nights exploring the city and, almost always, finding ourselves on Dizengoff beach where we connected and explored our minds. It was through my friendship with these four incredible young gentlemen that I was able to learn almost everything which I had yearned to know since I had left my sad home. Dreadlocked Adam was the spiritual centre of our group, he did not lead or follow and spoke of "the death of the ego". Simon was the poet and the intellectual, Kelly was the wise kid, always getting himself into some sort of humorous situation, ever forgetful, lost and smiling. Steve was the moral compass and the most gifted musician (he is now a professional drummer with the band Dark Horses).

Eventually, we drifted apart, I had a girlfriend who was grooming me for Israeli citizenship (ani rotze ze neshika, bevakasha (I want a kiss, please), and they were looking for a few last adventures before heading back to England. We reunited for a sad farewell on the bus to Ben Gurion airport, and I promised that I would do my best to join them for a trip to India. A year later I met my Luisa at the farewell party of my school friend Jonathan, west of Johannesburg and you know the rest of the story. Jonathan now lives in London, and due to our commitments of work, housekeeping, vehicle preparation and constant mobility, we never had the opportunity to meet up with even these dearest old friends. Unforgivable, I know. I should have made time. Maybe I wanted to forever remember them as the young men I had befriended all those years before, perhaps I was unsure of how a reunion would evolve, and I received an extended no invitations. Maybe it is best that the glory of youth in golden summer sunshine should not be tainted by ageing men battered by life under grey skies, real or imagined. Those of you who know me that I am not actively social, perhaps, in some ways, I am still that young man who emerged from five months of solitude mentally removed from society to the extent that I have created a world which I control and in which I feel completely comfortable and, on occasion, enjoy the company of those who are like I am today.

And what, you may ask, was the point of that story? Well, we never found the time to visit old friends or make new friends, we did so because we could not, and we hope that you will all forgive us. Thank you.

Unfortunately, we only had a few weeks to complete the work on the camper interior and reach Germany. We could not communicate our angst to Steve, but when we met, we were again under pressure. Steve is the kind of man who is infinitely patient and kind. He is the kind of man who cleaned out his workshop and gave us, four strangers complete access to his tools and materials, and we are the kind of people who would not take advantage of that generosity. And, when we stay in a persons home, yard or workshop, we like to repay their generosity by cooking dishes we have learned as we travel. For Steve and his wife Shelly, we made a few good, old fashioned South African braais with ribs, potato bake and salad, washed down with a few big, cold beers. Their neighbours Glynn and Dara joined us, and soon we were part of the family. Glynn was very proud of the fact that he could walk across the road at any time, through a line in the creek and pull out a fish for the grill, a large fish, a large and tasty fish, within ten minutes, every time, guaranteed. That night we all ate sweet ribs.

Each day the work continued on the camper. We built the beds and the kitchen cupboards (the frame was skew, none of the drawers or doors were square, so we called it shabby chic), built storage boxes for my tools, fixed the roof rack, installed European headlights, worked on the brakes and gave the Landy a full service. After his workday ended, Steve would join us in the workshop to help us out, he dedicated most of his efforts to welding two stainless steel end caps for the rear camper wall extrusions, and he did an excellent job. During a coffee break, I asked Steve why he thought the fuel tank was taking so long to fill. I had checked the breathers and had wracked my brain but could not think of the solution or find the problem. Steve took a puff on his vapouriser and had a think. He then grabbed a torch, took a look down the filler neck and gave me a "ya can't be that stupid, can ya?" look. He bent a piece of wire, fished around for a moment and pulled out the green rag which I had put in the filler neck to keep the dust out while we were doing the rebuild. For two months I had been filling the tank at a rate of a litre a minute, now she fills like a Formula One car.

Steve was a wonderful host, patient and full of good humour, even as time began to run out for us to head across from the UK to France. A relaxing BBQ with Glynn and Dara was what the doctor ordered and we feasted on lamb before relaxing in Glynn's little home pub with an excellent Irish whiskey and listened to Glynn's stories of playing in a chart-topping ska band, meeting many of my musical heroes and of course, the band he plays with today - The Ruffs. The Ruffs are pure Lincolnshire, and they insist that you should Never Wear Yellow in August because that is when the little bugs come out and molest anything yellow. I could have stayed in Lincolnshire, had a farmhouse near my new mates and shared a drink and a joke with them every other evening. "You know, you don't HAVE to live this crazy life, don't ya?".

Our last night in the UK was a rush. We drove down to Wales to visit Bearmach, the Land Rover's spares company which has been supporting us with parts, both maintenance and emergency parts since we were in South America. Our navigation system took us on little back roads through the Welsh countryside, and we arrived at the Bearmach offices late on a Friday afternoon to a heroes welcome. We like to work with companies who have a vision for long-term relationships and Bearmach as a company is growing significantly every year, which can be attributed to great product quality, market focus and excellent management. The Operations Director, Richard Green, invited us to his home for dinner and fantastic whimsical Welsh conversation. We wanted to stay longer but, as always, Luisa had already booked a non-refundable ticket (for the channel ferry) and we had to get moving. Luisa is our driving force, and she makes things happen but when Luisa; when will we be able to move slowly?!

That night we slept in Bournemouth, near my sister's house. We arrived at 2 am from Wales, parked on the side of the road and slept. I realised that morning that this was precisely why we had converted the Land Rover to a camper. If we still had the rooftop tent, we would probably be forced to find a campsite or a motorway gas station where we could open the tent to sleep. Or we would have slept in our seats, which is hell in a Defender. When we did the conversion many were unhappy that we had dismantled the beautiful double cab 130. I don't blame them. I too loved the original Mafuta and taking her apart was heartbreaking, but now we are reaping the benefits of all those months of back-breaking hard work, blood, sweat and tears. The original set-up was excellent and served us well for all those years, but it had its limitations - we were always outside, always. We had to cook and sit and work and relax and live outside in the elements. If it was raining heavily or very windy or scorching hot, we only had the rooftop tent for refuge and with four people in one small space, sitting either cross-legged or lying down, patience begins to wain. We would get on each other's nerves, we would cramp up and jostle for space. And eating meals in the rooftop tent is never a good idea, particularly when you have clumsy kids who regularly spill food and juice all over the bedding. And don't get me started on the heat in the there. In Northern Brazil we were camped outside my friend Elmer Brito's workshop, preparing the Landy for the Amazon rainy season crossing. It was 40C at night and, because we were camped between large avocado trees, there was only the slightest breeze. When the breeze did make it through the windows, we would arch our backs to absorb as much of the cool air as possible, "Daddy, you are blocking the wind!". Mosquitoes, the size of wasps, were eating us alive, so we had no choice but to close the mosquito netting which stifled the airflow completely. It was torture, like being locked in a hot box on a summers day.

Eventually, we resorted to wetting our t-shirts and cooling our bodies and faces, the shirts drying within an hour. In Bolivia, we raced up to watch the Dakar rally and became part of the madness of the event in Uyuni, a city which is entirely unprepared for tourism. No, wait, I lie. There is a half-built, tiny stadium with a battered corrugated roof flopping in the gale and which construction workers and unhappy campers have converted into one large toilet bowl. We camped beside the loo stadium to escape the ice-cold wind which blew so forcefully that it ripped the rain cover which flapped loudly against the side of the tent all night. None of us slept that night, or that stifling hot night in Brazil and many other nights of storms, heat and loud traffic. Many evenings were spent driving in circles searching wherever we were for a safe place to open the tent for the night and often there were not many options available. Some accused me of going soft when we converted the Landy into a hard side camper, well, guilty as charged. I would rather have a happy wife, comfortable children and a good night's rest. We lived in that tent almost every day and night for four years, I think we deserve a bit of comfort.

That night in Bournemouth, we parked outside a stately home, closed the blinds and slept with the roof closed. It was not ideal, but we all slept well, lying down, safe and secure and inconspicuous.

I woke my sister Nicky and her husband Stephen at 5 am; we had to get to the ferry in Dover by 9 am and, thankfully, they love us enough that they did not mind the early morning knock on the door. With hugs and promises to return, we made our way to the port, missing most of the traffic and arriving in Dover just in time to wait an hour for the ferry to board.

We were back on the road again! Living in the Landy and living every day anew, it was this that we worked so hard to achieve. Freedom!

Our time in England had been too short, frustrating, but wonderful. We had met such incredible people and fell in love with a country which we could have called home, we made the promise to return, and it is a promise we intend to keep. Perhaps later in life, we will have the resources to be able to travel at a more leisurely pace, perhaps in the future we will stop creating massive obstacles for ourselves to overcome, perhaps in the future, we will be able to live a life of philosophical exploration. This is what we are working towards, and it will happen.

Page 25 Quote

Page 30 quote.

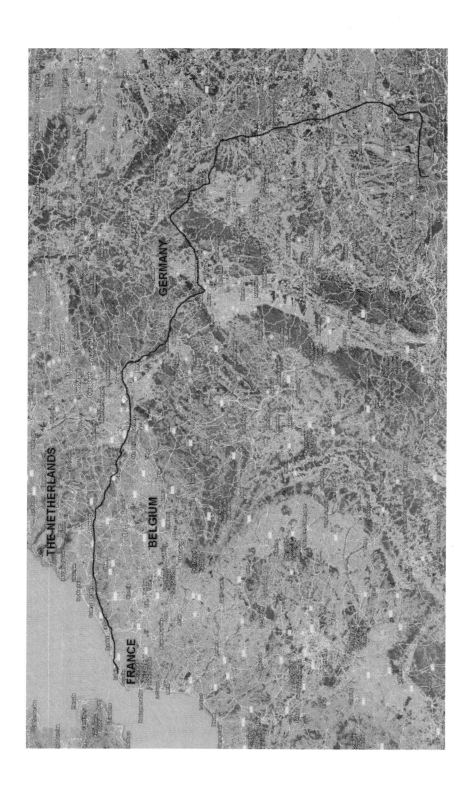

5

European Summer Paradise

Those of you who have been to French Guyana will know that it is a country which has been conquered by the French, not only by French armed forces but also by French culture and, even, French flora. Cayenne is a grassy city, windswept and relatively dry. Calais is almost identical! I joked that the ferry had taken us back to northeastern South America. And what a contrast from green, leafy England. Calais is shades of blown blue sea, grey architecture, brown grass, as is Cayenne. Refugees and migrants were scattered around the motorway leading to the port, sitting in the shade of trees and bridges, waiting for the opportunity to cross over to England, to begin a new life, to join family already there, to escape the French charity which gave them just enough to survive while they waited for the opportunity to prosper. 2015 had been the year of migration into Europe and, as migrants of a sort, we watched with great interest as Europe opened the gates. I was interested to see for myself whether the American media had correctly portrayed the situation in Europe as we had been in the US in 2015 and would watch Fox News or CNN and had been convinced that the end of Europe was near.

Luisa took over the driving duties, and I slept in the back of the Landy while she drove through France, Belgium (which has the most courteous drivers in the world according to Luisa and Keelan), Holland and into Germany where we slept at a motorway gas station before hitting the road to the Abenteuer and Allrad show.

What I did see of France, Belgium and Holland was surprising. I had been told by too many people that these countries were built up and congested, village after village after town after city. From the motorway, we saw only fields and crops and greenhouses and the occasional sleepy village. In

Germany, we witnessed green rolling hills, pastures and farms and quaint villages, perfect in every way, old but modern, rustic and functional yet beautiful and inviting. The autobahn was intimidating, but the rules simple. Go as fast as you want in the left lane or take it easy amongst the endless stream of trucks in the right lane and overtake only when you are 100% sure that an Audi, Mercedes, BMW or Porsche was not low flying, foot flat in the fast lane. The autobahn is an excellent example of common sense, you do not need a policeman to tell you that you are going too fast or whether your vehicle is roadworthy, if you are going to drive at 200 kph you will first make sure that your brakes are good and your tyres thick with tread. There are no goofy old ladies wandering into the fast last at 60 kph, they know better and drive better accordingly. We, limited by our common sense, mud-terrain tyres and a paranoid Luisa, cruised along at a respectable 120kph, relieved that our homemade camper roof had not flown off and killed everyone on the entire motorway and slip-streaming behind and past the trucks which carried the economy across Europe. Ausfahrt (which means exit in Germany) brought a childish giggle at every exit.

In good time we made it to Bad Kissingen, the venue for the Abenteuer and Allrad. The town is beautiful and quintessentially German. Each home is white with a dark roof and red flowers overflowing from windowsill flower pots. The streets are immaculate, clean and perfect, as are the houses. The good people go about there business as cheerfully as you would expect from the calm, curious and tensely relaxed German middle class. If anything, that was one of the first things that we had noticed about the United Kingdom; the class distinctions. In South Africa, I am from a middle-class family, but in the UK, we would be termed the working class (lower class would be the equivalent nomenclature in SA). The British middle class attend Eton and Oxford and go to school under the church tower in Adderley. In Britain, the middle-class are the bankers and artists and barristers and politicians and the landowners who are awfully polite while remaining frustratingly aloof. You can be a working-class millionaire or a middle-class billionaire, it is your accent and origin which determines your class, not your wealth. The upper class are the nobility, and the classes should not mix, Princess Diana was middle class until the day she died, and her ex-husband married a horse from his own class. In South Africa, or America, you can buy your way out of your class if you are wealthy and confident enough, you cannot do that in England, and in Germany, well, you do not need to. Germany, we would find, consists almost entirely of the middle class (of the South African or American variety). Sixty years of high-quality education and social responsibility have ensured that the Germans each have a piece of the pie and all enjoy the fruits of their labour while enjoying short work weeks and long holidays. The Abenteuer and Allrad show was interesting to me as much as it was an overlanding and outdoor adventure show, as a barometer of German wealth and health.

There are a few campsites at the event where you can park your rig. Those who arrive early enough at the five-day event will find a level piece of lawn to set-up on. Those who are late might park on a hill and sleep sliding. We arrived two days after the start of the event, assuming that the weekend would be the best time to present ourselves and hopefully sell some books. We were wrong, the busiest days are the first two, and we arrived to witness overlanders Woodstock with vehicles covering every inch of visible land as far as the hills permitted the eye to see while shades of khaki wandered about. Our friends Lukas and Eva were waiting for us and had fought tooth and nail to reserve us a slice of real estate next to their blue Mercedes camper, lovingly dubbed Diego. We had met Lukas and Eva in South America and had hiked to Machu Picchu with them, Lukas a great beer-drinking companion for the entire family and we loved Eva and her cheeky smile. Our laager was completed by another German couple, Bavarians Thomas and Sabine who had driven around the world in an old ex-military Mercedes truck, which was called an oldtimer in Germany.

Thomas had a simultaneously gentle but scathing sense of humour and his waist-length dreadlocks and hippy pants disguised a keen mind. We settled quickly into overland festival routine, meet old friends, make new friends, sip a cold beer while strolling around admiring every shape and size vehicle imaginable - from rolling apartment blocks to Mini Coopers with tiny hard shell roof tents, from ex-military personnel carriers to old hippy buses and an assortment of motorbikes, quad bikes, dirtbikes and tricycles. Next to a beer tent stood a food court and next to that stood the free toilets and hot showers. Each morning a bakery opened a stall in the middle of a roundabout and served chocolate croissants, baguettes, bagels and coffee.

In the evening's small elevated campfires grilled pork sausages and ribs and burger patties and vegetables. Strangers spoke as if they had known each forever, children happily went about their business, pets accepted endless affection and a cold beer was to be found at every turn. The German overland tribe is one, big, happy, comfortable family. Nobody is too impressed by the 5,000,000 Euro camper trucks except for those with mere 4, 000,000 Euro camper trucks and that guy with the Mini Cooper is everyone's friend. And Germans have been everywhere on this planet, it was difficult to impress them with our exploits except for the fact that this was our full-time lifestyle and that we had raised our kids on the road, homeschooling them. Homeschooling is illegal in Germany, and it is therefore impossible for a couple with young children to commit to a life on the road like we have. Many asked us if we knew how and the only real option for them is to emigrate to a country which allows homeschooling and then hit the road, an incredibly costly and complicated procedure. So, Germans are very well-travelled, but many travel by conventional means and only the retired or childless can travel the planet overland. Which might partly explain why the vast majority of our German friends do not have children, they want to see the world, dammit!

We joined the magazine at their stand to promote ourselves and our books and spent the days telling our story, meeting old and new friends and occasionally finding time for a beer and a bratwurst. Most Germans speak English but many do not, which made selling our English language books a challenge, but we did sell the vast majority and had time to walk around the show which is incredibly well organised and attended, with exhibitors selling everything from the massive, go absolutely nowhere trucks to stickers, patches and tools. South African exhibitors were there in their droves selling trailers, recovery gear, roof tents, clothing and outdoor furniture. We have been to overlanding events in South Africa, South America and the USA, and none can compare to the German event. I believe that boils down to a combination of expendable income, a culture of travel and a lust for adventure. And it is not just the die-hard overlanders who attend the event; people visit from across the country and are bussed to the event in a fleet of air-conditioned buses which circle the route from the parking lots and the campsite to the exhibition located on top of a hill. Up to 20,000 people attended the show in one day, now that is good business.

The campsite is, for us and many others, the highlight of the event. The only people selling are the beer and wurst vendors, and you can walk all day every day and not see all the overland vehicles, you never know who you are going to bump into and did I mention the cold beer? Delicious, cold, German beer. The Germans have a very high standard for beer, it is called the Rheinheitsgebot (literally - purity order) which limits the ingredients which can be used in German beer and the states of the former Holy Roman Empire (water, barley, hops and yeast). As a result, the beer is smooth and tasty, and you feel great the next morning. There is no corn in German beer, and it is the corn which really fattens you up and leaves you feeling like you have been drinking toilet cleaner (I am talking to you Coors Light).

And you learn the most interesting things about Germany when talking to well-educated and well-travelled Germans. For instance, did you know that all Germans pay an obligatory church tax which is 8 to 9% of their monthly salary? It is called the Kirchensteuer (church tax) which is quite bizarre in a secular state, but the good news is that you can pay a small fee to de-register from paying the tax, you just won't be able to marry or baptise your children (which you aren't having anyway) in the church.

Word spread that there was a South African family grilling meat and people joined us for a beer and a chat. Our small American BBQ was overflowing with excellent pork ribs (which I smoked over the course of a few hours) and friends from Poland, Holland, Belgium, Russia, Turkey, Austria, England, America, Italy Czech Republic, Portugal, Spain, Norway, Denmark, Sweden, South Africa and France showed up to shoot the breeze, some bringing our books for us to sign and others bringing gifts. In-between festivities, we were interviewed for documentaries and magazines and eventually ran out of words and energy and sat back to enjoy the flicker of the campfire and the conversation around us. We were overwhelmed by the camaraderie and affection we were shown and again promised that we would try to return the next year.

Sunday night was a late night for us, and we went to sleep, smiling and awoke to find an empty, clean camp area. It was like aliens had visited during the night and absorbed all but a few Defenders and a Spanish hippy van. Keelan and I did some work on the Land Rover, installing a rear bumper and checking the oil levels before heading south to Nuremberg where our friends Markus and Katherin lived.

I had wanted to travel to Paderborn, the German city where my maternal grandmother had been raised, to meet family long forgotten and to establish if there were any family traits which transcended the decades and continents. After a conversation with my now deceased friend, Torsten Delventhal, he offered to contact the Thebille family for me, to see if he could arrange a meeting. He messaged me the next day that he had found a valid telephone number and phoned, then spoke to an elderly lady. Unfortunately, the inquiry was not well received. …"I was trying to explain the reason for my phone call, trying to find something out for you, as soon as I mentioned the words "war" and "after the war may be to England", she stopped the communication instantly with the words, "I'm not answering these questions any more". Never one to beat a dead horse I left it at that.

We could finally relax after the show and had no real plans to be anywhere in a rush, so we took a slow drive. We had met Markus and Katherin in Jericoacoara, Brazil the day we completed our circumnavigation of South America back in 2014 and had celebrated with them well into the wee hours. I still have not forgotten how bad that hangover was or how fantastic earning it had been. Markus, a freelance filmmaker, was waiting for us with a fridge full of Hell beer but unfortunately, beautiful Katherin, a teacher, was away on a school training trip. Markus cooked us a Nuremberg speciality of roasted pork and fed us an endless supply of beer before taking us on a tour of the city the next day. Nuremberg (Nurnburg in German) had been an important part of the Nazi infrastructure before and during World War 2, and the Allies razed much of the city to the ground with endless bombing raids and during the Battle of Nuremberg when the American forces fought bitterly against the entrenched forces. The old town was destroyed but was painstakingly rebuilt after the war, stone by stone, restoring the pre-war appearance including the reconstruction of several medieval buildings. Markus was born and raised in Nuremberg and was an excellent guide, giving insights into the city, and it's past. We have learnt that a local is always the best guide. Bavaria itself proved to be the star of the show though and after leaving Markus (promising to return, as always), we headed further south to hang out at a community where dreadlocked Thomas and his wife Sabine lived. We arrived in Sulzbrunn, at the foot of the Alps, surrounded by green hills which fed fat cows wearing large bells around their necks. Bergtesgarten lay only a short drive away, and though I have been obsessed by the Second World War since sitting on my paternal grandparents flokati rug watching The World At War at the age of five, I had neither the appropriate time nor the resources to tour the battle sites and historical sites, that would have to be done another day, in the future, when I have the time and resources.

Thomas and Sabine live and work in a community of new agers, people I would call hippies, but these guys are not listening to Jefferson Airplane and smoking massive amounts of pot daily, that I knew of. They are more interested in a life which is peaceful and sustainable. Some meditate the day away while others work the gardens and take care of the large commune buildings which used to be a hotel and a residence. We set up camp outside the work area, near the vegetable gardens and compost shower and continued working on a few of the jobs which needed to be done on the Land Rover. Back in Arizona in 2016, we shared a meal with the legendary Jan and Leonie Vorster in their self-built Series 2B Forward Control Land Rover. I was discussing the plans I had for the rebuild of our Landy and Jan cautioned me. "The work never ends when you build a camper". He was correct, of course, and we were spending a lot of time correcting mistakes we had made and getting to jobs which we had neglected to do. And we found the one thing in Germany that the USA and UK severely lack; a decent "Big Box" hardware store. In both the former countries we spent a fortune on online purchases and wasted too much time searching for the products we needed. Home Depot in the USA stocks everything you need to build a house, but very little else. Screwfix in the UK has a massive range, but you need to know precisely what you need and have the time and energy to go through the 2,000-page catalogue to find what you need, then either order online or visit one of their warehouses where you give the code to a blonde woman with brown hair who takes a tea break while looking for your rubber stoppers. I want to walk into a hardware store and take my sweet time choosing the things I need and when you spend a lot of time fabricating you want to take a product designed for one purpose and adapt it to be used for your purpose. And to do that I need to hold a product in my hands, measure it, weigh it, ask it some questions. The German hardware stores such as Bauhaus and Conrad have a vast range of products at reasonable prices, if we had done the entire build in Germany, we would have saved a fortune.

Our few days with Thomas and Sabine and the peaceful people was a great experience for the kids and us. It is good to know that there are places in this world where people can relax and go about their lives is a peaceful, gentle manner, being kind to each other and the planet, eating well and taking care of the bodies and souls. My soul is too busy rampaging around inside my body trying to make sense of it all, perhaps the answer is to stop asking so many bloody questions, to embrace a calm mind and lifestyle. One day perhaps.

Our next stop was Switzerland, and we had read that you can only take in one kilogram of meat per person, or that might have been one kilogram of meat per vehicle. Either way, we had been to a butchery in Nuremberg and had bought eight kilograms too many. One solution was to braai a few of those kilos of pork ribs at the commune before heading to the border on the banks of the Bodensee which lies between Germany, Austria and Switzerland. Sitting on the patio outside the commune apartment block, we sparked the fire and slowly started to grill the extra meat, preparing a feast. Slowly but surely the smell of grilled pork attracted recently reconverted vegetarians, the benches around us filling with drooling, thirsty, peaceful people. Unfortunately, Europeans are not accustomed to the South African braai and the three-hour-long process of making fire, drinking beer, adding fuel to the fire and having a few more cold ones. The peaceful droolers began to stir and became ravenous, I began to fear for our safety. Eventually, there were so many people surrounding our little BBQ that I had to start grilling in earnest, and a reluctant Luisa had to fetch more meat from the Land Rover's large Snomaster fridge. Before the tie-dyed riot, I served the first racks of ribs and rashers coated in coarse salt with a BBQ sauce dip, all were gobbled down in a frenzy. Not everyone was fed, and hungry eyes begged me to cook more, faster! One young lady swallowed an entire rasher without chewing while we tried to placate the crowds, promising that they would be fed. By the end of the evening, we were down to one last massive rack of ribs and a few packs of rashes which Luisa refused to share. The night was a carnivore's dream, and we left the next day, headed towards Switzerland (promising to return, as always).

6

Yo Del Ay He Hooly Shit, That's Expensive!

We were sad to leave Germany, we had only spent 10 days in the country, and it had made a profound impression on us. Rural, green, beautiful, prosperous and modern, the people had treated us incredibly well, and I felt regret for all those times when I had allowed myself to brush all Germans with one broad stereotypical brush. By now, we should know better than to believe the notions of nations which others promote.

We were still not accustomed to this idea of driving from country to country without the massive hassle of immigration and customs. Before we knew it, we were in Austria which, let's face it, is Germany, and then made our way to the Swiss "border" where a blonde man with better things to do than look in my fridge waved us into Switzerland. I think the Defender has a hypnotic effect on people, they take one look and think, "Wow, you guys are legitimate, keep on trucking on, man".

Switzerland is not what you expect it to be. Yes, it is green and mountainous and picturesque, but it is also a bit old, a bit ramshackle, a bit odd. The houses, villages and towns are not as large and modern as in Germany or Austria, and the farms all have ancient sheds and wood stockpiles and implements. The secondary roads are narrow and forever winding, and everything seems somehow slightly small, almost compact. And Switzerland seemed far more multicultural than Germany which was monocultural in rural areas. We headed to Wil where we would be meeting with our good friends Ursi and Michel who we had first met in Argentina in 2014. Ursi was as feisty as ever, and Michel seemed happy and relaxed, of course, he was, he is married to Ursi! It was decided that we would head down to the river near their house where we would make a fire and skewer the large remaining rack of ribs on the Brazilian espata which we carry. At over four kilograms the rack was going to take a while, so we filled the time swimming in the river, drinking a few cold drinks and catching up. Jessie was in a black mood and slept in the back of the Landy, upon the bank, just out of sight. Usually, we would never let her out of our sight, but we had realised that Europe is safe (and we had a hard side camper with locking doors), not just relatively safe or quite safe but really safe. No-one would bother our child or try to break into or steal the Land Rover. Here people did not litter or break the law or rape and murder each other, they know better. That safety is rare in our home country, but we have learned that it is common throughout most of the world, which saddens us but is simultaneously encouraging. Maybe one day our people will know peace too.

The rack slowly grilled as we chatted about the past, the future and the present. Luisa had been doing some research, and it seemed like we might be able to apply for temporary residence in either Spain or Portugal, which would give us the freedom to travel Europe and abroad but which would also provide us with a home base in Europe. The situation in South Africa has been declining steadily since the mid-'90s, and if our children were to have an opportunity in this life, those opportunities would be found in Europe where they could be safe and prosperous.

Dark clouds began to gather over us as we sat by the river. I dropped the meat lower, closer to the coals and seasoned with coarse salt. Ten minutes later we were devouring the ribs with a dip of various sweet sauces. Other bathers considered us with interest, the meat we were eating would have cost almost $300 in Switzerland and would certainly not be grilled casually down by the river. As we finished eating the heavens opened, and we were forced to scramble with our belongings back up the slippery slope to where our vehicles were parked, and Jessica lay sleeping. It was then that a revelation dawned on me. Adventure is a choice.

You can live in the safest, warmest cocoon of luxury if you choose to (luxury is, of course, a relative concept). We could have grilled that rack of ribs in the oven of Ursi and Michels lovely apartment, we could have chosen to play a board game or watch a movie but, instead, we went looking for something different, we went back to nature. Adventure, like luxury, is a relative concept. The Camel Trophy teams had an incredible adventure out

in the jungle, but they did it within the secure confines of a corporate
They at times risked life and limb but, they did not have their family in the
Land Rover, and the vehicle did not belong to them, their risk was relatively
minimal. When they were finished competing in the jungle or desert, they
would return home to the safety and security of normal life (I assume) where
they would seek adventure again, this being their nature. I have great respect
for the Camel Trophy men, do not get me wrong, but long-term
overlanding is in itself an adventure and the more you risk, the greater the
reward. We chose this lifestyle, and we choose to live a certain way. We
chose to go down to the river and slide down the muddy bank, have a swim
in the fast-moving river then make a fire and have a cold beer while
watching the meat brown. We chose to do that because it is in our nature
to seek experiences over comfort and daily increments of small adventures
become, in totality, a great adventure.

The small city of Wil retains a rural atmosphere but is relatively modern, a
great place to live. Almost ten percent of the population is Muslim, but the
city is majority Christian, of various churches, a fact of which you are
reminded every 15 minutes when an electronic bell chimes, and when it
chimes it stops conversation. Not only did the fake bell chime every quarter-
hour it also clanged every half hour and on the hour when it would chime
each hour passed and then another ten times just to make sure you were
paying attention. At 12 am or 12 pm, all conversation stops, and you sit
staring at each other while waiting impatiently for the church to stop
interrupting, whichever great story was being told. Often the bells are
chimed for no reason at all, I imagined the priests playing cards, or truth or
dare, or drinking games, and every time someone lost they had to run over
to the bell button and give it a few thumps, then run back to the table
cackling. Sundays are the worst - the chiming, and presumably, the drinking
games goes into overdrive forcing the good people of Wil to escape into the
countryside where they can spend $20 on a beer and $15 on a bratwurst and
mashed potatoes. $2 on a litre of fuel.

That morning the bells drove us crazy and out of town towards the Santis
mountain. Crystal clear streams and acres of green escorted us through
valleys guarded by intimidating snow-crested mountains, winding past
wooden homes, barns and massive stockpiles of winter wood. Rural

Switzerland is not as modern as I imagined it to be, but it is ancient. This is a country which managed to remain neutral for 200 years and through both World Wars, while the rest of Europe was being levelled by industrial killing machines, Switzerland continued with a relatively healthy daily life thanks to a government with vision and a plan for self-preservation. No armadas of B52's carpeting bombed the major cities, and no armies chose to fight their battles through the densely populated civilian areas. Switzerland made compromises and a profit in fact. Switzerland passed The Swiss Banking Act in 1934, which guaranteed anonymous numbered accounts which were available to *anyone* with sufficient resources. Though the Swiss were neutral during both big wars, they had foreseen the coming of the second war (the Swiss' strategy for survival is to prepare for the worst-case scenario, and their motto is "In time of peace prepare for war") and further reinforced a policy called National Redoubt, which had first been conceived in 1880's to respond to foreign invasion. This defensive policy converted Switzerland into a fortress which would exact a heavy toll on invaders, a toll so heavy that invading the country would not be worth the cost of life and treasure. Essentially, the country today is a fortress, surrounded by the Alps and populated by a highly trained civilian army determined to ensure the survival of the nation.

Swiss men still serve in the Swiss army, it is compulsory to serve at least 300 days (women may volunteer for any position in the armed forces) during which they are compensated 80% of their salary (among other remuneration) and after which they are sent home with the knowledge that they are to "defend Switzerland to the last bullet and blade" and they know exactly how to do it. They are issued with a SIG SG 550 assault rifle which they keep maintained in their homes, ammunition will be issued upon request for target practice or in the event of an invasion or attack. In the event of an invasion, the entire relevant public transport infrastructure is rigged to be destroyed at short notice, for instance, where a railway line crosses beneath a bridge, a segment of the bridge is rigged with explosives to fall onto the railway, and artillery bunkers are situated nearby to prevent attackers from clearing the rubble. I imagine that most people on the planet imagine the Swiss as I did - neutral, peace-loving bankers. Well, the truth is they are warriors prepared for the fight! During WW2 they resisted Nazi attempts at

Anschluss (joining) and refused to become part of the Reich, even shooting down Nazi planes which violated Swiss airspace. In the late Sixties, shortly after the Cuban missile crisis, the Swiss passed a law which required the construction of ventilated nuclear attack and fallout bunkers. Every Swiss home we visited had its own bunker, designed and built to withstand a nuclear attack and provide refuge throughout a nuclear winter, there are enough bunkers to house every Swiss citizen. The military has built many thousand defensive bunkers throughout the country, and one young Swiss friend told me of driving a truck in a military convoy and how they approached the side of the mountain, a huge "rock" door slid open exposing a massive military complex within. Very James Bond.

There are other things about Switzerland which are incredibly impressive. The fourth-richest country in the world has relatively low income and corporate tax, they have seven state presidents (a few presidents use public transportation to get to work), are not part of the European Union, have four official languages and CH stands for Confoederatio Helvetica. Also, the country is overflowing with feisty, beautiful redheads. And the flag is square.

Michel and Ursi guided us to the cable car at the foot of the Santis mountain in the Appenzell region. The idea was that we would ride the cable car up and walk down, an idea which suited us perfectly - I had been drinking a lot of excellent German beer and needed to sweat some of it off. Keelan had still not recovered his athletic form after our stay in the USA, we don't talk about the girls, they are always in great shape. We were surprised to find herds of cattle at the top of the mountain, enjoying the summer sun while grazing on the sweet green grass. A red rescue helicopter wop-wop-wopped it's way close to where we stood and loaded a portly old man without landing completely. We could only assume that the gentleman had suffered a heart attack or similar when witnessing from an elevated position the beauty of Switzerland on a cloudless, perfect day. We were grateful that we were hiking down as I would probably have had my own heart attack if we had hiked up. We stopped at the Berggasthaus Aescher, a restaurant built into the side of a cliff where we were told, we could sample the world-famous Rosti, Swiss hash browns served with sausage and beer. We ordered two plates of Rosti and three beers and left the restaurant, with its breathtaking views, 60 Euros lighter. 60 Euros is almost an entire day's overlanding budget, and with fuel at $2 a litre we needed to save money. But, how often do you get to share exquisite beer and food with friends you have not seen since South America, all while hanging off the side of a cliff?

Not every day. The climb down the side of the mountain took a couple of hours, and when we eventually reached the paved road, it was so steep that we took to running down the road instead of labouring to control our balance with each step. More herds of cows munched at the inviting green grass and, now in a valley, we wondered how the farmers who lived up the side of mountains managed to get to and from their homesteads. As Switzerland is so tiny and ancient, farmers have long occupied any land flat enough to grow crops or feed and to support a house and barn. You can see why these people are gifted at winter sports; skiing is a way of life in the winter months and being impeccably organised ensures that after the hard work in the summer months, the winter months provide many opportunities for pleasure activities. Our South African minds imagine a white winter as a special kind of hell, when people are barricaded inside their homes, the wind howling, snowstorms barricading the doors, -20C at midday and a sky so grey and full of ice that all joy is ripped from your soul through your frozen eyes. Well, apparently not. It appears that the snow falls and the skies clear and many days, particularly at elevation, are sunny with perfect blue skies. The farmers go about their business quite happily during the winter months and down in the valleys the roads are cleared after each snowfall, life goes on. Like many Southern Hemisphere "Europeans" we have lost that winter culture. We do not have enough snow to warrant a sport and our winters in Cape Town tend to be half wet, windy Antarctic cold front assaults and half summer sunshine with a cool breeze. Down south we might surf in the winter swells or, if flash with old money cash, we might find a ski resort, but mostly we just bitch about the cold and wonder how much longer we can survive 15C while trying to braai meat on the patio and drinking copious amounts of red wine. For four months of the year, we are miserable, and Johannesburg is worse than Cape Town. Their temperatures drop to freezing in July, and every plant turns brown.

Johannesburg in winter is different shades of brown - dead lawn, naked trees, a layer of dust over everything. The air is so dry that your lips crack and everyone comes down with a strain of flu so debilitating that you can't even enjoy your sick day in front of the TV. And there is nothing to do all winter other than sit in traffic and wait for summer to return. Old houses were not built for winter, the glass is single pane, draughts of ice-cold airflow under the doors, and through the ceiling, there is no central heating. There you wear your coat inside the house and sleep under four layers of blankets, a woollen cap on your head, a scarf around your neck. We lived in Johannesburg for many years and winter was something to be endured, life did not begin again until the first rains came and the lawn recovered it's thick green wonder. A Cape Town winter is lovely by comparison and in general.

In Switzerland, winter is no longer as severe and, thanks to global warming, snow is not always guaranteed. But, they have a winter culture, the houses are built to be warm and cosy, there are activities and ski lodges and a multitude of winter sports to keep people occupied and smiling. Unfortunately, we have still not had the opportunity to enjoy a northern hemisphere winter (Baja California in Mexico does not count, neither does that hot, humid isthmus they call Florida), one day we will live through a real winter, six feet of snow, ice-skating, skiing, warming up by the wood fire, testing whether our European genes will reveal themselves and whether we can survive what tens of millions enjoy every year. Yes, we have many plans for the future.

We said our goodbyes to our wonderful friends on a blue, warm and sunny morning. Michel had given us a list of attractions to visit and advice for travelling Switzerland, but this time we were just passing through and would not explore, we simply could not afford to. Instead, this would be a driving tour. A reader of our books who we met at the Abenteuer and Allrad show in Germany, had invited us to his home near Interlaken overlooking Lake Brienz and Lake Thun. Philippe was in the middle of his military service and was stationed with the United Nations peacekeeping force (if the word force can be used to describe any UN military detail) in Kosovo. He was on leave and had arranged for many of his friends to join us for an evening of Swiss meat and beer. We usually do not accept invitations from people we do not know personally or are introduced by mutual friends, but we had a good feeling about Philippe, and we were not disappointed. His friends were mostly young guys who had recently finished their military service or were students and, as is the norm with young men, there was much banter, beer drinking and laughter. Luisa and I grilled the meat and enjoyed the view of the lakes while our kids disappeared to download the internet. That night Philippe and his friends explained to me what they had learned during their military service and how impregnable Switzerland really is. Later that year, I met with a friend, a former Colonel and Westpoint Military Academy graduate and we discussed "Fortress Switzerland". He was not convinced that Switzerland was as impregnable as I had been led to believe, but that just illustrated to me how efficiently and quietly Switzerland had gone about securing both its borders, and its reputation as a peaceful, neutral country. But, perhaps he knew something I did not know, which is likely, of course.

The next day Luisa plotted our course towards France, and we crossed the border without any problems at all except that it was raining heavily and the road along the French coast of Lake Geneva was in a state of disrepair. The contrast between the two countries is immediate and profound. France seems weathered and worn, less organised, with more evidence of urban decay. Our route was direct to Northern Spain, and we might have stayed longer in France had it seemed more welcoming. Perhaps the fault is ours that we try to stay off of toll roads and freeways and therefore experience parts of a country which most don't see. As in the USA, the construction of highways and freeways had taken the arteries of supply and demand away from the smaller towns and cities and rerouted them from large city to large city, industrial areas to ports. Many of the villages we passed through were charming and relatively well maintained, some were crumbling and inhabited by rusting Peugeot and Citreon shells. The decision had been made to get to Spain quickly and then to make our way across to Portugal, we were not exactly sure what we would do when we got there, but we had heard that Spain was large, beautiful and relatively cheap. We also had friends in Portugal who invited us to visit them. We were eager to see the Mediterranean coast of Southern France and took a few highways to get there, paying huge tolls to drive very well-built roads. Unlike most of Europe, parts of France are considered to be unsafe, and the motorway rest stops were to be avoided at night unless they were 24-hour stops with gas stations. We stopped at one rest stop and found free wifi and self-cleaning toilets and ignored trash bins. We decided not to stay the night. Luisa had read stories of thieves filling campers with gas to knock the inhabitants out, after which they were robbed of everything, she had read this on many forums and we decided that, for once, we would do what everyone else does and seek a gas station which we found not too far down the road. I parked the Land Rover close enough to the gas station to be visible but far enough that we could sleep peacefully. Waiting for the sun to set in summer Europe requires patience as it can be light until 10 pm. While Luisa and the kids cooked dinner and chatted, I drank a blonde French beer and watched a well-groomed Labrador try to escape through the fence which separated the gas station from a field and the nearby town.

I had a plan to chase the dog away if it figured out that the gate was high enough off the ground for it to crawl under but, luckily, he was not the brightest pup, and he continued to dig at the base of the fence, between two bushes, until a voice called and he rushed off to greet it. A young man with a shaved head, build and attitude of a Mixed Martial Arts fighter arrived at the gate in a small red Peugeot. He unlocked the gate, drove through, locked the gate and begrudgingly tidied the gas station forecourt, emptied the trash cans, fiddled with the locks of a metal cage storing replacement gas bottles and disappeared into the station building for a few hours. Early the next morning his car was still there, but he left not long after a group of young German men arrived and stood outside the Land Rover competing to impress each other with jokes and tricks with a football. "Hey, bugger off!". Silence. Hahaha, they laughed and buggered off.

After coffee and baguette, we continued to drive down the A7 and joined the A9 to Montpelier. French cities have such romantic-sounding names, but the entire cities are not the Parisian culture you might expect. Search Google images for Montpelier, and you are met with astonishing images of architectural beauty, of culture and monuments and blue sea. Which is what you can expect to find when paying five-star prices for accommodation, tours and food. What we found are the areas where normal people live. A slightly dusty and bright city of roundabouts, speed bumps, apartment buildings and shopping complexes. Us overlanders see the belly. Which is fine, I much prefer to see how real people live now to how the wealthy live and lived back then. We found a post office to send out a few books which had been purchased online. We Will Be Free and Travel the Planet Overland continue to sell very well, and often we try to carry stock of the books with us. They are heavy, but worth their weight, our problem is often trying to find a post office from which to send them and which did not charge us the equivalent of the books retail value.

We have sent books from most European countries and, if you ever intend to post a book, I would not send it from Switzerland, The Netherlands, Italy, Hungary or Greece. Germany has by far the most efficient, cost-effective and reliable post office. France is second but, unlike Germany, France has two price lists for books - one for the French and another for foreigners. To be more precise, there is a low-cost postal price for books in France but, we were informed by a middle-aged blonde lady with large glasses circa 1985, *that* price was for French books, written in French. Interesting. "Well, I have ten books to send, and some of them are going to Frenchmen, does that count?". No, it did not. We stood and debated our situation for a moment until a large man (large in every way and, he told us, of Algerian descent) suggested to 1985 that the books did not *have* to be written in French, they just needed to be books and only books. She shrugged sour shoulders, "If you want to take the risk", she implied. "What risk?". 1985 then informed us that the postal inspectors might open the packages to make 100% that some belligerent English or God forbid, German writer was not trying to illegally post non-French books in France and from France. I could imagine the inspector's reaction at finding a copy of We Will Be Free in the French language book only discount price sack. Sacre Bleu! Criminals! "We have caught you now, Monsieur Belle!". Off to the Bastille with you!

"Negotiations" continued for half an hour until the large guy gave 1985 an eye roll and took the books, all ten of them and charged us the lower price. So, if you received one of our books from France, this is what we went through to send them to you. A mild inconvenience, I assure you.

Montpelier is a tourist city, and we struggled to find free camping, we did find grimy campsites overflowing with vehicles but were also very expensive. We eventually realised that 30 Euros was the going rate for a crap, cramped campsite or you could pay 35 Euros and have a relatively nice campsite with a private toilet. We had not paid for camping for one night in the UK, so we decided to treat ourselves. That night we camped between tall hedges and amongst dry, brown grass. There were two types of campers surrounding us; the miserable happy camper with fully equipped RV/caravan and the unhappy camper with the under-equipped Citreon, flappy blue ground tent and wailing kids. The reasoning is quite simple - you can pay a lot to have a nice camping holiday, or you can pay a lot to have a crap camping holiday while trying to save money. I related to the blue ground tent guys, that is pretty much how we became overlanders, except we had cool Land Rovers and we soon learned how to camp happily - pro tip - avoid crowded, middle of the city, coastal campsites.

We waited until the very last moment before checking out the next day, Luisa gets every cent worth what she has paid for. When we did leave the park, we parked outside the gates under a palm tree and continued to use the wifi. If you remember one of my Instagram posts from sometime in August 2017, well one of those was probably posted while sitting under that tree borrowing wifi. This is our reality, we borrow wifi, scour the land for cheap or free camping, we sometimes shower only once a week but seek a large clean water source to wash in daily. We count the pennies, are forever trying to earn more, we make all our own food and are forever looking for a place to make a fire, grill some meat and drink a cold beer or a few glasses of wine.

That day we drove down along the coast from Montpelier to green, forested Perpignan, close to the Spanish border. That night we again found a campsite, Luisa had work to do distributing books from the USA internationally, and this camp, though ancient and crumbling, was literally deserted and had a braai area where we could celebrate our last night in France. The only other inhabitants of the campsite were old or young couples who occupied stark white, made-to-order holiday units with small verandas, minuscule kitchens, tiny bedrooms and bad plumbing. The braai went well, and we discussed our plans for the future.

Luisa, Keelan and Jessica had been granted three-month Schengen visas, and I held a British passport. We had planned to set ourselves up in the UK and establish a European base for further travel but, as you know, that did not work out for us. We had 45 days left in Europe and only a few options.

We had planned to drive to Asia, but we were encountering some very expensive and prohibitive red tape. Iran and India required a Carnet for the Land Rover which we could not afford and which the German automobile association, ADAC, had only recently stopped issuing to foreign vehicles. A carnet is essentially a customs document which allows a vehicle to be taken across a frontier for a limited period, this is done to ensure that vehicle will not be sold in the country illegally. The British would not issue a carnet either. Here is an interesting side story. I had been emailing ADAC for a while trying to negotiate a carnet, but they flatly and politely refused. I then posted on social media that we were struggling with ADAC, hoping that someone might have an idea or experience which might help us. A day later I received an email for an ADAC employee named Anna stating that as I had been told that ADAC could not issue the carnet, I must please provide my bank details for the refund of the deposit of Euro 3,300 which had been made in my name. Had my mother not raised me well, I might have been tempted to provide the details and accept the refund of fees I had not paid. I asked them to check their information as I had not paid a deposit and a day or so later received an email claiming a mistake was made and apologising for the inconvenience. I had a theory that an anonymous friend had made the deposit, and if you are reading this, I thank you, and I am glad that you, I and ADAC are all secure in the knowledge that we may be rogues, but we are honest rogues.

The quest for the carnet continued and we were instructed by the British RAC that they would certainly not be able to issue a carnet and that we would have to ask the AA in South Africa, who in turn insisted that we had to return to SA with the vehicle in order for them to issue the carnet, which required a deposit 100% of the value of the vehicle. Six months of digging came up with no alternatives. Apparently, there is a fixer in Iran who will take $3,000 and can get you into Iran without a carnet, but that is a massive risk, and we would have no way forward as we would still need a carnet for India. To add to our woes, half of South East Asia had recently put a blanket ban on self-drive tours (thanks to the Chinese tour operators and second-hand cars salesman who were flouting local laws), and some countries had banned right-hand drive vehicles, no doubt to stem the flow of cheap second-hand Japanese vehicles. So, driving across to South East Asia was becoming virtually impossible for us, simply because we did not have $20,000 to $30,000 to throw at the problem. A path of least resistance would be to drive across Europe to Turkey, up through the Stans to Russia then across Russia into Mongolia then back up through Russia from where we could ship to Alaska and do the Pan American drive again. We were just in the Americas. We needed a miracle. And we needed another plan.

Luisa had been discussing the idea of applying for temporary residence in Spain, or maybe Portugal. As I am a British citizen, it is possible for me to apply for temporary residence in those Iberian countries, and therefore, in terms of EU law, my African family may also apply. If we did this, we would have to make a paradigm shift in our thinking as long-term travellers. We often had to stop in a place for a while and work, sometimes stopping for a month at a time, if not longer, what if we just returned to one place instead of stopping en-route? A new idea was born - fly and drive. If we could obtain temporary residence, then we could travel with the Landy for a few months then return for a few months to work on our books and video projects, fill the coffers, then return to wherever the Landy is and keep going. It would be a new lifestyle completely, but there were distinct advantages. The kids and Luisa would have an opportunity for European residence, we could have an adventurous life and enjoy European comfort, and Keelan particularly would be able to study once he decides what he wants to do with his life. The disadvantage would be that we would have to fly and drive, and flights are expensive.

Another option, which Luisa was pushing for but hated the idea of, was to go to Ireland and live and work there as South Africans are visa-exempt. I would find a job (postman, Land Rover camper builder, tree surgeon, barman) and Luisa would probably revive our immigration business. After two years of working, selling our books and saving we could hit the road again.

Or, we could drive down to Morocco and then try and tour Africa but, again we needed a host of visas and Africa requires serious preparation and should not be attempted lightly.

We could play the lottery and win a million bucks.

None of these options suited us perfectly (except the last option, but the odds were against us) and we had committed ourselves to drive to Asia. With the pressure mounting, we packed up the Landy that morning and crossed over into Spain.

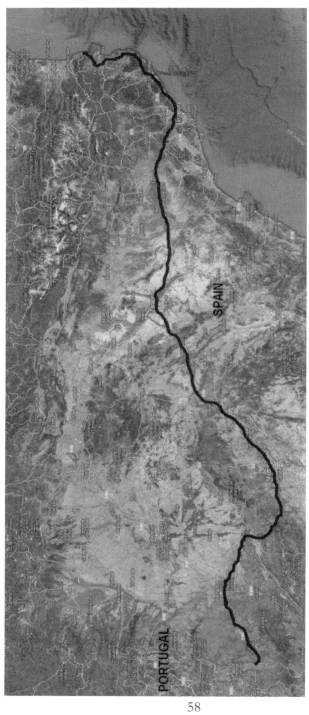

7

Spain

This European Union concept is quite amazing, the idea of being able to cross international borders without the tedium of customs and immigration is fantastic. And it never fails to amaze me how one country can be so very different from another - socially and geographically. The first thing we noticed crossing into Spain was that the road deteriorated quite badly as it wound through dry, windswept hills. We then passed the old immigration and customs buildings and a few abandoned truck stops. Luisa spotted a person standing on the side of the road, maybe a hitchhiker, but as we neared it appeared that this person was looking for a ride of another sort. A girl stood on the verge of the road, surrounded by uncut grass and the litter of careless motorists. She stood there alone, talking into a headset, she turned to face us. She wore a glamorous, glitzy miniskirt 100 fingers from her knees, her hair platinum blonde and waist-length, her feet tortured by six-inch stilettos, her face painted with the warpaint of a nightclub, breasts straining to be released. She had the thousand-yard stare of someone who has seen too much and soon we passed the person she was talking to on the headset. This girl was dressed exactly the same, but she had jet black hair down to her waist, the next girl had flaming red hair down to her waist, and the fourth girl was African. Simon Cowell would have formed a new girl group if they could sing, we all know they can dance.

The first town we drove into was wealthy and sleepy, as was the second. Eventually, we drove down into Palamos looking for camping. Palamos is a beautiful coastal city just north of Barcelona, and it was obvious the wealthy Catalan Spaniards favoured the city for their second mansion. The Land Rover broke necks as we potted around the city, she gets a huge amount of attention wherever she goes. It was also abundantly clear that the Spaniards have a very different style of camping than the French do, the Spanish campsites offer a selection of pools and activities, have restaurants and games rooms and bathrooms with granite countertops, laundry rooms and immaculate campsites. All of this at the same price as a dirty, depressing French campsite. Why the French do not drive an extra 60 kilometres and have an excellent holiday, I will never know, but I understand that, even without official borders, for some, the idea of leaving their country is too daunting to contemplate. We are all told how dangerous or expensive or horrible the country next door is. It is not usually. We found a campsite with a huge, sparkling pool and the owner, impressed that we had driven so far, offered us a campsite at the off-season rate. We accepted and settled in for a few days, we had work to do, braais to make, and a route to plan.

The Catalonia region of Spain is situated in the northeast corner of the country and is autonomous but not independent. We soon discovered, after many conversations with fellow campers, that the Catalan people are fiercely independent and it was not long after we drove past Barcelona on our way to Madrid that the Catalan parliament announced an independence referendum. We had found the people of Catalonia to be cultured, compassionate and generous, and it was with mixed feelings that we witnessed the Spanish response to the referendum. Madrid declared war on Barcelona and riot police from the Guardia Civil and National Police Corps were bussed to the region, with orders to crush the "uprising". The good people of Catalan were shocked by the heavy-handed response of the police who considered the movement as treasonous. The riot police beat the stuffing out of anyone who stood in their way as they sought to shut down the referendum offices. Women, the elderly, local police and even the much loved and respected fireman found their skulls introduced to a heavy, rubber baton. It was heartbreaking to see the videos and images of people we may have befriended being treated with such passionate, organised aggression, but we understood why Madrid felt justified to behave the way it did. If the Spanish government had allowed the independence referendum in Catalonia, they could soon expect the same from the Basque country (the ETA terrorist group is Basque and had waged a bloody secessionist campaign for many years) as well as the regions of Andalucia, Aragon, Asturias, the Balearic Islands, the Canary Islands, Cantabria, Castile, Galicia,

Leon, Navarre and Valencia which each have a secessionist movement. To allow Catalan independence would be to endanger the Spanish state itself and by crushing the Catalan independence movement, they sent a very clear message to the other regions that Spain will remain intact. While we were sympathetic to the will of the Catalan people, we had recently witnessed the prosperity of the region and, though the police action reminded me of the heavy-handedness of the Venezuelan police, the Venezuelan people are starving, their government wholly and completely corrupt. And since Catalonia forms part of Spain and Spain is a member of the European Union, the Catalan people have all the rights, protections and privilege of any EU citizen. Catalonia is an industrial powerhouse contributing to 20% of Spain's economic output (and the Basque Country contributes 7%), Spain simply could not afford to lose the area and ultimately the territories which would follow suit, particularly as the country continues to struggle through a recession.

Overlanding across Spain is sublime, and soon you come to expect a few things; excellent roads, the cutout of a huge black bull atop large hills, castles and cathedrals overlooking prosperous and beautiful towns surrounded by hills and fields of dry grass. Finding free camping is relatively easy, and we often found ourselves camped next to a river, cathedral or castle. The food is excellent, the beer is great, the wine is great, and the prices are pretty good. Often, we would drive into a village and locals would beckon us to join them for a beer and tapas (finger snacks served with the beer or wine). Our route took us from just west of Barcelona to the city of Zaragoza and then on towards Madrid where we would need to get some new shock absorbers installed on the Landy. We stayed in an area of Madrid known as Alcala de Hernandes, and it rained heavily for two days. Apparently, it had not rained properly there for almost eight years, and our presence ended the drought. It happens like that you see, extreme things happen when we visit a country. During our time in the USA, they experienced the greatest amount of mass shootings, and Donald Trump was elected President, Baja Mexico flooded, while in the UK they had the worst terror attacks in many years (and a great summer), in Spain they had the greatest rain and the Catalonia rebellion. Later that month Portugal would suffer the worst wildfires in history, shortly after we arrived.

Our stay in Spain was brief, the first time around but, within a few months, we would return, and return the next year again.

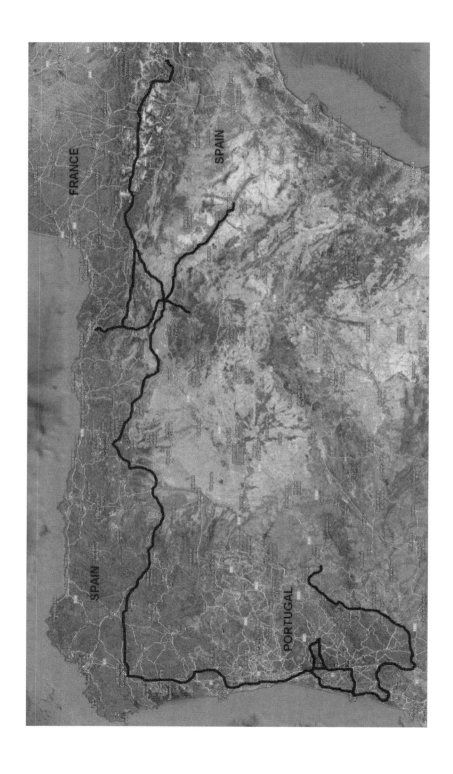

8

Pure Portugal

Portugal is a country which exists quietly next to her big sister Spain. Spain gets all the tourism, terror attacks, illegal immigration, headlines. Portugal goes about her business and being here I feel as if I am in South America, specifically Argentina or southern Brazil, not western Europe. The Portuguese (together with the Spanish) discovered the New World and once controlled many times the size of Portugal. One of the first Portuguese people we met was in a small city called Figueira da Foz (where we rented an apartment for a couple of months), and his name was Ruben. Over a glass of wine and after a scrumptious meal in his restaurant, Abrigo de Montanha (translated "mountain shelter", overlooking the Atlantic and considered the most beautiful restaurant in Portugal), Ruben explained to us how Portugal is the centre of the Universe. He had maps, charts and an encyclopedic knowledge of Portuguese history to back up his claims. Portugal became the first global empire in the 15th Century and after handing Macau to the Chinese in 1999 became the longest-lived colonial empire. Portugal possesses the greatest history, finest wines, most beautiful women, most beautiful landscape, finest people, best sailors and most delicious food. Ruben is a patriot.

Before we arrived in the country, Luisa found us a house-sitting assignment in the north of the country, and we arrived at the house on a Monday morning at 11 am expecting a relatively quick handover, a nice home and pooches to take care of for a month. We were in for a treat. The owner, Patrick, answered the door three long minutes after we knocked, standing on the hot, untidy patio waiting patiently with our best-trusted house sitters smiles fading. The house itself was cosy and beautifully decorated by a woman, had a swimming pool and a large kitchen and many attractive details, the dogs were old but energetic. Patrick had a red nose tracked by veins, short white legs, a potbelly and a thatch of silver-blonde hair. He sat down on the couch and spread his little legs, shouted at the dogs and began to tell us a long, sad story. His wife had left him and returned to England. She was a very bad person, apparently - deceitful and unkind. She had left him a few months before, and now they were fighting over the house - she wanted him to leave so that she could sell the house and he refused to budge. He then stood up and disappeared into the kitchen for a minute and returned to again sit on the dog hair leather couch. Legs splayed. He thought that she was just bored in Portugal and missed her family back in England, he thought she would come to her senses once the English weather drove her batty and she would return to the sunny house. I think she escaped. And Patrick was not leaving that day or the next or next week, maybe the week after that. He had hurt one of his skinny, pale, varicose ankles tripping over one of the dogs and the doctor had told him to rest and not to travel.

He then gave us an example of a limp we had not noticed before and a tour of the house, kitchen - large and strangely built, a half-empty beading plastic jug of wine stashed next to the fridge. The pantry - empty. The main bedroom - off bounds. Downstairs was the guest area - large airy bedrooms, a games room, a kitchenette. Outside a rusted imitation, Harley Davidson leaned next to an inviting blue pool. Keelan had a swim and Patrick invited us to stay as long as we wanted, before excusing himself and wobbling back to the kitchen. He returned with a crooked smile, heavy eyelids and no limp. He was cured! "Stay as long as you want". He seemed to be paying a lot of attention to Luisa and Jessica. Luisa and I began to bristle. Patrick then walked us across the road to a dead vegetable garden and a shed, "You can camp here as long as you want". What I have not yet told you is how the man loved the sound of his own voice and constantly chatted, sometimes incoherently. He was looking for ears. Ears to listen to his stories, ears to listen to his opinions, ears, no mouth. Patrick was drunk, and Patrick was lonely, and Patrick thought he had found a great way to find free ears. We left before I could make his ears ring. We had been so sure that we would be settled for a month that we found ourselves parked in the Landy wondering where exactly we would go, where we would stay for the next month, our funds were running low, and we had given ourselves a massive mountain to climb.

Portugal is rustic, ancient, progressive and modern. Whitewashed houses with terracotta roofs, a dry, temperate climate, friendly and most welcoming people, beautiful cities and ancient villages. Portugal does not have a powerful economy and wages are low, many young Portuguese travel to Northern Europe in search of higher wages and greater opportunities. The result is a country which needs immigrants to help boost the economy. We judge a country by a few simple criteria, and you can tell a lot about a nation by the state of its rivers and public areas and in a small town called Constancia, we found the best of both. The campsite was a mere 13Euro per day and was very well maintained. The river (Rio) Zezere flows past the campsite and joins the river Tejo (or Tagus, the longest river in the Iberian Peninsula) on a course for Lisbon and the sea. The water of Rio Zezere is crystal clear and ice-cold, revitalising and rejuvenating after another long, hot day, the sky at times grey with smoke from a million blazing Eucalyptus trees. The fires threatened to engulf the small town, and we all watched which direction the wind blew. We drove to a town called Avis, where the Land Rover club was holding a meeting.

We parked the Land Rover in the camp area, next to a road and not too far from the electricity box. A few people recognised us from our books and social media presence, and we were invited to join parties as we walked along admiring the Land Rovers. The Portuguese have their own style, and we soon learned that the braai was made to cook large, fresh sardines which are served on a piece of firm "integral" bread. The idea is that you use the bread as a plate and eat sardine after sardine after sardine while sipping on Super Bock beer (which is made from the water of the river Tejo) and Sagres beer (which is made from the water of the river Zezere) or sipping on a glass of cold Vinho Verde (green wine). The sardines, beer and wine are consumed all day and into the night until, at the stroke of midnight, the men, women and children will wander up to the little campsite coffee shop and drink strong, sweet espresso. Never in my life have I ever seen men swop drinking booze for coffee unless they had a very, very good reason. After the coffee, some went to bed, and others continued to party until the early hours of the morning. We have grown up in the last few years and called it quits after the coffee, headed back to the camper and hit the sack with a smile. The next morning, we swam in the large, cool pool and continued to wander around the campsite photographing the many Land Rovers, most of which were stock standard. I asked a middle-aged man standing next to a pristine green Range Rover Classic why the vehicles were all factory standard. He told me that it is illegal to modify a vehicle in Portugal. The entire vehicle must be factory standard, and that law applies to every vehicle registered for use on public roads. No wonder the Portuguese were regarding our Defender with such amazement - the large tires, camper conversion, LED headlights, bull-bar, winch, etc., are illegal, and if the Defender had Portuguese PT license plates the vehicle would be impounded faster than you can say Uma Sardinha mais por favor (another sardine please)! Only very few of the Land Rovers in the campsite that weekend had modifications, and it was understood that the owners were taking a huge risk driving the vehicles on public roads. One young Series owner had been pulled over by the police and fined 2,000Euro for having a military-style bumper which he had bought with the vehicle and was approved for military use. He paid the fine and sold the Series.

Our goal in Portugal was to apply for temporary residence, we had approached a Spanish immigration department but had found the requirements and process to be too uncertain and the waiting period too long. In Portugal, we decided to take the opportunity to apply for European residence, based on my British citizenship. The decision was made because we wanted the best possible future for our children, and despite the hype, Europe seems like one of the most stable regions on this planet earth.

The temporary residence process was not simple at all (reliving the stress and worry of this period gave me a mini-mental meltdown, and it has been a week since I have been able to force myself to sit down and continue writing this book). But, after two months of bending backwards, our spines did not break, and we were eventually rewarded with Portuguese residence. The immigration officials asked us, "Do you want to travel or do you want residence?". We responded, "We want both!".

Not long after the residence was issued, we were back in the Land Rover heading east. Our goal was to drive to Asia, and we were determined to make it, even though the residence application and process had drained most of our resources, we were confident that the sales of or books would

continue and we would find a way to pay for the carnet we needed to le
enter Iran and India. We headed up to northern Portugal and the Geres
National Park - we were on the road to Asia, perhaps!

Can Overlanding Europe be an Adventure?

This is a question I had asked myself repeatedly over the last few years. It
seems that most dream of overlanding the developing world, but what of
the developed world. Does a country need to be poor and dangerous in
order for an overland journey to be exciting and rewarding? We were
determined to find adventure in Europe.

Using the Wikiloc app, we plotted a route across northern Spain, through
Galicia, Leon, Castille, Navara, Aragon, the Basque Country, over the
Pyrenees mountains to Andorra and back to France. Our goal was to drive
on dirt roads and trails as much as possible and revert to paved roads only
when we had no other option. From the Geres National Park, we re-entered
Spain and headed northeast and found ourselves in mountain country. For
a week we simply followed our Wikiloc route and found ourselves driving
through picturesque villages which gave access to the mountain trails which
led to more picturesque villages. The food was superb, bearing in mind that
we do not eat in restaurants but make our own food using local ingredients.
We enjoyed steaks which rival Uruguayan beef and we enjoyed prices which
were lower than we had paid since South America. I suppose that is the one
benefit of enjoying locally grown produce. At night we camped either in
free camper zones or up in the mountains. Almost every town or village has
it's own allotted area, called aire, where campers can park for free. The idea
being that the campers are allowed to park for 24 or 48 hours and they will
spend their money locally, which they do. Most towns also have paid
campsites with amenities whose business does not seem to be negatively
affected by the free camper sites. But, overnighting on concrete is never our
first choice, and we were often able to camp on the trail, alone and
surrounded by stars, overlooking a mountain village, listening to the
cowbells ring while grilling some food on our little braai and enjoying a
beverage. We were falling in love with Spain.

Southeast of Bilboa, we came across a peculiar area nestled between low
mountains in the La Rioja region. The town of Mansilla de Sierra had been

flooded when a dam was built downstream in the late '50s. A drought had caused the water to recede, leaving the ruins of the old town exposed when we arrived. A hot spring full of naked bodies bubbled under a high road bridge where tourist vehicles parked. We drove down the steep dirt road leading to the water's edge and camped next to the ruins of a large house. Surrounding us were the campers of overlanders and hippies, young and old but we were able to access the most remote waterside camp because we drove a Land Rover. I prepared a fire for a braai overlooking the lake while Luisa prepared Keelan for a haircut. Keelan had not cut his hair since 2014 and had finally decided that it was time to remove the thick, blonde ponytail. With the family watching, Luisa took a handful of golden hair and cut off the ponytail. My boy looked like the man he was becoming, and we shared a cold beer as the sunset over the ruins. We were parked in what had once been someone's living room or bedroom, making a fire where their child's cot had once stood, washing our dishes where they once washed their clothing. The ghosts of the town surrounded us and joined us as we were entranced by the flickering flames, to look out across the water and ponder existence. The men and women who built that home could never have imagined that one day the fruits of their labour would be submerged in water, a disaster dictated by their government. They could not have foreseen that strangers from the other side of the earth would make a fire where their walls once stood. They had lived their lives in the pursuit of survival and success, never thinking that the river, which was the source of their hydration and nutrition would one day be forced to destroy their homes. I despise those who are forever warning of the end of our world and the end of our civilisation, their warnings keep us from either fully investing in our lives or granting us the peace to live as we choose. Since 1947, armageddon has been predicted more than eighty times by "credible" sources, many of whom have a Wikipedia page. Hundreds of thousands were duped by these con men and women and made terrible choices to ensure either their survival or everlasting life. The people of Mansilla de Sierra received notice to evacuate, and their world was destroyed for the benefit of others. The night sky was full of glistening stars which reflected off the lakes mirror flat surface. The fire flickered, we were warm, comfortable, fed and relaxed, but there was a sadness in the air.

I wanted to stay another night, there were no toilets or facilities, but a walk took care of bodily needs. Luisa wanted to move on. What Luisa wants, Luisa gets. We drove up, out of our near-perfect camp and came across a Defender 110 which had been parked overlooking our position. The British owner ran tours in the area and suggested that we take a drive to a desert called the Bardenas Reales, which was not too far away, apparently, and well worth the drive. We left the lake and drove past an ancient castle and along twisting mountain roads with very little traffic. The 200-kilometre drive took a few hours as we drove slowly, enjoying the countryside, small villages and comfortable temperatures. As always, we avoided toll roads and highways and rolled through towns which entertained few tourists.

Spain wears her history on her ancient sleeve. Castles dominate the hills and churches dominate the villages and towns, and it is abundantly clear that the royalty and the clergy were working hand in glove. The "Catholic Monarchs" booted the Islamic Moors out of Spain entirely by 1692 and had already begun the Spanish Inquisition in 1678 ostensibly to oust heretics, Jews and Muslims. Apparently, the inquisition was not nearly as horrific as we are lead to believe, the British are charged with starting a "Black Legend" as the Spanish were their political and religious enemies. Two worlds, the ancient and modern, live together peacefully throughout Europe and we marvelled at ancient buildings wearing neon signs as we filled our water tanks from a courtyard water fountain.

The Bardenas Reales would be relatively unremarkable elsewhere on the planet but are peculiar in Europe. The area is 100,000 acres of semi-desert which was an inland sea until the water drained into the Mediterranean 10,000,000 years ago. Together the water and wind eroded the area into an incredible collection of canyons, plateaus and isolated hills. The largest military zone in western Europe is located here, and Game of Thrones fans will recognise it as the Dothraki Sea from season six. There are limited areas of agriculture on the plateau which are a stark green contrast to the dry, chalky vista. We left the dusty main trail through the badlands and set off to explore on trails, which see almost no traffic. Luisa and Keelan filmed the Land Rovers progress as Jessica, and I drove through the most challenging sections of the trail. Seasonal rainfall had over the years eroded the trails, but even the deepest ruts did not pose any challenge for the

Defender. Tall, brown grass bowed in the stifling afternoon breeze as we explored further into the park but, eventually, we turned back to the main road when we found that the trail ended at the base of beautifully eroded ridges.

The fesh fesh dust covered the Land Rover in fine dust as we made our way back through the Bardenas, looking for a place to camp for the night. This would be the perfect place to free camp, but there were signs forbidding camping, so we continued to a town called Arguedas where an Aire free camp area was offered by the local community. We arrived and parked surrounded by French and Spanish camper vans, the area was paved and surrounded by trees and sandstone cliffs. The cliff was fascinating as it was dotted with caves which I imagined were inhabited by an ancient people. A quick search on the free WiFi revealed that the caves were dug in the late 19th century by locals who could not afford homes, each cave had its own living area, grain storage and garden, we were camped where their corn once grew. The caves, which retain a year-long temperature of between 18C and 22C, were inhabited until the 1950s when the state began a social housing project. Apparently, many troglodytes were reluctant to leave their wonderful cave dwellings, and I could imagine why, would you rather live in a cramped council house or live free surrounded by rock, with a view of the world? At night gaudy coloured lights lit the cliff faces and Luisa, and I had a chat while the children mainlined WiFi. So far we had some wonderful experiences driving trails and back roads and had managed to cross most of Northern Spain far from the beaten track, and our goal was to now reach Andorra via the Pyrenees mountains. What could go wrong?

Driving towards Bilboa the next day, the Landy began to misfire. At first, the stutter was gradual, but by the afternoon, she reminded me of K K K K Ken from A Fish Called Wanda! We tried to drive some logging trails, the misfire was at high revs, but at low revs, the engine seemed fine, the hope was that there was some gunk in the injectors and the recently added injector cleaner would help the engine to run smoothly again. The logging trails were up in the hills and very muddy after some recent rains. Sections of the road had been washed away, and the loggers had filled the holes with branches, steep drop-offs to the right taunted me as I drove and Luisa filmed. In low range, we drove slowly but surely through the doomed

Eucalyptus forest until we reached a steep grade. I slipped the Defender into second gear low range and began to ascend the slippery mud track. It was here that our problems started. The Land Rover would not rev freely, and we found ourselves idling roughly, unable to continue the climb. I tried again in low range first gear, but the fuel was obviously not reaching the injectors. We had two choices - reverse and return 20 km's to the main road the way we came or, Luisa advised while looking at the map, we could get over the hill and rejoin the road in 1 km. I shut off the engine then turned the ignition back on and began a bleed/purge cycle by pumping the gas pedal five times (one of the advantages of an ECU controlled Td5). After the last purge cycle, I started the Landy and drove her slowly up the hill with enough fuel in the fuel lines to get us up and over. At the top of the hill, we hit a large bump in the road and plume of smoke entered the cabin. "That smells like an electrical fire!" warned Keelan from the back seat. He was right. Stop, drop and roll! I had no choice but to continue driving up to the crest of the hill, if we stopped we might lose momentum and struggle to get moving again. Also, I was in denial and was hoping that a clump of muddy oil from the leaking transfer box had fallen on the exhaust. Luisa reacts like she always reacts when there is a problem - by screaming and predicting the very worst-case scenario. This is not helpful. At the summit, I shut the engine off and slid under the Landy to inspect while Luisa and Keelan sniffed the dashboard and battery box like bloodhounds seeking a burning fox. I saw nothing but an oily splodge on the exhaust, which might confirm my oily clump theory. Keelan insisted that the smoke smelled electrical and after checking all the visible electrical wiring we decided to keep on going with spanners to disconnect the batteries and the fire extinguisher in Luisa's lap. Bilboa was a 100 km drive away, and we decided to head there, find a campsite and work on the Landy. I suspected the fuel filter was blocked and needed to find a spare. We made it to Bilboa with the Landy shuddering along at any speed over 80 kph. It was nerve-wracking to drive in city traffic, concerned that the Landy might either stall on the highway or burst into flames! Our priority was to find a parts supplier and immediately contact our friends, and parts sponsor Bearmach, who did not have a distributor in Bilboa but had one in Vittoria, a city 80 km south on the road to Pamplona. A beautiful Brazilian called Sandra is the Iberian Bearmach representative and, despite the fact that it was late on a Friday afternoon, made some calls to arrange a service kit for us. By some miracle, she found a kit for us and told us that we could collect it the next day in Vittoria. Now, this sounds like a simple process, but it involved us driving around trying to find free WiFi we could connect to, at the same time hoping that the Landy would not die on us. While Luisa chatted to Sandra, I drained the fuel filter and did another bleed/purge cycle hoping that we could remove the gremlin without too much of a fight. Gremlins like to fight.

We camped in an Aire surrounded by large French motorhomes. Tucked between the big white rolling palaces, I found a Polish couple who were, like us, fighting to find a way to stay on the road. They had opened a mobile surf tour company (including rental surfer vans) which operated in Portugal and Spain and, while they had been able to live off the venture for almost two years, they struggled with the proclivities of their clients. Most of their clients were young Europeans, some of them were wonderful people, but many of them were very hard work. There were the party animals who just wanted to surf all day and get numb and happy all night, there were those expected to be pampered and served hand and foot, there were those who were so incompetent that they struggled to enjoy an easy life. We clicked with our new Polish friends. Often success only comes after many failed attempts, and it is the fight to face failure and start anew, which presents the most challenges. She was an elegant former model who could have quite easily chosen a life of leisure on the arm of a wealthy man. He was a former advertising executive, talented and full of ideas. They, like us, had been incredibly successful back in the "real" world, and they too had chosen the hard path and, like us, they had paid the price of serenity. I tried to help them with ideas. Write a book - done. Do a crowdfund for a great product - done. Write articles and sell images - done. Make awesome surf videos - done. I researched the couple later, and the quality of their work was exceptional. So where were they failing where others had succeeded? I had a theory, and I asked their opinion. The theory? It had occurred to me that nationality plays a huge role in social media following - people like to follow those to who they relate, they like to see those who have the same background and opportunities succeed, because that success is attainable for themselves. We are relatively unknown in South Africa. The thumb suck maths is thus: we have fifty million citizens in South Africa. Of those fifty million people, perhaps ten million would be considered middle class with expendable income. Of that middle class, perhaps 1% is interested in the great outdoors, camping, overlanding and vehicle-based travel. It all boils down to economies of scale. The off-roading and overlanding community in South Africa is relatively tiny, and of that community, there is only a small percentage of people who are interested in international overlanding. Americans make up the largest percentage of followers, and we did not really spend that much time in the USA. Our journey has been covered by international overlanding and Land Rover magazines, the BBC, Petrolicious and Gear Patrol and Uncrate and Outside magazine and if we were ourselves American, I truly believe that we would be in a league of our own. Think about it... A hypothetical family from Oregon gives up their successful business to travel the world in a Land Rover Defender. They drive solo from Argentina to Alaska, circumnavigate South America, tour east and southern Africa and drive from the UK to Turkey, all while homeschooling their children and writing three (or four) great books and making original and entertaining short travel documentaries. That family would be having a glass of cold water with Ellen Degeneres and interviewed by the New York Times. Our Polish friends are faced with the same dilemma. Germans follow Germans, the British follow the British, the Spanish follow Spanish speakers and the Portuguese love the Brazilians but not all English speakers follow English speakers. I also like this theory because it exonerates me of blame for the success which we have not yet achieved, I have an in-quantifiable, indisputable and wholly plausible excuse to give my wife when she asks for one.

And if you are to be an independent content producer, you need to have a large and engaged social media following. That van with a girl whose ass you follow on Instagram is distracting you from what I am trying to impress you with. A picture of my Defender on top of a mountain in Mexico or Peru, or Turkey, or Tanzania, my family raised on the road, the sacrifices we have made to get to where we are, all pale in the face of a Tacoma with an ass pretending to do something with an engine. Facebook and Instagram then keep flip-flopping the algorithms so just when you start to make headway, they shift the goalposts. I respect my new Polish model friend because she has the integrity to not prostitute her feminine gifts in exchange for likes, hearts and thumbs up. She could quite easily do that, no-one cares what language a body speaks, but, like us, she prefers to inhabit this world in a way which will continue to serve her as she ages gracefully. What will the ass with a van be doing in ten years? Hating gravity and dreaming of who she used to be. What will our Polish friends and we be doing in ten years? We would have refined those years of struggle and hard work into long term success. And this is why I am incredibly grateful for the type of people who choose to follow our journey. The people who follow us now will be there with us in ten years, they are the lifers, not just interested in overland travel as a fad. Thank you!

Back on the road we drove to Vitoria and made it to Aegis 4x4 ten minutes before they closed and a friendly, tall young man called Hector presented us with a box containing a fuel filter, oil filter, rotary oil filter and an air filter. Bearmach to the rescue. Unfortunately, the misfire remained even after changing the fuel filter and Luisa and I decided to make our way to a campsite in Pamplona where we could work on the Landy. The campsite was dull, and fallen leaves covered the ground. Our first priority after checking in and handing over 30Euro was to check the facilities and found what we were looking for - a covered braai area. With the kids comfortable and settled with the Land Rover in a corner of the campsite (far away from everyone so that we could work on the Landy without managements knowledge) Luisa and I engaged in that most enjoyable outdoor activity. With the fire going and a cold beer in hand, we discussed our options. Our many friends from around the globe responded to our social media posts asking for advice. Many suspected the famous Td5 "oil in loom" problem, many said the fuel filter and/or fuel pump, and some suggested the injector seals may be kaput. We had had a fuel pump fail in Argentina in 2015 and had wisely decided to build an access hatch into the floor of the camper when we did the conversion in Florida. We had been pressed for time, and I had come close to not building the hatch in favour of more pressing jobs but now was relieved that we had taken the time. If not, we would have to jack up the vehicle, remove the back tyres and drop the fuel tank to access the in-tank fuel pump, a process which can take a full day in a campsite. We had a spare fuel pump with our spares in the Land Rover, and it was decided, after the third beer, that we would replace the fuel pump, inspect the ECU for oil and check the entire electrical system. The next morning we got to work - removed the camper floorboards, opened the hatch, removed the fuel hoses, opened the top of the tank and replaced the fuel pump after inspecting the fuel tank for sooty black build-up which would suggest that the evil diesel bug (which we had suffered in England) had returned. The entire process took an hour (as opposed to two days thanks to the access hatch) and confident that the fuel tank was clean we took the Landy for a test drive. The misfire was gone! While others run with bulls with Pamplona, we run with Gremlins and bugs. The rest of the day was spent going over the Landy with a fine-tooth comb and the next day we hit the road to Andorra, our confidence growing as the Landy performed excellent at any speed. We headed back into the Pyrenees and enjoyed a few days of uneventful trail driving until we reached Andorra.

9

Andorra

Andorra is a tiny, wealthy, mountainous country sandwiched between Spain and France. It is not part of the European Union, but the Euro is the official currency, and the duty-free zones are a magnet for woman like Luisa who imagine everything they ever wanted, half price. I had a feeling this little country (the sixth smallest in Europe after 1. The Vatican 2. Monaco 3. San Marino 4. Lichtenstein and 5. Malta) was going to be expensive, as Luisa had an eye on a drone for our videos. We made our way up the mountain passes to a small village called Norís where men worked plastering a new boutique hotel, while locals and tourists sat drinking coffee outside a cafe, enjoying the warm autumn sun and blue skies. Luisa hacked into the WiFi to confirm the route on her various navigation apps while Keelan and I took a walk around the village. Jessica slept. It was the end of the summer season, and soon the pass would close as the snow began to fall. We drove out of the cobbled village, the paving giving way to an unpaved road and the road narrowing. We passed a few farms and farmhouses before entering a tiny stone village called Tor which boasted a café offering coffee and cake. Tor has only twenty-five inhabitants, but recently the village gained notoriety as during the Spanish real-estate bubble, locals came to conflict over the ownership of a mountain within the municipality, the conflict led to the murder of three people and is the subject of the book, Tretze Cases i Tres Morts (Thirteen Houses and Three Dead). No wonder the locals seemed miserable. I also suspect that the complete lack of sunshine for all of winter and 80% of summer has a role to play.

Turning left we crossed an ancient stone bridge over a wood strewn river and climbed up into the dark forest. This route was used to smuggle tobacco for many years and, whereas the major paved routes into Andorra have customs and immigration facilities, this route (known as Caraterra de Tor in Spanish) is not controlled. There are limitations as to how much electronics, alcohol and tobacco you can buy duty-free in Andorra but if you are willing to drive out of Andorra via the Smugglers Route, you can take as much as you can carry. Illegally. Eventually, we emerged from the tree line and back into partial sunshine, surrounded by green rolling hills and rocky peaks, grazing cattle and a few scattered stone buildings. Most of the road did not require 4x4, but we engaged low range for the steepest parts of the climb. I used to believe that low range was for tough stuff 4x4 work only, but since driving a lot of mountains the last few years, we have learned that low range is perfect for high altitude steep gradients whether ascending or descending.

We encountered no other humans on the road and within two hours had reached the summit where the dirt trail became perfect paved tar. Ski lifts and lodges dotted the slopes surrounding us and at 2,500m we had entered Andorra at Port de Cabús and began a descent towards the capital city, Valle de Andorra on the CG4 road. We passed villages where they used dollar bills to wash windows and wipe their tanned and toned bottoms. Each large, wooden house boasted a Porshe Cayenne or a new Range Rover, the workers drove Land Rover Defenders and new Discovery's. Ducati's and GS motorcycles dotted the countryside, and glum people in designer clothing lamented their horrible existence. Big money makes people miserable, it is a fact, particularly if the money is old. How old money works is the patriarch dies at 75 leaving behind his younger, bitter 60-year-old wife and greedy, aloof offspring which he hardly had any time for and who were raised by staff and schools. The matriarch now plays the miserable siblings off each other and exacts from them everything which she desires with the unspoken promise that the most favoured child will inherit the most. The siblings hate each other, their mother and their siblings' children. They compete with each other for favour, and the matriarch dispenses lashings of sour scorn on her sons and daughters-in-law. The old mother divides and bonds the entire family and only dies once most of her male offspring have themselves died. This is Andorra, and here they do not need soap operas.

Valle de Andorra's city centre reminded me of an upscale Las Vegas and by upscale I mean designer coats, designer jeans and designer shoes and not a red cap or pair of shorts and flip flops in sight. Until we arrived. We flip-flopped our way into a supermarket and searched for bargains. Leaving the kids in the Landy, Keelan on the WiFi and Jessica sleeping, we flip-flopped our way past Gucci and Armani and Bleh and made our way to every department store in the country, looking for that elusive "cutting edge but half price" drone. Luisa had loved Venezuela - back in 2014 you could get 75 Bolivars for a Dollar and there were still a few products on the shelves which you could buy at the same price as anywhere else in the world but at a great price by Venezuelan standards. As you had exchanged Dollars on the black market and everything is a tenth of the "actual" listed price. For hours we searched and Luisa, fearing the dreaded "buyers remorse" could not make a decision, of course, and told me to make a decision. "OK, is this a good price and a good spec? Yes? Then buy this one. But, if it is cheaper on Amazon, why don't you just buy it on Amazon? How much cheaper is it? $20? But this one is here in your hands now. Buy this one. No, we have searched Andorra, there is no better price. Buy this one. I don't know what the return policy is, ask him. He says it is 3 years in Andorra. But we won't be in Andorra for three years. What if it breaks? I don't know. Here, buy this box of chocolates and this bottle of whisky and this pair of headphones and this case of imported beers and this phone charger and this bottle of wine. Happy now? No? I give up".

That night we gorged on Kit Kat and Snickers while parked in a massive supermarket parking area surrounded by French and Spanish camper vans while Luisa scoured the internet for that elusive top-spec half-price drone. She did not find it, of course, and we left without a drone. I was relieved and disappointed. Relieved to have not parted with $500 of fuel money and disappointed because we really do need to invest in a decent drone if we are to elevate our documentary making. But, many of the countries we plan to visit do not permit the entry or use of drones which would present serious problems if we were to try and smuggle one across borders. Iran, Morocco and Kyrgyzstan are just three of the countries on our eventual route which had imposed outright drone bans and to fly on in the country is illegal. My strategy will have to be to buy footage from people who we meet on the road who have drones. Keelan has suggested that if we hand him $100 and some confidence, he will be able to build us a drone. I am sure he can do it.

It was a cool night parked sandwiched between the multitude of white box campers, the large three-story supermarket complex and a forest. In the morning, we rode the escalator up to the third floor where we were able to use the bathrooms, Keelan and I finished in five minutes then spent the next twenty minutes watching the world go by, waiting for the girls. Before hitting the road again, Luisa turned her attention to finding a "smugglers route" back out of Andorra. And she found one! Using the Wikiloc app, she plotted a route up out of the valley to a national park which shared a border with France, the route is nearly impossible to find, and we were not sure if we would be able to cross back into France, but we decided to give it a go. It would be worth the effort to avoid Andorran customs finding Luisa's illegal extra bottles of wine. It was a crisp, blue autumn day as we wound up above the city and back into the mountains. There was little traffic except for the odd Range Rover or Ferrari, and soon we entered the national park, which had no gate or staffed entrance. The road turned to well-maintained dirt, and we drove up to a plateau where a man and a jeep stood staring off into the distance, a couple of grumpy lycra runners worked for endorphins, and two elderly men encased in vintage leather rode ancient dirt bikes rapidly in the direction of Andorra de Valle. The trail forked ahead of us and our navigation system stalled in the rarefied mountain air, we had to make a choice based on instinct, and we chose to go left, down the trail from which the old bikers had emerged. It seemed that we were driving a trail known to very few (an Andorran friend who had explored Andorra extensively had never heard of the trail into France) and we had the suspicion that we might be heading for a dead end. The trail dropped into the shade of the mountain and continued to descend until we passed the gates of smallholdings, yellow and orange leaves on the ground, an icy stream flowing in the shadow of rock beside the trail which was slowly becoming a road. One vehicle squeezed past us, a French farmers Nissan SUV and rounded a bend to be met by a herd of longhorn cattle. Luisa was driving the Land Rover, and she moved over as far as she could to allow the beasts to pass. They stopped dead in their tracks and eyed us uncertainly. The cattle's colouring was similar to that of the African Brahman cattle, sandy grey, but they were shorter with rounded bodies and rectangular heads. Luisa turned off the diesel engine, and Keelan told to put his big blonde head back in the vehicle, a cry from behind the herd motivated and they shuffled forward, reached the Defender cautiously and broke into a trot as they passed the vehicle. Large bells hung from their necks, and they clanged past us.

We had seen those cowbells in Germany, Switzerland, Portugal and France - the bell ensures that the farmer is always able to find his stray animals when they are left to graze in the summer fields. The weather was changing gradually, and soon the mountains would be covered in snow, and the cattle would be warm and bored, safely inside their barn chewing on the hay which the farmer had worked all summer to grow and preserve. They will stand in the dull light and chew the cold winter away until eventually, the summer sun returns, the snow melts and the sweet green grass grows. It is the cold European winters which forged the Europeans into the successful people they are today - if you do not work hard in the summer, you will perish in winter. Cheese, sausage and marmalade are inventions of necessity which allowed the farmer to preserve food over long periods of time. Unfortunately, in this lonely, mountainous corner of France there were no procession of people in cultural attire to welcome the livestock home, no drinking of beer or eating German sausage - the farmer herded the cows, his Nissan led the way, and they live happily ever after, many miles from the nearest town. We had heard rumours of people who had disappeared into the Pyrenees and Alps to live uncomplicated lives as their ancestors had done many generations before them. They grow what they eat and eat what they grow and survive with little contact with the outside world. I never imagined such places could exist in modern Europe, but now I can.

Lunch was eaten next to a French motorway, little black sedans speeding past us as we ate brie and camembert cheese and sausage called fuet and fresh baguette. Our route was now direct to the ocean and on towards Italy.

10

The French Riviera (aka Cote d'Azur)

With no option to wild camp or explore mountain ranges, we joined the French motorway and blasted along the coast. We stopped outside St. Tropez and paid an exorbitant amount to rent a small holiday bungalow. Luisa needed WiFi as we had a few hundred copies of our second book to send out, we did not carry physical stock but had to facilitate the printing and delivery. It took a while, but every book sale was absolutely necessary for us to keep the wheels rolling. It is our lifeblood. There are a million experiences to be had along the French Riviera, but if you are reading this book, you are most likely not interested in that crowded, expensive part of the world. As overlanders, we enjoy seeing the sights and visiting places we had only ever heard of, but this coastline is the haunt of the wealthy, tanned bodies, expensive clothing, jewellery, perfume, yachts, sports cars and restaurants. We break the mould. After a couple of days of work, we were ready to leave the horrible bungalow with its tiny plastic everything, and head to the coast for a look at how the 1% live. We drove into Cannes, the sight of the world-famous film festival, and trundled along the beachfront, admiring the beautiful white penis' floating in the bay while old men with young wives stopped chewing crayfish to sit up straight and watch our hand-built Land Rover Defender camper roll by. I was expecting to be envious of the lives of the rich and famous, and while I admit I envied their wealth, it seemed they were equally, if not more jealous of my perceived wealth and our obvious freedom. The Land Rover bore no stickers or flags and the only hint of our origin in the mysterious number plate - CX34225. I imagined the diners debating or quietly considering where we might be from. Some would instantly recognise the CX plate as being from Knysna as that is another rich man's playground, but others would have been completed perplexed. And this gave me joy, a huge bubbling fountain of happiness. The wealthy envied us! They had everything, but they could only imagine what personal freedom we must enjoy. The Ferrari's, Porsche's and Lambo's did not get another look when the Defender is in town. I was reminded of parking the Landy in the middle of an exotic car show in Redmond, Washington surrounded by some of the most expensive metal on the planet, and the Defender stole the show - completely.

In Nice, we stopped to buy groceries in a neighbourhood which, though only a few kilometres from the coast, could have been on another planet. Moist, grey apartment blocks surrounded the supermarket, and an air of quiet desperation hung in the air, not dissimilar to the atmosphere you are served with your watery burger at the Denny's on the Vegas strip. A coin's throw away, people either fortunate or incredibly intelligent were spending a year's wages for a night of extravagance while here we bought groceries with the cleaners, cooks, waiters, servants and day labourers. We are of the people and can enjoy lunch with a king and dinner with his staff, we have no delusions of class, we have no airs, we have no graces. We ask nothing from either and try to give more than we take.

The road looped down towards Monaco, and we felt as if we had been transported back to our beloved Cape Town. It is no wonder that so many wealthy Europeans have chosen to make that incredible, mountainous African city their summer home. An investment in a mansion in Clifton will buy you a broom closet in Monaco, and this tiny country stopped shopping and preening and strolling to watch us drive by. We were lost in the maze of the cities narrow, perfect streets and shimmering tunnels feeling like the boys from Top Gear driving one of their mad inventions. A well-heeled man offered directions as we sat idling outside the white walls of an opulent hotel, our phone frozen by built-in redundancy and Angry Birds which had sensed a WiFi connection. It had taken a day to drive from St. Tropez to the other side of Monaco, and we looked down from the top of the mountain, once we had negotiated the maze of roads which led up from the bay below. Again I was reminded of our beloved Cape Town, and we were homesick, we had left one of the world's most inviting cities to travel the world unknown. At that moment I could have clicked my magical fingers and returned the family to our little, breezy home in Melkbosstrand, lit a fire and called the friends to visit - "I have some stories to tell".

Rain began to fall as we drove the highway which swept over bridges and through tunnels to Italy. Luisa's maternal grandmother was Italian and in some ways driving to Northern Italy was a homecoming for Luisa, as much as it had been for the kids and me to finally step foot on British soil. We stopped at a wet and windswept Italian gas station to check our maps and make plans for a place to park and sleep that night. Well dressed but miserable people arrived to drink coffee and smoke cigarettes. Such a concentration of wealth renders those who live on the periphery dissatisfied and bitter, eager to establish their social standing above others. We rejoined the Italian motorway where Fiats and Alpha Romeos drove either way too fast or much too slow, off-ramps and on-ramps to the highway were too short, and I soon understood why Italian cars drive fast and stop well. An old lady tried to drive us off the road, a young man overtook us but did not bother to leave our lane to complete the manoeuvre, the rain continued to fall, and we searched the countryside for signs of the serenity for which Italy is famous. We did not find serenity. Instead, we found wet, cold, old houses and industrial towns. We camped that night in an area designated for campers, outside a sports complex. Park 4 Night is an excellent app, and as many Europeans tour with campervans, there are often places to park legally and safely in most large villages and towns. Luisa and I sipped on a freshly purchased red wine, and the kids made themselves comfortable. Young and old locals heading home for the night would race anything with a motor up and down the road which was fringed by tall, thick reeds. That morning we entered a coastal village where we stopped to stock up on supplies. The Italians seemed friendly enough and well dressed, but hell-bent on getting a deal - if I stepped forward to inspect a loaf of bread, a little old lady would zip in front of me to establish what had caught my eye. It happened almost every time I became interested in any kind of produce. In a quiet Carrefour supermarket two weeks later, I stood alone in the capacious butchery considering the protein for that night's meal. I stepped forward to inspect some chicken carcasses and as if from thin air, a woman suddenly emerged and stole in front of me, leaving me standing mouth agape, staring at the back of her head. I could not control myself. "Hey, Luisa", I called with mock cheer, "can you believe this, an entire butchery and this old dear has to zoom in front of me, no-one else in sight and three tons of meat but she has got the chicken before I do. Incredible!". The perfect pile of blonde hair turned within its supple brown, fur-collared jacket, cream slacks and leopard print shoes to glare its painted wrinkles at me. How rude? "Seriously, Luisa, I mean is this an Italian sport of some sort, they shop as they drive!". Another old lady stopped pushing her cart to witness the commotion - perhaps there was a really good deal on chicken, she would not want to miss out. We are never disrespectful of the cultures we visit but sometimes enough is enough.

We were invited to Tuscany by a Facebook friend. Nigel had a beautiful home in Tuscany and took us to tour the Ferrari museum in Modena, he worked for Ferrari as an F1 buyer, and we were in good hands. Again, the Defender stole the Ferrari's glory as she had done in the USA. I am not making this up, a Ferrari is a Ferrari, but each Defender is unique, and ours stood out that grey day, dripping oil on pristine red-painted tar, not smug, just superior. If a Ferrari is the bull's balls, Defender is the entire bull. In my former life, I was employed by a young Greek oligarch, my job was to make him a lot of money, and I did my job very, very well. He dreamed of owning a Ferrari and a Toyota Land Cruiser, and I knew he had once stood in the same museum drooling while I was merely curious. I had my dream vehicle, and I had driven it all the way here via the Americas, no Ferrari can do that while accommodating a family of four. I knew my vehicle was not nearly as expensive as a red Italian but, this British African was far more valuable (I too am a British African, my "parts" came from the UK, but I was assembled close to Johannesburg, as was my Land Rover Defender 130).

That night we cooked a feast of beer chicken and roasted vegetables while Nigel fed us beer, wine and whiskey and we left the next morning to camp at a sosta near Bologna. A sosta is a camper parking and storage area which allows campers to park for a maximum of three or four days at a reasonable 15 Euro a night. We stayed there for 15 days. And in those 15 days, we saw the sun twice. It rained, hailed, snowed and sleeted. The sosta had a large heated recreation area and heated bathrooms and the elderly caretaker who took a liking to us friendly and polite South Africans. During the day Luisa and the kids sat in the rec room and did schooling and computer work while

I sat in the Land Rover and wrote Overlanding the Americas. Some days were more productive than others, but I was comfortable sitting in the corner of the camper, plugged into the camp electricity, a 15 Euro heater keeping the cool at bay. Snow piled up on the roof of the Landy and drifted past the windows as I recalled our experiences in the Americas, trying my best to write an account which was fair and honest, exciting and engaging.

Every moment of those fifteen days I was vindicated in my decision to convert the Defender into a camper, I could not have written a book sitting in a freezing cold rooftop tent. Every other night we would take advantage of a gap in the weather to grill some meat on our little braai. Every morning I would walk to the supermarket and would sometimes set off on longer walking journeys to explore the rural outskirts of town, a journey made difficult and dangerous by reckless drivers and a lack of pedestrian infrastructure. We had entered the sosta with no real plan for the next few months and left with a set destination - Naples to house sit a villa for a week and then Greece to care-take a private island for two months! While Luisa had been searching the website Trustedhousitters.com for a long-term house-sitting gig to sit out the winter she had come across a listing for a private Greek island. We knew that we were perfect for the assignment as we had taken care of an isolated farm in Baja, Mexico and were not afraid of being alone, in fact, we preferred to be alone. Luisa applied for the assignment knowing that there was a slim chance we could get the assignment as there were bound to be hundreds of applications. A few minutes later Luisa refreshed the island listing on the webpage and found the listing had been removed. She looked like someone had stolen her puppy. A message notification popped up on my computer. The message was from a handsome Namibian we had met in Malawi in 2010. Corné had since fallen in love and married. Last I had seen, he was living on an island. In Greece. Corné had pulled the listing as soon as he had seen our application and was sending me the information about the island, within five minutes it was decided. We were heading to Greece! This is the reward of freedom.

Naples was rough, littered, unkempt and unloved. The house-sitting gig was for an American military family who were based in Naples. Winding our way through twisted, filthy streets, we eventually found the house and a strange little woman from Oregon who was taking care of the villa until we arrived. The house was dusty but beautiful and cosy. The cupboards full of American brand food and a bag of Kingsford BBQ coal under the BBQ. It seemed that the American homeowners bought only fruit and vegetables from local markets, and everything else came over to Naples from the states on air force planes. For a wet week, we settled in and finalised Overlanding the Americas, me proofreading and researching to confirm my most controversial opinions while Luisa worked on the cover and the layout. We settled on the first edition which had been crowdfunded and which was called La Lucha, the cover four Mexican skulls representing each member of the family. One day, those first editions might be worth something, let's hope. At night I dialled into Radio Eagle and listened to a modern-day Lieutenant Steve (hohoho Frenchy) on American Forces Network Vicenza 106 bringing news from the states and playing mild pop. The kids played with the two old dogs, and the black cat with a crooked tail decided it wanted to live in the Land Rover. According to the homeowners, the local council was run by the mafia, and the streets were never cleaned, garbage infrequently collected. Each home in the area was beautifully painted and decorated, each had a well-maintained garden and a shiny car, but not one of those homes took care of the street in front of their home. The garbage piled up against garden walls, weeds grew to lie on the road and were trimmed only by passing car, trees scratched the roofs of taller vehicles, and at first glance, the area resembled the apocalypse. We left the evening the Americans returned, the lady of the house did not look well, and a week later, she messaged Luisa that she had just been diagnosed with cancer. Life is too short.

Recently I read a book titled Tribe: On Homecoming and Belonging. The more I read, the more I became convinced that I was reading a revelation, a manifesto for the modern man (and woman). Essentially, we are collectively miserable because our lives lack the meaning which motivated our forefathers to hunt, farm, wage war, and die happy at the ripe old age of fifty. Modern men have become complacent; we push shopping carts around overstocked stores, we sleep in a house we did not build, we hardly know our neighbours and the last time we had blood on our hands was when we slipped while shaving our vaginas. Life has become too convenient yet complicated, we are challenged but not in a way that satisfies us. In the endless pursuit for happiness we make ourselves miserable simply because "happiness" is overrated, wouldn't you much rather be satisfied?

A particularly interesting chapter in the book describes how many European pioneers abducted by Native Americans (who apparently prefer the name "Indian" because all people born on US soil are technically native Americans) eventually refused to return to their Euro American societies when given the opportunity and many of those who were forcibly returned, escaped to return to the tribes of which they had become part. Benjamin Franklin, troubled by the circumstances of white children captured by native tribes wrote, "They become disgusted with our manner of life and take the first good opportunity of escaping again into the woods, from whence there is no reclaiming them".

For almost all of human existence, young men were forged into men in the heat of battle. Many these days do not have the "opportunity" to go to war and earn the respect of their communities. I was raised in Apartheid South Africa and chose to wear a military uniform of some sort until I was 12 years old. It was only once I realised that I was part of a tribe but spoke the wrong language and would therefore never be truly accepted that I swopped my "browns" fatigues for a leather jacket and a pair of black boots. During high school all white boys were given military training but, when I received my call up papers at the age of 19 (until 1993 military conscription was compulsory for all white males), I decided to become a conscientious objector. I have always been fascinated by military history and would have benefited greatly from military discipline, but I did not have anything but contempt for the Apartheid government, how could I offer my life to their service? I missed a rite of passage opportunity (and a few years in jail but, fortuitously, the Apartheid government was elected from power and conscription was ended). Within two years I found myself sleeping on the beach in Tel Aviv, I had travelled as far from as home as I could afford and was determined to fend for myself until eventually, I returned home, a new man.

I had changed, but my society had not.

I escape into the woods every chance I get. It used to be that a man could claim a piece of land build a home and live a simple life, hunting, fishing, farming. Chopping wood for the fire which warms your home and cooks your food is immensely satisfying. Catching a fish or providing meat for the table is the most natural thing a human can do, and it earned a man the respect of his family. But once the home is built and the meat preserved and the crops planted, a man realises that he needs a community. A human needs a tribe, a tribe which allows him to be himself and offers him the opportunity to participate in the joys and sorrows of a large family which loves him as a brother, son, father, uncle. We gravitate towards those who are most similar to ourselves because, instinctively, we know that we need to be part of a community. The nation-state is too large and diverse to be considered a tribe, and when the interests of the leadership supersede the needs of the people, divisions are created (which the leadership then exploits). Sports fans and religious adherents are similarly united but separate. A tribe is a large family, democratic by nature, settled or nomadic.

We are the overlander tribe, and we are nomadic. There is something within us overlanders which drives us to explore, we are drawn to the open road, to the wild, to places most others will never experience. Overlanding, particularly the international variety, is addictive simply because the experience is so difficult but rewarding, your soul is satisfied, and your psyche sated. However, we are a tribe which does not live together, the very nature of our pursuits keeps us apart, but we understand each other's motivations and pursuits. Some of us choose not to live in a community.

Seven years ago, I sat on a comfortable couch looking through a wall of glass at the ocean which almost surrounded my home. At the age of 37, I had all the security a man could ask for, but I was miserable. Why was I miserable? The year before we had driven our Defender from Cape Town to Kilimanjaro and back. A trip which took almost six months and which had been incredibly difficult but intensely rewarding. We had escaped our comfort zone, and we had met incredible people, the kind you can only meet on such a journey, the kind of people who instantly become friends for life because we are part of the same tribe. Returning to the dull daily routine, the repetitiveness of which reduced weeks to a blur, the suntan faded, the fat returned, the hair turned grey and the skin sallow. I had found myself (and my tribe) out on the road, but here I sat, a shadow of the man I had briefly become. I eventually came to the conclusion that we needed to live a life of purpose, to live in the pursuit of knowledge, experience and love, not in the single-minded pursuit of wealth. I am writing this while living temporarily in Greece, surrounded by the ocean. Our lives lack security, but they are full. Each day is unique; we are challenged to grow, adapt, perform, learn and succeed. I am discovering who I am by living a life in search of knowledge and the satisfaction earned through adversity. I am meeting members of my tribe and communicating with them, we may not be together, but, we are not that far apart.

A traditional relationship between man and woman has roles and duties assigned to either based on their gender. The man took care of household and vehicle maintenance, brought home the bacon and flipped the meat on the Friday night BBQ. The woman took care of the man, the offspring and the home. But, this is not 1952, woman have liberated themselves from the kitchen and are taking over the corporate world. Yet, it amazes me that there are still men out there who cannot cook the simplest meal, it is a fundamental skill we should all possess, the ability to feed ourselves.

Young men need role models, and that should be their father.

My father left when I was ten. He was not a great role model, and we only really spent time with him on weekends as he was a travelling salesman. My mom, who had been a housewife, had to suddenly learn how to drive, get a job and provide for her three children while their father was off making himself happy. She worked long hours and returned home every evening exhausted. We soon learned to repair and iron our own clothing, cook meals and clean the home (mom will laugh reading this, she had to beat me with a wooden coat hanger to get me to clean my room).

"Humans don't mind hardship, in fact, they thrive on it; what they mind is not feeling necessary. Modern society has perfected the art of making people not feel necessary.

It's time for that to end".

Mr Unger should have written Tribe twenty-five years ago.

We left Naples at 11 pm and drove through the night to the port city of Brindisi where we would be taking the ferry over to Greece. It was a long night of driving, but we were determined to get the early morning ferry as the ferry ride itself was to be twelve hours long. Night driving can be enjoyable if you have a good flask of coffee and an audiobook or podcast to listen to. At 4 am, we arrived at Brindisi before having two hours sleep and driving to the port to buy the ferry tickets and board the ferry which had seen better days in the 1960s. Most of our ferry companions were hard-drinking, heavy smoking Bulgarians, and we took up positions in the quieter section of the restaurant where we would sit impatiently and wait for Greece to arrive. The engine throbbed constantly, and a storm broke on the Mediterranean. My fear of ferries returned in full force, and we took a walk to ensure that we knew where the exits and lifeboats were located. At night we arrived in Igoumenitsa, Greece and I drove the Defender out of the ferry, collected the family and drove straight out of the port - the only semblance of passport control had been the two friendly Italian policemen who had inspected our vehicle documentation that morning in Italy. Greece might share economic woes with Italy but seems to be in much better condition - the infrastructure modern and maintained, beautiful new roads, tunnels and bridges and not a piece of litter in sight. We parked outside a gas station, restaurant of glass and fine wood and slept lying down for the first time in two days. The name of the island we were headed to was Silver Island and it lies north of Athens in the Aegean Sea. Rested and eager to get onto the island, we drove across inland Greece and were surprised by the beauty and rustic charm of the interior. Everyone visits Greece to enjoy the coast, but we found places which were hardly ever visited by foreign tourists and we were treated with genuine affection by people who did not view us as walking wallets. That was still to come. We arrived at the town of Gilfa at 2.10 pm and missed the 2 pm ferry. We knew Corné and his wife Lissa were waiting for us and they were concerned that the sea might become rougher later in the afternoon. At 3 pm we caught the ferry across the Aegean and then drove to Oreoi where we met Corné and Lissa and bundled our belongings onto the cold dock before taking the Landy to be parked in front of a small supermarket. The Landy was to be parked for two months of winter, and I removed both batteries and all the jerry cans from the roof. We would have loved to take the Landy to the island, but the Greeks have cornered the market on sea transportation and would have charged close to 3,000Euro to take the Landy on the 7-kilometre sea journey to Silver Island. Had I been able to take the Landy, I would have rebuilt her interior while we waited for winter to pass. We joined Corné and Lissa on a small fishing boat and pottered out to meet our new home.

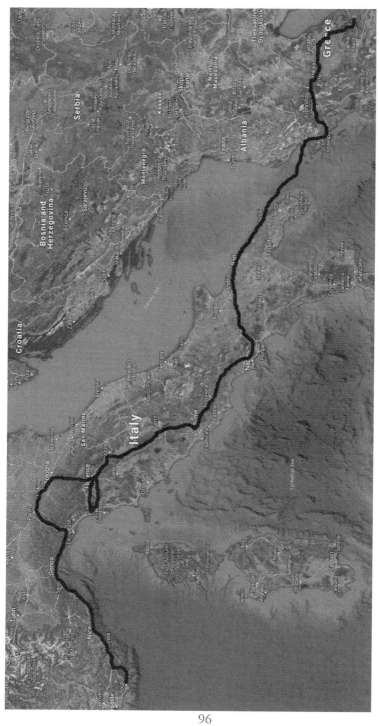

11

The Island

The island has an atmosphere and a personality. Shaped roughly like the number 8 (the symbol of eternity) it is just under a kilometre long and just over 400 meters wide at her widest point. The southern point houses a temperamental abandoned lighthouse where Leonard Cohen would have sat in the evening drinking red wine and writing songs about his broken heart left in New York. The northern half of the island housed the main buildings - two small villas and a workshop area. The western half of the island received the most sun and was dry and covered with olive trees, the eastern half wet and bore completely different flora, these two halves are the split personality of the island - the joy and light, The Sadness and cold. Corné and Lissa had resuscitated the infrastructure after many years of neglect, rebuilding the old houses with their own hands before opening a highly praised yoga retreat. To quote the Silver Island website:

"Much of the magic that is Greece lies in the names of the islands. Many of these sun-soaked jewels of the Aegean were named after the gods of Greek Mythology. Silver Island is no exception.

In the ages now gone by and shrouded in magic and folklore, Silver Island was known as Deucalion – a semi God. Deucalion and his wife Pyrrha were credited in Greek mythology as being the re-creators of the human race after a great flood; their story has certain parallels with the story of Noah's Ark. This is the story of Deucalion and Pyrrha. Zeus, ruler of Olympus, God of gods and men, and god of the weather, was angry with Prometheus, the god of fire. Deucalion was the son of Prometheus.

The use of fire had been the privilege of the gods alone, but Prometheus had given this gift to a human whose inadequacy to handle it had turned humans evil and wicked.

Zeus became angry with Prometheus and all humans and thus decided to create a terrible storm to end the human race on earth. But Prometheus intervened, and Deucalion and Pyrrha (daughter of Pandora) were chosen by him to recreate the human race.

They made and provisioned a great Ark from Silver Island, where they lived and rode on the fury of the storm, sailing for nine days and nights and found themselves on Mount Parnassos.

It was here that they gave thanks to Zeus for their deliverance and they made an offering to Zeus and asked that a new generation be born. While doing this, they heard a voice commanding them to "cast the bones of their mother over their shoulders" – the stones of mother earth. They do as the voice commanded and all the stones that Deucalion threw became men and the stones Pyrrha threw became women and so mankind was reborn.

The modern-day Greek word for people is "Laos" which is derived from "Laas" the ancient Greek word meaning pebble and stems from the myth of Deucalion and Pyrrha. It is said that Helen was born of the union of Deucalion and Pyrrha and that all kings and queens and noble people of Greece are their direct descendants by union.

In the Greek Encyclopedia and in numerous references, Silver islands latitude and longitude are listed and confirmed as Deucalion and the little island a few hundred meters off the north of Silver island, as Pyrrha. It is also thought that the temple of Demeter may be found in the peninsula called Agios Demetrios some 900 meters North of the island".

There are rumours of Nazi gold, as three German soldiers had been stranded on the island at the end of WW2. I searched but found nothing.

We settled into the island and were instructed on how to maintain the water and solar system, given a walking tour and after a hot shower, enjoyed a night falling asleep to the sound of waves. Within two days, Corné and Lissa sailed off towards an adventure, and we made ourselves at home - the island was now ours and for two months, we would become part of her history. Keelan and I worked with the ancient tractor and hand saws to clear many of the tracks which circumnavigated the island. The western side hot and dry, the eastern side cold and damp. A large pile of logs and sticks was our woodpile, and we took the time to prepare a few loads of wood, enough fireplace wood for a week. The wood was a mix of pine and olive, and much of it was rotten, but we found plenty of stumps which needed to be chopped or long branches which needed cutting with the small chainsaw before being reduced to chunks with the axe. This was to be my weekly workout, apart from the daily walks around the perimeter of the island to check the small coves for sea litter and that there were no unwelcome visitors. There are no private beaches in Greece, they are open to all, and sometimes hunters would visit the island to hunt grouse. Fishermen would sometimes moor at one of the two small jetty's, and there were workers scheduled to arrive the next week to work on new workers quarters. With my Brazilian machete in hand I would walk the lesser-explored paths and cut back the overgrowth, a small quad bike with a plastic bread basket strapped to the rear was my main source of transport and every morning and evening I would ride around the island inspecting the water tanks and solar panels, the lighthouse and the water supply from the mainland. We soon settled into a routine - I would wake up early, usually before sunrise, and prepare breakfast after a walk. Luisa and the kids would do their chores and settle into their work and schooling in the small but cosy lounge area where the fireplace was the only distraction. In the first weeks, the weather was pleasant, and we would eat lunch at the large, white outside table listening to the chickens argue while watching the seagulls soar above us and boats pass below. At sunset, we would prepare a simple dinner or make a braai of rich loukaniko sausage and lamb, served with ripe tomatoes, onions and delicious feta cheese. The local rosé wine welcomed the stars and Luisa, and I would sit quietly and discuss the future, the past and the present while enjoying the calm and solitude. During the quieter evenings, I sat alone and restored an old SOS signal and a ship to shore radio and used my wood carving knife, a gift from Canadian Bill, to transform driftwood into figments of my imagination. The kids and Luisa would watch a series or a movie on a laptop.

We heard that the winter storms could be quite violent and that we might receive snow. The buildings were built for hot summers, and we had to be prepared for the storms when they came. Corné and Lissa made certain that they had left us with enough gas, diesel and water to wait out the storms and the solar system was the best we had ever seen with a bank of batteries and a large diesel generator which would kick in automatically if the power was low. We would not be suffering through the winter. A week after arriving on the island a storm swept slowly across the Aegean, there was no snow, but there was a lot of rain, and we were able to keep warm and busy with the fireplace heating the lounge and the WiFi providing contact with the outside world. Our pantry was stocked with a week's worth of canned food, rice, pasta, sugar, vegetables and a bag of chocolate - all of which Luisa rationed with the discipline of a military quartermaster.

The only drawback of being on the island was the reliance on unreliable and extortionate fisherman who doubled as water taxis. Evangelos and Giorgios were our lifelines and connections to the mainland. We had agreed with Corné that they should take their small speedboat in to dry dock as I was not comfortable piloting a boat across a tidal strait and the storms were sure to break the boat from the anchor in the small bay. Evangelos charged 70Euro for a one way seven-kilometre trip to town. Giorgios charged 50Euro as he had a much smaller boat. So we either had to pay 140 or 100Euro return if we needed to go to the Lidl supermarket or to check on the Landy and explore the town. To put this in perspective, a couple of young locals had arrived on the island in the summer offering take-away food to the guests - even with a significant mark-up you can only pay so much for souvlaki and the delivery costs from the mainland could not eat all the profit. The local grocer had an arrangement with Corné and Lissa, and he provided the groceries to the island at a significant markup - a tax which our friends were happy to pay for as long as they were contributing to the local economy they would be welcome in the community. If they had to buy a large boat to ferry clients and supplies, they would infuriate both the grocer and the fishermen who had come to rely on the island for a constant and healthy source of income. They would find their guests unwelcome on the mainland, their water supply cut off, the beaches crowded with fishermen and the island regularly trampled by trespassers.

They would be driven mad by a population who relied on the pockets of tourism which fed foreign reserves into villages which would be otherwise destitute.

We sent a grocery order to the grocer, and Evangelos delivered four bags of basic supplies for which we were charged 300Euro and a delivery fee of 70Euro. At 370Euro a week for the food we would soon be burning through all our cash even though Corné had given us 1,000Euro for food. We were not obligated to pay the "gringo tax" and arranged for Giorgio to collect us on a calm, sunny day. We walked around Lidl and filled three shopping carts with supplies and paid a total of 400Euro for a month's supply of food plus Giorgios 100Euro for the round trip. As we were loading the food, the grocer arrived to witness our treachery, a look of stunned betrayal on his face, he was deeply hurt. Well, he had his chance, and he blew it, I knew that not shopping with him would not damage his relationship with Corné and Lissa and felt no obligation to pay exorbitant prices. We were caretakers, not guests.

A week before Christmas, a Texan family flew into Athens and drove a rental car over a snowed out pass to enjoy the island with us. We had met Scott at an overland rally in 2016, and his wife Kacy and daughters Kiley and Charlotte joined him to visit the crazy African family on an isolated island. There were two ways this could go - we could either murder each other or we could become one big happy family. The first few days would tell. Kacy and Kiley would go running every morning after a hearty breakfast of eggs, toast, muesli, sublime Greek yoghurt and sweet oranges. Charlotte and Jessica would play while Luisa worked and Scott would join Keelan and I as we worked the paths surrounding the islands, clearing the brush and trimming the trees. There were three quad bikes on the island, but only one was working properly, Scott and Keelan worked together and were soon able to get all three bikes running properly. We soon fell into a rhythm and became good friends.

Scott was not the kind of guy who could sit still and he was forever busy exploring the island, flying his drone, taking photos, working on a treehouse, working with us to maintain and prepare the island for the summer, teaching me how to take better photos and turning down yet another offer for an evening beer or glass of wine. Christmas came, and we enjoyed a simple celebration and the giving of simple gifts, (the way Christmas should be) and a quiet New Year. Kiley inspired Jessica to run, and Charlotte (who whistled constantly) played boule and helped her mom with the handwash laundry and adopted me as a jungle gym. The family are scientists, engineers, runners, the best example of America with a deep sense of morality and community. We knew we would miss them when they left, which they did after Scott travelled with us and, without being asked, restocked our pantry (Evangelos arrived to take us to the mainland a day late which infuriated me, what if we had a medical emergency? This perhaps was the price we paid for not greasing the grocer's palms).

We waved goodbye to our friends, standing on the small jetty where I had pushed Scott into the freezing sea, and he had narrowly missed stepping on a spiky black urchin. We had swum together while the girls explored the rugged coastline on the kayak's we had brought down from the work area with the leaky old tractor. We waved goodbye on a crystal clear blue morning, the same blue skies which greeted us every morning during their visit and the next day the clouds moved in, the storms rolled up, the winds howled, and we did not see blue sky for two long, wet, frigid weeks.

The island takes on a new personality in late December. Every last glimmer of summer heat and glamour is scrubbed from the surface, the cold west is the front in a war of wind and sideways rain and occasional hail. We had to ration wood, and the generator ran for an hour every day, water began to flood the villa from its foundation. Keelan and I took turns every morning and evening to trudge up the path to the solar and water system to ensure that all the levels were healthy. The rain was filling the grey water tanks and I proudly reported their levels to Corné, as if I had some hand in ensuring that they filled sufficiently for him to have a moist summer garden (I had a small role to play, ensuring that the gutter system which fed the tanks was in good condition and free from debris). And when there was a problem with the water supply from the mainland, I sent videos and photographic evidence of a forensic audit of the pump activity and tank levels over a ten-day period - I had a lot of time on my hands, it is true, but I also wanted to be sure that we handed back the island in better condition than we found it.

When there was a break in the rain, Keelan and I would take the quad bikes for a ride around the perimeter ensuring that all was in order and enjoying the muddy roads. One morning, after a particularly violent storm, I found a Terrapin turtle washed up on the jetty. I then found another and another and another, six in total varying from the size of a saucer to the size of a side plate. We did some research and discovered that they were freshwater turtles who must have been washed out of their river by a storm. They stank like open sewers (a defence mechanism) and would shit on you if you picked them up. They would search the island for freshwater and would die if they did not find any. The only freshwater on the island was an ancient natural well next to the tiny church/smoking area, and they would never find that, or they might, but I could help them along. Back at the jetty, we rounded up the foul reptiles and carefully scooped them into a bucket which we then strapped to the back of the quad bike and rode them up to the well while gagging. While lowering the turtles into their new home I fell into the deep, dark, muddy well, balancing the turtles bucket in one hand while trying to scramble up the muddy banks which caved as I clawed at them, an ancient Greek water beast speeding up from the depths to devour me like a snake eats a mouse, the stinking reptiles falling out of the bucket onto my clothing. Keelan laughed and laughed and did very little to save me from a wet, painful, stinking death. Eventually, I saved myself, and though I checked on the turtles every day, I only saw them once again, perhaps the water beast had snacked on them.

A hawk pair shared the island with us, but we only ever saw them briefly, harassing the colony of seagulls on which the predated. Occasionally we found the furry white skeleton of a young gull and once stumbled across the male hawk in a field near the main water tank. He was hopping on the ground and jumped into an olive tree and vanished before our eyes as if he had never been there and was only a figment of our imagination. Another day the earth began to rumble to deep booming explosions. The booms would vary in depth and frequency, and Luisa became paranoid, fearing an earthquake. We rode around the island (by now the storms had passed, and we were again enjoying blue skies) and tried to establish where the noise was coming from, we emailed a Greek contact we had been given in case of emergencies and he had no idea where the explosions were coming from and Corné and Lissa had never heard the mysterious noises before.

An old fisherman appeared on our doorstep one misty morning, his face wrinkled and creased by decades at sea, his hand's crooked claws leathered by ropes and nets and hooks and scales. His name was Papu, and he had brought us a gift of blue and yellow fish. I offered him coffee, and we sat together in the breezy living room, the temporary plastic winter blinds flapping in the breeze. Papu lit one cigarette after another while he sipped on his coffee, an arthritic hand balancing the mug more than holding it. He spoke no English, and I spoke no Greek but many years of travelling distant lands had taught me how to communicate without the reliance on words. Words sometimes cause problems. Papu was married, and his wife lived alone near the port in Oreois most of the year while he searched for ever-dwindling fish. Huge schools of tuna mocked the fisherman as they thrashed through the water, but they were protected by law, and they seemed to know it. The small colourful fish he had brought as a gift were known to cause hallucinations, we needed to cook them properly, boiled for five minutes then grilled or baked. His boat was moored at the western jetty, and that was where he spent the night, protected from the swell by the island. He wore a thick woollen jersey and an old fisherman cap, I asked him if I could take a photo of him and he posed - V for victory, the cigarette smouldering between his wooden fingers. By the time he left, the mist had cleared and we had enjoyed another pot of coffee. Papu returned to visit once every two weeks, and when I ran into him in town, he greeted me warmly - he did not make a living from foreigners and could afford them genuine friendship.

Our family was temporarily extended by the two pets which we were caring for - Lulu the long hair German Sheppard mix who Corné had rescued and Cosma, a dominant tabby which ruled the island with ferocity. Cosma left his mark on all of us, long, itching scratches. He took two weeks to warm up to us (except Jessica who he loved from the first day) and would come and go as he pleased, lying for a long tummy rub before being spooked by an ancient ghost and shooting out of the room, leaving the rubber tending a bloody wound. It was his party trick. Lulu was the most silent dog, and we only ever heard her bark once on a dark, stormy night. Her party trick was to scratch on the door, wait to be let in, lie down for a minute then stand at the door to be let out, repeated throughout the day and late into the evening. Lulu was Corné's dog, and she sought out the men in the family, loving and affectionate her Kryptonite was thunder. She would pace in circles endlessly even before the thunder began and once the rumbling started she was consolable only by me, perhaps I smelt like Corné. After an hour trying to placate her, I took a mattress into the living room and lay with Lulu, rubbing her as she shivered and moaned, her butt in my face. We stayed like this for eight hours until eventually the storm passed and we were both able to sleep, exhausted. At least we had the fireplace to keep us warm.

Cosma chased rodents in the late afternoons and sat on the roof when the sun shone - scanning the island for intruders. There was a second cat on the island, a stray which had been dumped by a fisherman and I would leave food for the cat near the staff quarters, behind the small villa and adjacent to the workshop where the quads and tractor stood. I only saw the stray black cat twice; once after a huge storm and the cat had not eaten in three days (I knew this because the bowl had not been emptied) and once again on a warm afternoon. Cosma had followed me up to the workshop and spotted the stray just as I did and attacked, chasing the stray up a tree and then into the bushes. Cosma was a dick.

The days I enjoyed the most were the wood chopping days once a week when the sun was strongest. It was on these days that we would all go about our chores and I would often come across Luisa or Jessica as they hung washing to dry (hand washed) and I walked past with a wheelbarrow full of wood. Keelan would sometimes join me to work the wood, but often his mother would have him doing other work, so I worked alone. The cutting pile sat at the top of the hill surrounded by tall green grass, ancient grape vines and knobbly olive trees. I checked the chainsaw oil and fuel before sharpening its blades, the axe and my machete. Wearing gloves, I would sort through the pile of branches, looking for logs which I could chop into 40 cm lengths and split with the axe. The best logs lay wet beneath piles of branches, driftwood and planks and some would be rotten, by the end of our stay on the island we were reduced to burning branches and the larger sections of logs which were impossible to split with an axe. After sorting the logs for cutting, I would lay them across two logs and cut the sections with the small chainsaw, before splitting with the axe I would take a break and look out across the island to the lighthouse, to the islands in the distance and to the fishing boats which anchored nearby.

The future was uncertain for us, we were planning to drive to Asia, but it did not seem like we would be able to afford the bureaucracy - Iran and India demanded carnets which could only be issued where the vehicle was registered (South Africa) and which required substantial deposits. Some Asian countries had shut their borders to overland vehicles (the Chinese had started running their own tour groups across borders which undercut local tour agencies), and other countries did not allow right-hand drive vehicles. Our books had been selling well, which covered almost all our expenses, but we had recently seen a massive drop in sales. We had self-published all three of our books through Amazon. I regularly search our titles on the internet, and I found two sites selling our books new, which was impossible as only Amazon and we had the original book files. I researched the websites and discovered that both were owned by Amazon who I emailed to enquire whether we were earning a commission on our books sold through their other sites. Amazon responded by asking me to prove that the books were our intellectual property! I suspected that Amazon was directing the sales driven by our social media work (we do all the marketing for our books) to these other sites and processing the sales there without paying any commission which equals pure profit for them and sleepless nights for countless other authors and me. At the same time, Facebook adopted a "pay to play" strategy and the social media platform into which we had poured thousands of hours of work based on, "It is free and always will be" now demanded that we pay to boost our posts which were now hidden from our followers. So, I pay to boost the post on Facebook which drives the sales to Amazon, who directs the sales to other websites and steals our profit. Now I am just waiting for Google to screw us. I would rather live on that island forever, growing our food, tending a herd of goats, fishing every day and living a simple life. But that is not an option. Instead, I enjoyed the time I had there, the sun on my back and a cool breeze blowing through the long grass. A boat heading for the horizon, the hawk hunting seagulls, my family working together to ensure we had all we needed, two weeks of paradise left before we were back on the road, heading optimistically into the unknown.

Corné and Lissa returned and told us of their adventures. The island was ready for them, all the buildings had been cleaned and repairs done (the roof of the massage room had blown off during the storm which scared Lulu, and we had nailed it back on and reinforced it). The roads had all been cleared, the trees trimmed and the debris moved to piles, the stone walkways had been weeded, the gardens cleaned and maintained and all the propane tanks, water tanks and fuel tanks had been swopped out or topped off. All they needed to do is walk back in, put their luggage down and get busy with the projects they had planned for the new year. Before they had even reached the main house, Lissa asked us to return to take care of the island the next year. In my heart, I knew we would not be able to, but I told them that we would if we could. Nothing would make us happier than two spend another two months in paradise. We grilled lamb and drank the last of our wine and the next day we handed over the island.

The boat came to fetch us in the morning, and we drove the tractor down to the jetty, full of our meagre belongings. The jetty was barely big enough for the tractor to turn and I had nervously driven it there half a dozen times without driving into the sea. This time I let Corné do the driving. Lissa waved as the boat departed, Lulu by her side and she continued to wave until she was a mere speck on the horizon. We were all quiet, subdued, sad to be leaving, anxious about the road ahead. We had driven the Landy once during the two months, and she had developed a misfire, which I treated with some German diesel treatment. While the family and Corné waited at the jetty, I returned to retrieve the Landy from where she had been parked in front of the angry friendly grocer. I installed the batteries and was relieved when she started up on the third turn of the key, then drove to the jetty to collect the family, pack the Landy and say goodbye to Corné. He left with hugs after securing a promise that we would return. I said I would do my best. We drove the Landy to the ferry and made it across just as the sun was setting but could not leave the town; the misfire had become so bad that we could not drive up hills and Gilfa town sat surrounded by tall hills.

With the sun setting, we decided to sleep near the ferry dock and tackle the hills again in the morning, which was wet and windy. We had asked Bearmach to send us a box of parts and filter items, and in the morning, we changed the fuel filter and bled the fuel system before attempting to make it up the hill. We did not make it. The Landy made it halfway up before misfiring terribly and stalling in the middle of the road. We rolled back off the road and bled the fuel system twice before the Landy would start again and get us back down the hill. Driving in low range did not help. We tried to get up the hill again, getting some speed up which was sapped by a sharp corner at the base of the hill. Again we stalled. Perplexed and pissed off we returned to the town and found a small gas station. The owner said we could use his oil pit to service the Landy if we bought the oil from him. While Luisa researched our misfire and gleaned advice from the online tribe, I serviced the Landy, and the rain continued to fall. We changed all the filters and the oil, replaced the air bleed valve and filled the new fuel filter with injector cleaner as advised by an Englishman called Nick. We added fresh fuel and a pint of diesel treatment. The Landy made it up the hill, and after driving for half an hour on the freeway the misfire began to disappear, but a warning light appeared on the dashboard - water in the fuel. Pulling off the freeway, we drained the fuel filter and continued to drive to a small tourist town and camped outside a wet and empty campsite. Luisa made dinner, and the kids chatted and played with a stray dog. We would soon be in Turkey where we could hopefully escape the frigid weather and have an adventure. Back on the freeway the next morning, the Landy was driving beautifully, with plenty of power; hopefully, we had solved our problem!

With a few things to do before we left Europe, we camped at Zapatero and Sons, a camping store which allowed campers to stay for free. For three days it rained, and we made friends with an Australian couple who knocked on our door one night, offering sweet treats and conversation as if they had just moved into the neighbourhood and were putting their best feet forward. They provided a welcome distraction from our daily routine of self-inflicted isolation. We really should be more social Luisa, I agree.

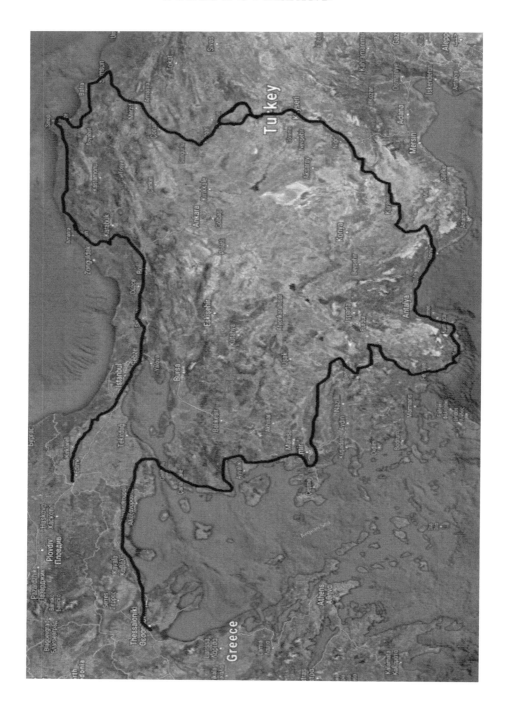

12

Turkey - The Land of Blue Water

The border was as cold and frigid as the political relationship between Turkey and Greece - a couple of Greek soldiers had the week before wandered onto the Turkish side and had been promptly arrested and detained. An icy wind howled as we drove out of Greece - a miserable border guard shouting us out of Europe. The Turks seemed as miserable. We paid for three-month visas though we only intended to be in Turkey for a month, it is better to give yourself breathing room, who knows, you may fall in love with the country, or the shit might hit the fan, and you need more time to clean up. The Turkish customs guy had a look at the Landy and a look at the vehicle registration papers which read "pick-up". As we had converted the Landy into a camper in the USA there was no way to change the registration documentation besides, in South Africa, a vehicle of 3500 kg GVM or less did not have to re-register when converted into a camper. "Pick-up or caravan", the official asked impatiently. I pretended not to understand, how would I explain the South African law to a man who spoke no English other than "pick-up or caravan!", which he asked again, loudly. "Both, pick-up caravan, no problem", I replied. "Pick-up or caravan!?". He was starting to lose patience with me. "Pick-up caravan", I insisted. He conferred with a colleague and told us to sit down and wait. The wind blew through us as Luisa, and I sat and mumbled to each other in Afrikaans. What if they did not let us in because of the vehicle? We would have to go back to Greece. And then what? We would have to head up through Bulgaria to Georgia. And then what? Don't worry, we will figure something out. The official returned to glare at us for a few moments then had a look at the Landy. Perhaps he spotted the kids through the window, I am not sure what changed his mind but, he returned and muttered something to his colleague. A few minutes later, we were called to the office and handed our paperwork along with a temporary import permit. Relieved we headed out of the border area, showed our papers to one last policeman and drove into Turkey!

It was bitterly cold, wet and grey as we drove down a wide avenue towards a shopping complex where dejected but friendly people drank coffee and bought groceries. The sun was setting, and we were all hungry and tired after the drive to the border and the stress of the crossing. As rain fell, we decided to not head to Istanbul but to instead drive down to a ferry crossing near Gallipoli. It was too cold, and the weather forecast predicted an Arctic freeze, we had no idea what that was, but we decided to head south and find the sun. That night we parked outside a clean and modern gas station and ate a meal of hotdogs before dressing in warm pyjamas and going to sleep. The wind blew ice cold and gale force all night long, and in the morning the Defender refused to start. I had recently changed the glow plugs, the batteries were fully charged, and the fuel pump was working as it should. For half an hour we tried getting her going, but not even a push start would get her started. Eventually, the battery wore down, and we were cold and exhausted from pushing the Landy. I talked to Mafuta, I asked her to please start, explained that we could not sit here at the gas station and fix whatever she needed fixing if she would just get us down south to the warmth we would give her all the TLC she deserved. I patted the dashboard and gave the ignition a turn. Rrrr, rrrr rurr ruuurrr. Then suddenly diesel ignited, the engine turned and turned again and burst to life belching a large cloud of blue-black smoke. Mafuta! After warming the engine up for five minutes, we continued the journey to ferry at the end of Thrace, the European part of Turkey. We visited Gallipoli where the Turks repelled the Allies during WW1 and where many New Zealand and Australian soldiers perished. It was a solemn scene, wet and dreary. We then visited a Turkish monument to the Turkish soldiers who had perished. Gallipoli changed Turkey itself as it was there that Colonel Mustafa Ataturk made a name for himself and we would later learn that Ataturk was our ally as we travelled to Turkey. The ferry crossed the Darnadelles, and we sat astonished as our ferry played chicken with an oil tanker and a container ship. In maritime terms, we missed the tanker by a hairsbreadth and thankfully made it to the banks of

Asia unscathed. Yes, we had made it to Asia after leaving the USA almost a year before, and we had accomplished so much in Europe.

We drove through the city of Canakkale and were amazed by the relative modernity of the city and by the massive concrete mosques which called us all to prayer. The Landy was misfiring again and we dared not stop but had to, not far from the famed site of Troy. A gas station allowed us to park in their covered wash area and work on the Landy. Luisa and I checked the Crank Position Sensor and the loom to the ECU for oil (there was none), we checked the fuses and relays, the MAF and MAP, the fuel pump, fuel filter, fuel cut off switch, glow plugs, alternator, starter, oil, coolant and filled the fuel filter with injector cleaner. We ran out of ideas and decided to press on, we were driving the coastal road and hoped that the road would be level and not too steep, as it was when the engine was under stress that the misfire was worst. We drove on and immediately encountered a large, steep hill - the Landy reduced to crawling along in second gear, hazard lights on. The misfire worsened, and after four hours of mountain passes and steep roads, we descended into a coastal plain and glimpsed blue skies and sunshine, the mountains holding back the European winter.

In the city of Burhaniye, we stopped at a supermarket and bought some food, there was apparently a campsite nearby, we needed to get there and get busy working on the Landy; hopefully, the repair would be simple. The Landy limped into a wet neighbourhood and rolled in a campsite called Altin Camp. A kindly old man directed us to a site near the ablutions and told us that the fee was 30 Lira a night. I parked the Landy and turned the engine off, Luisa asked me to move the Landy to face away from the sea as we were parked twenty meters from the beach and the wind was cold. The Landy would not start. She had done her job and had fought her way over the mountains to get us to a camp where we could fix her. She did not often refuse us and had never let us down but now she needed some love. Luisa and I made dinner in the enclosed wash area, shared a bottle of wine and planned the repairs. We had narrowed the possible fault to one of the following: fuel pump, fuel filter, crank position sensor, injector loom, fuel relay, fuel pressure regulator, ECU, Mass Air Flow Sensor, Mass Air Pressure Sensor and injector seals. We had already sent an email to Daniella at Bearmach in Wales, and they asked that we send them a list of parts we needed and they would see what they could do. We have been working with Bearmach since 2014, and our relationship grows stronger every year - we never ask for more than what we need, and they never ask for more than is reasonable. They are our back up team in some ways, and I know that if we are up a creek without a paddle they will send a paddle and the paddle will be perfect for the job. Yes, they are part of the journey. We sent through a list of the top suspects (we did not want to ask for too much) and set about working on the other little jobs which needed to be done on the Landy and work on the book sales.

The strangest thing had happened. The day we crossed into Turkey, we stopped receiving book sale orders through our website. It was as if someone had turned off the light and our revenue stream trickled to a stop. It was only months later that we learned the true extent of Facebook's algorithms and the Amazon treachery. It was only the articles which I sold which paid our way and all our attempts at merchandising seemed to fall flat because we were not located in the USA or the UK. We were in one of those situations which test us completely, it is when times are tough that we have to fight and fight hard - to retain our motivation, to solve our problems and to get the wheels rolling again. With no other choice, we focus and fight!

The weather was indeed better on this side of the mountain, we could see the north shrouded in dark grey clouds while we enjoyed a braai on the beach, or while we worked on the Landy. A short walk from the camp; a small store sold booze, cigarettes and bread and we soon learned that the cheapest food in Turkey is pretty much bread, eggs, mayonnaise, herbs and chicken. Every day we ate huge boiled egg sandwiches for lunch and a chicken meal for dinner. Every day Keelan and I walked to the shops, and we prepared for the arrival of the parts. Time has a way of slipping by when you are broken down in a campsite; by the time you have finished your initial repairs, diagnosis and ordered your parts, a few days have passed and then the order needs to be confirmed, processed, dispatched and inspected by customs and delivered by a local courier company who don't speak English (not that they are expected to) and somehow manage to continue to attempt to deliver to the wrong address. Two weeks fly by. We replaced the fuel pump and fuel filter, the Crank Position Sensor and the Mass Air Flow sensor and the injector loom and the rocker cover gasket. The Landy started and ran beautifully. Yes! Luisa began packing, but I asked her to wait until I had done a test drive. I started the Landy again, and she ran like a lumpy old tractor. Damn! I drove her out onto the narrow straight road, and she ran beautifully in all the gears except fifth, then she ran like a pig. We turned into a neighbourhood and then Landy engine slowed to a stall. I ran the TD5 bleed process (ignition on and pump the accelerator peddle five times) and limped the Landy back to the camp, defeated. A British friend Mike suggested that the fuel relay could be the problem. We nursed the Landy to the nearby industrial area and bought a relay from a kind man who ran a small store and played guitar when there were no customers. We installed the relay and VRRROOOOOOMMMM the Landy drove perfectly! A $2.00 relay fixed our problem! We drove into the town in search for an ATM (which in Turkey are stand-alone block units on a street corner), and after Luisa drew some cash we headed out, but as soon as we turned onto the road back to the camp the misfire returned and we almost stalled before reaching the campsite. We asked Bearmach to send us a Fuel Pressure Regulator and injector seals (I did not believe that the injector seals were the problem because the goddamn misfire was intermittent and a mechanic and engineer agreed with me) and they sent the parts out the next day. A week passed while customs held our parts hostage and we prepared for the repairs, watching repair videos on the internet and studying a step by step guide sent by our mechanic friend in Cape Town. When eventually the parts arrived, we had settled into a new camping spot in the middle of the camp. An elderly German couple arrived and stayed a few days. They drove an orange Land Cruiser and commiserated, they too had had fuel problems and had waited a month in Kathmandu for a very expensive fuel pump, yes Toyota's suffer from failures too and when they do, the repair is often not cheap. With our injector seals in hand, we set about the repair. We waited for a day with warm sun and little wind, as opening the engine in a windy, forested campsite would hardly be a sterile environment. Cautiously I worked to open the top of the engine while Luisa provided back up and queued up an injector seal repair video she had downloaded. We did not have the necessary special tools to remove the injectors but found that we could lever them out with a large Allen Key after unbolting each individual bracket. Working methodically we removed each injector and the offending seals (which had given us over 300 000 km of service each). Each injector was then cleaned and fitted with new seals before being replaced in the engine, working with the patience and care of a heart surgeon - if I messed this up, we would be in for an expensive repair which we simply could not afford. The camp owner brought us a few steaming glasses of sweet tea and the sunset. A large, fat dove flew over and crapped directly into cylinder three! Fat bastard. We cleaned and worked until late into the night and around 11 pm, finally replaced the rocker gasket and bolted down the head. Now the moment of truth. Would the Landy start? And would she run well without misfire? I cranked the engine a few times and she started! I had been instructed to hold the ignition open for twenty seconds at high revolutions to be sure that the injectors seated. I hope our neighbours did not mind the late-night noise, but we really had no option. It was only the next morning that we were able to test drive the Landy and with the kids fed and sitting under a tree surrounded by tools, tarps, cardboard boxes and cans of motor oil, Luisa and I drove out onto the road where all other test drives had failed. But not this time. We had succeeded. Well, she had not misfired, but the true test would be fully loaded, out on the freeway, driving up the side of a large hill. The camp staff gave us a one-week discount on our four-week bill. They had been incredibly patient with us and had made us part of the family, the Turks deserve the reputation of being wonderfully hospitable and caring.

Finally, we drove out of Burhaniye, heading south along the coast to the city of Izmir which is wealthy and growing wealthier by the minute, if the amount of high-income residence construction is any reliable indication. The city itself is built on wide avenues, and we camped that night in a parking lot next to an auditorium and a park where couples lounged on the lawn, and lycra-clad soccer moms pounded the pink rubber pavement. Apartment blocks overlooked the parking area, and we had a few visitors who welcomed us to Turkey, one gentleman gave us a few loaves of fresh bread and another gave us each a hand made bangle. The Land Rover had performed excellently on the 200-kilometre drive from Burhaniye and Luisa and I celebrated with a few cold Efes Pilsner, which is brewed in Izmir. After a dinner fed to stray cats, we sat on the lawn, parked between buses and trucks, and contemplated our existence. The morning came bright and sunny, we packed and continued our drive south along the coast to where

Luisa had found an area of coastline where we might find somewhere to camp and continue our existential ponderance. It is worth mentioning that Turkey is incredibly easy to overland. There are many clean, modern gas stations and each town has a branch of the Swiss grocery store chain Migros, which sells a large variety of produce including beer and wine (at the time of writing we are in Morocco which should invite Migros investment). The roads are also very good, and the country is as safe as any of the countries we have toured.

With Luisa directing, we headed down to the town of Demercili and drove out onto the beach, following a trail on the app Wikiloc. There was a large rocky hill in our path, and the app suggested that we would find a beautiful beach to camp on. We drove along the track which led away from the beach and between low hanging branches which scraped at the side of the camper. In low range, we tackled the track up the side of the hill, but it soon became apparent that the trail had not been driven in a very long time, long enough for the trees to reclaim the path. It was at the point that we had to machete through and we decided to head back to the beach, rather than to hack at the flora which we did not *have* to chop on a farm and where we might not be welcome. Back at the coastline, Luisa spotted a beach which connected a small peninsula to the mainland and pointed us in that direction. We drove across the beach, up a 4x4 trail and found ourselves in a perfect location for a bit of wild camping. Rocky coves and clear blue water invited us, a shepherd tended her goats, and a couple of curious dogs trailed the Defender until we found a level area to camp above a small beach. We were in paradise, apart from the plastic which litters almost every coastline. While Luisa set up camp, the kids and I took rubbish bags and collected the litter which seemed to grow from the ground. It took an hour and more than a few rubbish bags, but soon we had the area within sight of the Land Rover almost as pristine as Mother Nature intends.

Amongst the litter, we found many shoes, mostly sandals, which at first we found interesting from a survival perspective - if Tom Hanks had this many shoes on his island he may have not been as depressed. But then an even more depressing thought occurred to me - from our peninsula camp we could see a large island, and this was the Greek island of Lesbos (almost every island surrounding Turkey is claimed by Greece, 156 in total according to the Turks). Greece is European Union and Syrian refugees wanting to make a new home in Europe needed "only" to make it from Turkey onto a Greek island and claim asylum. Human traffickers were more than happy to load Syrians onto barely buoyant crafts and smuggle them to Greek islands in exchange for huge sums of cash. Many of those crafts did not make it across the Aegean and, it occurred to me, that the shoes we found on the Turkish shore had likely come from the drowning feet of Syrian refugees. As if to confirm this suspicion, a Turkish military helicopter arrived and dropped orange marker dye and two divers into the sea, who they later retrieved. Luckily no-one was drowning, it was purely an impressive training exercise.

I made a campfire, and we watched the sun set over Lesbos, fishing craft cruising by. One of the shepherd's dogs adopted us and spent the evening curled by our feet and the night sleeping under the camper. We fed it bones and leftover food, it fed us love and joined us as we explored the peninsula the next day, marvelling at the beauty which the locals took for granted. A small restaurant surrounded by fishermen shacks clung to the hill on the mainland, fishing boats bobbed moored to the beach. From a cliff edge 50 metres above the sea, we could see deep into the water where schools of small fish enjoyed not being large and delicious. A small forest grew at the centre and the highest point of the rocky isthmus where young couples could picnic privately. Ancient ruins kept their secrets and provided shade as we rested and looked out across the blue. We could have stayed there a week, a lifetime, but left after two beautiful nights and days.

Driving away from the coast, smiling, the Landy hiccupped. And then on the next hill, she stalled and came to rest on a dirt road. Not again! Luisa and I bit down hard on a shit sandwich and dug around the engine looking for a fault. Perhaps there was a bad earth, maybe the injector seals had failed, maybe we had to re-solder the exposed wires which we had found in the loom during the injector repair. A grey-haired man driving a new Audi stopped and offered assistance. He had a Defender at home and knew a good mechanic, maybe he could call his mechanic? We remained determined not to rely on mechanics and took the man's number, promising that if we could not fix the Landy, we would give him a call. We had passed a roadside restaurant on the way up hiccup hill and decided to get the Landy back there and borrow some electricity to re-solder the loom wires which we suspected had created a short. At the restaurant, which did not seem open though a few men ate lunch under a tree, we asked for power. The men joined us, and we watched as Luisa soldered the wires which were hardly accessible behind the engine. A young man named Khan offered his assistance, but we were sure that we could fix the problem. We could not. We then removed and inspected the Crank Position Sensor, and Khan noticed that one of the contact pins within the CPS was bent, he straightened it, and we plugged the sensor back in. That worked. Khan was our new best friend, and he invited us to his home, a few kilometres down the road where his wife prepared a selection of pies, cakes, olives and fruit for us to eat. Khan offered us showers and a bed for the night in his modern home. We declined, it was still early, and we wanted to keep on driving despite the Landy giving us a heart attack. Khan then offered us ninety eggs from his hatchery, and we accepted thirty and took a photo of our families together, his pre-teen children shy and surprised by the large, blonde, unexpected guests who claimed to be from Africa. We should have stayed the night.

Pamukkale is one of Turkey's greatest tourist attractions and lies inland near the city of Denizli. There was no way for us to know that the journey there would be of the most memorable experiences we have had, and little of that had to do with the travertine pools or the ancient Greco-Roman city built above the shimmering white pools. We arrived at the base of the pools after an uneventful day driving through beautiful countryside. Tourist buses, touts, and police jostled for attention in the small, busy village. Pamukkale (or Cotton Castle in Turkish) is pronounced pama-coolair with the annunciation of the third and fourth syllables, and we found a large, dusty parking area where we could spend the night. But, Luisa had other ideas. A road ran to the right of the pools, in a valley between two large hills, we decided to explore, and we noticed a steep dirt road climbing the side of the hill overlooking the World Heritage Site.

Luisa ran up the road, camera in hand (as she was determined to film all our adventures) and once she reached the top of the hill, she stood there, looking confused. She tried shouting at us, but we could not hear her though I knew exactly what she was saying - " I don't know, it's really, really steep!

And there are really big holes! And when you get here, I don't know if you should turn left or right!". All of the shouting was accompanied by the waving of arms, bending of knees, pointing and head shaking. "It's up to you!" she shouted, but I could not hear. The kids assumed the position for off-road driving and I engaged low range first gear and headed up the hill, which was tricky but worth the effort. I steered the Defender right at the rise of the hill, and we found ourselves on a hilltop overlooking the entire tourist attraction, the perfect site for a hotel. It was late afternoon by then, and we set up our chairs and took in the sights. We could see hundreds of ant-like people clambering the slope surrounding the pools on a path which led all the way to the ancient ruins which were at the altitude to our camp. We had a 270-degree view which extended to the valley and the city of Denizli, and as the sunset, lights were lit, and the call of the muezzin floated up to us, the scene became magical. Spotlights lit the white framed pools and the ruins, and we experienced Pamukkale the way very few have before us, we knew this because there was very little evidence of human activity on top of the hill. We had found that all-natural public spaces are badly littered in Turkey (the only irritant in an otherwise spectacular country, if they could address the litter mentality the country would be almost perfect for exploring) but here there were only two very old plastic bottles and no other litter. This free/wild/bush camp was the perfect example of why independent vehicle-based travel has so many advantages over other forms of travel - we were having a unique, life-altering experience at almost no cost, we did not have to share that experience with strangers, and we were free to come and go at will. Nothing else comes close!

An anxiously excited dog approached the vehicle, it must have sensed that was inside. He was a large dog, a mix of an Anatolian shepherd and a smaller creature, and he and Jessica fell in love with each other immediately. This is not a rare occurrence, all animals love Jessica and she loves all animals, they connect instantly. After dinner, we fed the dog and he adopted us as his family, he sat with us as we watched the stars brighten and he stayed with us all night, occasionally barking at a perceived or real threat, we will never know. Once we are settled into bed, the camper takes on a different character. It is a cosy nest, we each have our own space, and we can lie and talk, joke, listen to a podcast, watch a movie, read a book or browse the internet if we have an internet connection. The challenge when building the camper was to have it comfortably accommodate four adult people, and we succeeded. In the morning, Luisa will lie on my bed while I prepare coffee and breakfast and then we pack up and leave, or stay depending on the plan for the day. We could be camped on a magical hill or in a gas station parking lot, it does not make a difference when the doors are closed, and the shades are drawn, our little bit of paradise is in between those four walls. But, it is not always peaceful, sometimes we are having fun, sometimes we are arguing, sometimes we drive each other to distraction and sometimes it is the best place to be on earth.

I did not see the need to join the tourist hordes and assault Pamukkale that morning, we had an amazing experience, and it was decided that it was better than that should be our lasting memory of the site, not an expensive, distracting jostle. Instead, we drove out of town and towards Denizli, where a new friend awaited us. Ergun had sent us an email inviting us to stay at his home, and we accepted. Sometimes there is a tone in an email or a message, something which entices and sets your mind at ease. We have made the mistake in the past of visiting people who extend the hand of friendship but are really only interested in business opportunities or exposure to our followers on social media or who want to impress their circle of friends with world traveller guests. Ergun invited us to meet his family and have a shower, a meal if we are hungry or a washing machine if we needed, the type of invitation one traveller would send to another.

We met Ergun and Huseyin as they waited for us parked next to the road into Denizli. Ergun was driving his orange VW bus, and we followed him through the city and up the side of the mountain to his home in an up and coming neighbourhood. Ergun's house had stood alone on the mountain for years, but as the wealth of the city grew, developers moved in and built beautiful double story houses worthy of Conde Nast. Huseyin is Erguns neighbour and is the kind of neighbour you want to have; cheerful, generous, incredibly kind and intelligent. We met Erguns family - Asli (pronounced Asla) his son Arda and his daughter Ezra. The home western in decor - peace symbols here and there, a collage of family photos, colourful rugs and a large white sofa, a new, large kitchen from which the aromas of cooking food wafted. We took turns having a much-needed shower (it had been a week since our last proper soap scrub), and we changed into fresh clothing while Luisa stuffed piles of dirty clothing into the washing machine. The family spoke wonderful English, and Asli's sister cruised around the kitchen with purpose.

By the time dinner was ready, we were all drooling, and we were not disappointed. The food came and kept coming - meatballs stuffed with peas and onion, mashed potato, boiled eggs and salad. Then a course of minced meat and rice wrapped in vine leaves and then a huge platter of fried meat, vegetables, onion and tomato which one ate like a taco. Homemade lemonade was served with the meal along with homemade beer, wine and cheese. It was a feast which Asli and her sister prepared and served with no fuss. We made sure to wash the dishes after the hours of conversation came to an end, and the children prepared for bed. We spent six days with Ergun and his family and became part of the community. Every morning Huseyin would pop in before work, as he always did, had a cup of coffee and joked with the kids. Every evening we would take a walk after dinner, and we were delighted that the community was close, so close that we miss-took them for one large family. Two blocks from Ergun's house the government had built a large community vegetable garden, professionally designed and equipped and subdivided into small lots each with its own shed, which the community could rent for a pittance. The gardeners could grow whichever fruit and vegetables they chose and were encouraged to trade with others, the government posted notices and advisories of how to grow the plants, which fertilisers and insecticides to use (if any) and they provided seeds. The whole community could be fed by their own labour which freed up their income for other purposes. We tried to do our bit around the house when not working on our various project (writing books is easy compared to selling books, and everyone wants a pound of flesh) but Asli ran her house with such quiet efficiency that there was hardly ever any work to be done. We did make a South African braai, and some of our favourite desserts and the kids washed dishes whenever Asli turned her back. It was while we were with Ergun that we installed the rear air suspension to deal with the horrible body roll we have struggled with since the rebuild. Ergun suffers with quiet dignity with a strain of muscular dystrophy which was slowly eroding a tall, powerful man who had conquered mountains and had been a mountain rescue volunteer in his youth. Ergun never said a word about his disease other than to explain what it was, and he was completely self-sufficient despite limited mobility. He walked with the aid of crutches and had to consider each activity in advance. Together Keelan, Ergun and I spent the afternoon installing the airbags, and Ergun studied the camper we had built - he had recently bought an old Turkish military Defender pick-up and had plans to build a camper similar to ours with which he could take his family around the world. Asli seemed to be inspired by our family doing what many consider to be extremely dangerous and realised, perhaps, that we are who we say we are - ordinary people who do extraordinary things. Ergun, we would later learn, was considered the best VW mechanic in all of Turkey and he was the best because he was university educated. He had chosen to restore old VW vehicles instead of pursuing a corporate career, and this set him apart, most mechanics in Turkey are from the working class, and they do business accordingly. Ergun taught us some tricks while we installed the airbags and asked a hundred questions about our camper build, and it is when the build earns the respect of technical professionals that I am really proud of what we have conceived and built.

We settled into the neighbourhood and could easily imagine a life living there. An empty lot stood between Ergun and Huseyin's house, the perfect place to build a home with the mountains on our doorstep, a deep blue sky and a city below, friends on either side. Asli took us to the supermarket in her old VW Beetle. "Hey, Asli, does this thing have brakes?" I asked, filling the back seat. She sped into a traffic circle and rocketed out the other side. "Sure, it has brakes, but no fifth gear and I have to pull this string to use the window wipers", she demonstrated the window wipers, pulling on a string as the world blurred past. "There is the fabric factory, and there is the university and here is the hospital where other Asli works". She piloted on auto, curly hair bouncing on her shoulders, a stream of information burbling as we slid around corners, taking short cuts around congested traffic. The city could hear us coming and hid. It was amusing that the mechanic's car had no fifth gear, but the brakes were great, perhaps definitely Ergun did not repair the fifth gear so that Asli could not achieve mortal maximum speed. We were grateful. Asli slid the Beetle into a parking spot outside the largest Migros in the city, and we extracted ourselves with giddy laughter, like children from an olde world roller coaster.

Food is mostly affordable in Turkey, some imported goods and technology are expensive, but Turkey is similar to Brazil in the 80's and the old South Africa in many ways - degrees of political isolation necessitates self-sufficiency, and resourceful people will find ways to provide for themselves. Turkey is a country of two worlds, the old and the new. Cities like Izmir and Istanbul and Antalya are wealthy and modern, European to a degree, but the cities and towns of the interior are closely connected to the past. Denizli is a city in the middle, caught up in the development of the new Turkey but happily holding on to her identity. That day at the Migros we bought meat for a South African braai and ingredients for desserts and sides, that night it was our turn to take care of our hosts, and we hope that they enjoyed it, the photos suggest that we all had a wonderful time. Shortly before we left Ergun invited Keelan and me to visit his workshop but I, regretfully, was working to a deadline and was not able to take the time that day, so Keelan joined Ergun for the day and returned enthused. Ergun was impressed with Keelan's acumen and work ethic and offered the 18-year-old an apprenticeship. Keelan promised to consider the idea.

We left reluctantly but understanding that we would one day return and, if I have my way, we will meet on the road one day. After we finish touring Africa, I would like to ship the Defender to Turkey and then drive up to Russia and across to Alaska. We will have to see what the road has in store for us over the next few years. Regardless, our time with the family had left a profound impression on us, and we are forever grateful for their hospitality.

Leaving Denizli, we drove to Lake Salda, a 196m deep crater lake which lies in the southwestern Anatolia region. The lake is surrounded almost entirely by a pine forest, and we arrived expecting the "Turkish Maldives" as the locals call it. A small town claimed the lake as their own, and I wish they would love the lake as it deserves. A dirt road rings the lake, and we drove for many kilometres searching for a place to camp, but every site which looked perfect from afar was strewn with litter - bags of plastic bottles, nappies, food and sweets wrappers - while the large bins provided stood empty. Ergun had told me that there is a name for theses polluters - Gunubirlikciler - the day campers. We call them the Goonies. The Goonies descend on a beautiful beach or forest or picnic spot and let loose. They make fires (burn tyres in extreme cases), play music as loud as possible, dance and drink and grill and laugh and shout and terrorise nature. And when they are done, they leave a pile of plastic, bottles, cigarette butts and general destruction. The Goonies do NOT represent Turkish culture, they are the remnants of poverty, their thinking that of those who need to be disrespectful to nature to elevate their low social status, they are clothed in ignorance and bravado and are an anomaly who without the Turkish overland experience would be completely blissful. In Brazil, we saw similar behaviour, particularly north of Rio de Janeiro. The lowest of society know that there is someone lower, and that is whoever has to clean their mess. To find a clean area to camp, we had to leave the forest and follow a 4x4 track onto a large sandy beach where we filled a large bag with strewn plastic bottles before having a swim. The shore of the lake is rimmed by clear, blue water and white sand but as you swim deeper the water darkens, and suddenly you are floating above a black abyss. A 200-meter deep swimming hole is absolutely terrifying, Keelan is braver than I.

The next day we headed back towards the coast and the city of Fethiye, camping along the coast as we drove, finding secluded coves and bays where we could sleep peacefully after a swim and a braai. Turkish beer is good, particularly Efes and it is the perfect late afternoon drink while watching the fishermen go about their business. Fethiye is a tourist trap, and after a drive down to the main beach we decided to head back to the main town where we spent the night sleeping in a noisy square, and Luisa found an apartment to rent for the equivalent of a days camping in Europe. It took a while to find the apartment, and once we found it Luisa declared that she was not happy - large bouncer looking types hung around the pool, a weathered blonde woman sucked on a long white cigarette, and the apartment itself was as worn as the bottle blonde. The landlord had another option, an apartment down the road, only $5 more per night but better suited to a family like ours. He was right. The second apartment was better in every way with no long-term residents, and we settled in to get some work done. The most common question we are asked is how do we afford to travel like we do, we must be very rich. The answer is we work hard to keep going, the book sales account for half of our income, the videos bring in a small amount, but we are working hard to change that, and the articles I write account for the other half of our income. We do also have some small corporate income, but that is difficult to come by and voluntarily limited. I am sure many have this idea of us lounging around most days, driving from beautiful location to beautiful location and having an easy life, being lucky. Well, the harder you work, the luckier you are, and we work almost as hard as we did when we ran the immigration firm. We are building towards the future. And our expenses are relatively low. The point is, we need to work, writing books is much easier than selling books - especially when you write books like mine which do not fit neatly into any pigeon hole, and you have controversial opinions which are reasonable and not extreme enough to be revolutionary. It is a quiet revolution. We have to keep to our schedule of 5 days overlanding and three days in a camp or apartment working to put together all the media which we have gathered during the 5 days of adventure, or misadventure.

It was while in Fethiye that Keelan decided that he wanted to return to Ergun to do the apprenticeship. We messaged Ergun and Keelan began negotiations. Ergun offered to provide room, board and training and a small allowance. Keelan was satisfied, as were we, and almost two weeks after we had left Denizli we headed to the Fethiye bus station where Keelan would catch a bus loaded with snacks, instructions and his mother's tears. Keelan had been growing restless for a while - he had grown up on the road, travelling as we do, living in the Land Rover, a different country every other month. While others dream of that existence, his dreams were leading him in another direction, towards his future. Keelan is mathematically minded and enjoys mechanical work, he dreams of building everything from overland vehicles to tanks and aeroplanes and zombie-proof fortresses. A mechanical internship, free from the constraints of mom and dad and little sister would allow him to be the man he wanted to be and for us, at least, we knew that he would be safe in the arms of a family which would treat him with love and respect. He will inevitably seek to find his own path, and this is what we have raised him to do - to find his passion in life and to pursue his own dreams while employing the principles learned from a courageous life as an explorer. Sometimes his quest for liberation caused tension, and we had to be patient with each other, which is not always possible.

Momma bear was not happy sending her son off on his own. This would be the first time that he would travel alone, and it would not be a soft journey in his own country. He was not fazed at all, and I filmed the girls crying as he sat on the bus waiting impatiently for his own little adventure to begin. The ticket seller, who Luisa had earlier given a plaster for a cut finger, noticed Luisa's sadness and popped his head out of the bus window, pretending to cry, "you can take me instead mommy". His gentle teasing reassured Luisa, Keelan was in the hands of good people, and he would be just fine. The bus pulled out of the station carrying its precious cargo and headed out of town while we headed in the other direction, quietly.

With Keelan in Denizli, our entire dynamic changed. Keelan is boisterous, he is noisy, opinionated, clumsy and affectionate. He listens to the Pixies all day long, enjoys arguments about politics and culture and can talk for hours about aerodynamics, rocket fuel and lightweight alloys, turbo construction and the physics and efficiency of turbojets. And you must pay attention - there is always a quiz at the end. The girls are far quieter (when Luisa is not on the warpath) and will sit quietly and chat or read a book or watch a series on the computer. And man, can he suck up WiFi, it is as if he absorbs it through his skin.

From Fethiye, we drove up to visit the home of a man who had come to visit at the apartment. Engin has hosted our friends Luis and Lacey (Lost World Expedition) and Brad and Sheena (Drive Nacho Drive), and we were amazed by his collection of Land Rovers. On the steep, narrow road to his home, we stopped to check our directions and watched as a road worker piloted a new blue digger. One of the digger's tyres exploded while we sat waiting for the navigator to wake up and the explosion was so loud that Luisa screamed out loud, imagining that the end was near. Up at Engin's house, a day was spent working on the Defender, giving her a service and attempting to cure a transfer box leak which we had been struggling with since before driving up to Alaska in 2015. Engin lathed the main seal collar but doubted whether the leak would be cured, he was right. That evening we drove with Engin to Gocek, a playground of the rich and famous yacht crowd where our old overlander clothing clashed with the expectations of the restaurant peddlers and gift shop owners. We bought an evil eye, that blue glass charm which is synonymous with Turkey and which held the promise of good luck (it broke a year later, which is apparently a good luck omen as opposed to the western broken mirror superstition). Engin was accustomed to the peculiarities of long term overlanders and knew that we would not be sitting down for a five-course meal, but patiently waited for us to by some supplies for dinner at his home in the hills. Gocek sits at the confluence of the Mediterranean and the Aegean in the shadow of the 4th-century tomb of Amyntas and is paradise for anyone with large piles of cash, the sea turquoise and the hills green, the villas exclusive and the smell of lobster, crayfish and expensive perfume in the air. It always amazes me how the wealthy can seem so completely miserable on vacation, so aloof and dissatisfied, bored and irritated with the company of their friends and family while desperate for the approval of those richer than themselves. We have had a few opportunities to study these fascinating creatures and, I have to tell you, wealth seems wasted on the wealthy as much as youth is wasted on the young. What saddens me is that these people are held as a goal for us all, idols of success and confidence. I would rather have a simple lunch with the working class than a feast with the wealthy. Wealth isn't the problem, of course, it is how some people wear it, and the desperation others have to possess it. I will admit to jealousy, the food coming out of those dockside restaurants smelt absolutely delicious, and I knew I could not justifiably afford to feed my family those meals, which would cost the equivalent of a weeks travel. But, we have experiences which the white shirt wealthy could never have.

Engin bode us farewell, and Luisa directed us down the coast, and the coastline was as beautiful as any we had ever seen. Turquoise waters lapped against sandstone cliffs and pristine white sand, boulder-strewn beaches. Slowly we meandered along the D400, oohing and aahing until we reached the tourist mecca of Kas where we bought supplies and headed back up to a cove we had spotted which might be suitable for a nights camping. The cove was hugged by the road and a camper parked above the beach while women in burkinis played with small children on the beach and in the sea.

We parked behind the camper and popped the roof of the camper. "Hello, is it safe to stay the night here". The owner of the camper was a Turk who lived in Izmir and holidayed on this coast every year. "Yes, of course. The road can be noisy, but you can stay here as long as you want". This was great news. A fishing boat slid into the small bay and anchored, the fisherman repaired his nets while listening to pop music and then took a nap in a hammock while his boat rocked gently, the Greek island of Kastellorizo in the background. The girls and I swam in the cool sea, we could open our eyes underwater, and the small waves broke onto the pebbled beach, rolling the pebbles against each other creating a hypnotic, rhythmic rasping. As the sunset, we made a small fire and drank a cold beer. The coastline reminded me of the road between Strand and Betty's Bay in the Cape, South Africa. But there the police would have told us to put out the fire and admonished us for drinking beer in public. And there we would not be safe sleeping alone next to the road. The Turkish police drove past our little beach once every few hours, but they were there to protect us, not control us if we behaved like mature tourists. A rental car arrived as the sunset, and four Chinese tourists emerged and made a beeline for us, cameras at the ready. "Where are you from, what are you doing here, where have you been, you are so big, your wife is so beautiful, can we take a picture, grrr you are like a wild man". I had not trimmed any hair on my head or face for three months in anticipation of the famous Turkish barber experience. They took photos of the meat roasting on Brazilian skewers, they took photos of the Land Rover from every imaginable angle, and they left us feeling overwhelmed. As the sunset we enjoyed the rasping of the sea on the beach, the colours in the sky, each others company and the calm still, which was only broken by the occasional passing car or bus. Across the road stood a newly built tourist information cabin, not yet occupied, a slightly dilapidated shack served as a change room and a hose provided fresh water. We could have stayed there a week.

The Turkish have a peculiar custom. After a wedding the bride, groom and entourage will drive their cars, blaring pop music, to beautiful and popular places. There the entire group will emerge from the vehicles, dance, sing and holler. The bride drowning in white lace and silk, loving every second, dancing and waving her hands in the air. Cameras film the roadside experience and, just as suddenly as they arrive, they all pile back into the wedding vehicles and speed away, leaving us wondering what exactly we just witnessed.

After the wedding party left the traffic thinned, the stars emerged and the moon reflected off the calm sea. We were completely at ease, there are few places in the world where one can feel so safe and relaxed, the Turks have every reason to be proud of their nation and culture.

On the third day we packed up and left, reluctantly but in the knowledge that once paradise becomes normal, it loses its shimmer. Best to keep going and seek another slice of heaven. Unfortunately, the cove and Kas were to be the highlight of our Turkish coastal experience. We spent a few nights camping on beaches in highly rated tourist spots, but there were touts, the water not as pristine, the beaches not as beautiful. The problem, it seems, is that guide books are written by fly-in travellers who do not have the freedom of movement which we enjoy. The busses and shuttles run from tourist hot spot to tourist hot spot and the best places are those who are often ignored. It was time to head for the mountains, but first Luisa had a surprise in store for me.

In Antalya, there is an internet-famous barber called Barberstown. Luisa had been chatting to them on Instagram for a while, since the Greek island where she convinced me to stop trimming my hair. For three months I had let it all grow, and I looked like a homeless man, a bush of grey hair on a body dressed like an overlander, at least. The barbershop is not at all what you expect. It is not located in the middle of a hip, expensive mall or on the outskirts of an affluent neighbourhood. The gaudy store is located under an apartment building, between an auto parts store and an insurance broker, near a school. Inside, the walls are painted in an extravagant 1980's tiger stripe scheme, the barber depicted in a clumsy mural as a bearded Turkish Edward Scissorhands, the ego is immense. We sat down with Omer to discuss the video both they and we would make. We agreed that he would tag my Instagram in his post and that we would pay him the normal fee for the haircut. With that out of the way, I showed him how I usually cut my hair. This was not our normal environment, Luisa cuts my hair and had done a great job on the Amazon river ferry, in campsites across the world and even, later in our journey, in the Sahara desert. Barberstown is a small kingdom. Omer is the king, and he struts around the small shop with its three work stations and a wash area. The other barbers are his minions, and he orders them to move, cut, wash, move! They obey. The errand boy is the lowest of the low, and he is not permitted to speak unless spoken to, to smile or join the conversation when the king relaxes. Omer the Ego rules absolutely. For three hours we sat, witnessed and participated in haircut theatre. The Ego strutted, eager to show the large foreigner with an exotic camper and amazing story who was the boss. Napoleonic in the comedic sense, the emperors' new clothes, Ego began an extravagant show. A minion washed my hair, I had to lean forward where I sat at the cutting station, my head in a basin, an act of submission. Ego pretended to chop at my neck with an imaginary scimitar. Choice. Ego then fluffed up all my hair to make me look truly ridiculous while his younger brother, the dark-eyed prince dressed in white, shot the video with an iPhone. Oder the Ego then set to work cutting and trimming and fiddling with razors and gold scissors and a cut-throat blade. It took an hour to achieve very little. Often the ego would stop and pour a white powder onto his black, thinning hair and puff it up into an impressive hipster side parting before sculpting his beard. We drank coffee, and the king resumed his vital work. Hot black wax was smeared across my cheeks and nose, paper tubes inserted into my ears and lit with a dramatic hairspray flamethrower performance. More hot wax was shoved in my nostrils and ripped out, the wax slowly peeled from my face for maximum cinematic value and extra pain. My eyes swelled with liquid. With great fanfare, the ego trimmed my beard, pretended to slice my throat, and spent an eternity spraying hair spray into my skull. Luisa filmed and the brother filmed and the king performed, and I squirmed. Eventually, the ordeal was over, I posed with the coiffured king under the Edward Scissorhands mural, we paid and left. The video, to date, has had close to 300 million views on Facebook and Instagram and, of course, the king did not tag my account as agreed. That is, in retrospect, a good thing. A very good thing, indeed. I poured a few cups of water over my head to rinse out the kings cockadoodle hairdo, as soon as I could.

That afternoon we headed out of Antalya to meet friends of Ergun and Asli. Abu and his wife Dorothy lived in a beautiful home built in the middle of a traditional village. The house was a wood, double story A-frame surrounded by a wild garden of fruit trees, vegetables and herbs. A small stream trickled along the border fence and we ate oranges, nectarines and plums from the trees while Abu gave us a tour. We sat and drank lemonade from a beading glass pitcher in the shadow of the house, grass tickling our shins, the heat oppressive, but the drink cool and the conversation entertaining. Abu had lived in New York for many years and was a journalist and photographer before returning to his native Turkey where he New Yorked through each day. Their passion was travel and Ergun had rebuilt their VW camper with which they often travelled to Greece where they would sit on the beach and eat fine food and drink fine drinks - as fine a pursuit as any.

From his balcony, we watched the scorching sunset over the mountains and listened as the village prepared for a wedding which Abu assured us would be the simple affair of simple people. He had lived in that village for too long and had never learned to appreciate the folk music. Abu explained that Turkey is a country populated by two groups, essentially. Ataturk was a visionary leader and his vision of a secular nation birthed modern Turkey. The country was changing rapidly under President Recep Tayyip Erdogan, who employs religion as a political tool. Abu did not trust that his neighbours would protect his freedoms if his ideas contradicted their beliefs. He warned that social media was closely scrutinised, the telephone calls were monitored and that an unpopular opinion could easily result in a knock on the door; the thought police. He and Dorothy kept to themselves when not travelling and only really felt free when they were alone together on that Greek beach. I asked why he did not leave. "Well, what would happen to the country if the educated, secular people had to leave? No, the followers of Ataturk have a duty to the country".

Dorothy fed us a meal of homemade cheese and potatoes, salad and excellent wine. She would return from Europe with various cheeses and would clone those into her own cheese. Jessica drank a glass of wine and blushed as we spoke of her fondness for Turkish boys. With the sun set, the evening cooled, and the song of the muezzin regularly joined the conversation. In Turkey the Muezzin call is incredibly loud, we have been told by a Swiss couple that in Iran the volume is half and later we would experience the same in Morocco. We left the next day after filling the

Defenders water tanks with water and the fridge with a few blocks of fine cheese, we made a promise to meet Abu and Dorothy in Cappadocia where they visited every year for the last 16 years to hike, explore and relax.

Alanya is a city of beachside hotels and resorts where Russians and German wake before the sunrise, mobilising the troops to compete for the most precious of resources - a sun lounger. A beach towel draped over the reclining chair wins the prize and competition is fierce. There have been bloody brawls over the furniture of sloth and, I believe, there are now some hotels which cater to Germans almost exclusively and others to their eastern counterparts. We drove past it all, past the sunburned blonde people wearing the forced smiles of misery and the water parks, shopping centres, casinos and gaudy restaurants. We drove for what seemed like an eternity past hotels which competed with each other in a phallic display of statues - Greek gods, mermaids and biblical legends. We drove past it all and found a road which would take us out of the city labouring under a grey sky and soon found ourselves driving up the side of the Taurus mountain range. As we climbed, the vegetation grew greener, and a drizzle began to fall between us and an astounding view of the city below. At the summit, the road plunged into a forest and into another world completely. We were in the Andes once more, in Colombia or Ecuador, the road narrow, wet and winding along a cliff's edge. Stalls which sold mountain produce hugged the precipice, closed perhaps because of the rain or perhaps because of the day. There are a few parking areas at trailheads where public toilets offered no relief, and the glass of broken windows littered the asphalt, accompanied by cigarette butts and broken beer bottles. It was the shattered vehicle glass which encouraged us to head further into the mountains, away from a short drive to the city and the types of people who do not know how to use a toilet and who break glass. Keelan was not with us and he was missed.

With the sun beginning to set, we found that we had climbed and descended one mountain and were halfway up another. Small villages clung to the slopes, and we realised that we would have to camp wild in the mountains - there were no suitable gas stations or camps nearby. I parked the Land Rover beside a fork in the road, to the left asphalt, to the right a dirt path. The path led to a river, and we had learned that where there is a river, there will be recreation areas, formal or informal. I made the decision to trust the good Turkish mountain people and to camp by the river which ran cloudy blue, and it struck me then that all the natural water in Turkey is blue and we dubbed it The Land of the Blue Water.

The drizzle became rain as I steered the Land Rover down a sloped track scarred with tyre sized holes which were full of mud. Beside a tree which grew out of the riverbank, I reversed the Defender onto a level patch. We would not lift the roof and if there was trouble we could drive the vehicle immediately out of the area. Luisa cooked pasta while Jessica and I read books and chatted. The rain fell, and the blue water gushed by, occasionally a vehicle would pass, slow and continue driving with the honk of a horn. As the sunset a white pick up crested the slope and stopped, rain illuminated in the streams of headlight. For a few minutes, the pick up sat menacingly, observing us, before sliding down the muddy path and coming to a halt directly in front of the Defender, blocking our escape. If I had to, I would put the Landy in low range and push the vehicle out of the way. But first I needed to confront our unwanted visitor, and the first weapon in my arsenal would be a friendly greeting and a confident handshake. Luisa knew what to do, if the situation turned bad she was to drive out of there and get to safety, I would follow when I could. I put on my old, black all-weather jacket, my Leatherman on my hip and stepped out of the habitat, closing the rear doors and reassuring the girls as I stepped out. With the rain pelting my back I walked through the mud beside the Land Rover and as I reached the front, a tall man with dark features stepped out of the pick-up, leaving the lights on and engine running. I stepped forward and smiled, my hand outstretched, "Salaam Alaikum". Peace be with you. "Aleikum a salaam" the man responded and stepped forward to shake my hand. And peace be with you. He asked my name, and where we were from, he seemed tense, but when I told him that we were from South Africa his body language changed in an instant and a smile of disbelief spread across his lips. Impossible, two fingers wiped against his cheek. You are white? He spoke in Turkish, but I have had this conversation, so many times, I could communicate the dialogue in sign language with my eyes closed. Using that sign language, I told him our story - Southern and East Africa, around South America, all the way up to Alaska (Alaska! He exclaimed) then across the USA, UK, Europe and now Turkey. I am a writer, my wife is a photographer, we have two children. Ali regarded me for a moment. Lit a cigarette and made a phone call. The area where we were parked was roughly 75 meters long and 20 meters wide, beside the Land Rover a bank had been excavated and the area was relatively flat. Ali told me to wait, then returned to his vehicle and reversed to the far end of the level area. I stood under the tree and waited. After a few minutes a large, new grader arrived and began levelling the area in front of the Land Rover, a truck arrived and waited at the top of the battered muddy track. Once the grader had finished levelling, the truck drove down carefully, Ali moved the pick up, and the truck lifted the rear and dumped the stones while driving towards our vehicle, hitting the brakes at intervals to bounce the stones out in heaps. The truck drove slowly up the track and parked on the level area next to the road. The grader then set to work levelling the stones meticulously and in a matter of minutes had created a near-perfect surface. "For you", said Ali, motioning towards the level stones. He indicated that he would return in the morning and we would have tea and while he was saying goodbye the grader set about levelling the muddy sloped track, creating a smooth path. We were astounded. Ali was the foreman of the extensive road works, and he had welcomed us to his country, expending resources and working in the dark and rain to ensure that we felt safe and comfortable.

The next morning he returned as we were preparing our morning tea and told us to follow him. We packed up quickly and drove out onto the road with Ali leading the way. The sun shone brightly, and the sky was a perfect deep blue as we drove down into a valley on a perfect new road. A compound appeared on the right, and we pulled up next to Ali's pick up outside a half square of temporary white buildings where a few men stood and spoke. Ali motioned to the bathrooms, which were perfectly clean and private and suggested we could have a hot shower. The girls and I took turns showering as the compound cook prepared a breakfast of cheese omelette and sweet tea. Ali stayed for a while and gave me a tour of the compound - an entertainment area had been built at the end of one wing and behind that stood large drum BBQ's, a heap of cut wood and a small vegetable garden where the cook grew fresh vegetables to feed the road crews. Ali showed me photos of his family on his phone, making sure that we had enough food and water for the Land Rover's tanks before rounding up his men, saying goodbye and heading out to conquer the mountains with tunnels, bridges, rock, stone and tar. His goal was to create a new modern road linking the isolated towns of the Taurus mountains and the interior with the prosperous coastal cities, and he and his hard-working team were doing an excellent job but with a heavy hand. If there were any environmental impact studies done, they were a formality to be ignored - rivers were dammed and rerouted, cliffs detonated and valleys paved. Mosques were built to line the route as part of the road construction, large concrete structures built with the efficiency of a relief structure.

Fresh and fed, we drove out onto that new road and headed further into the mountains, our hearts warmed by that legendary Turkish hospitality. The Turks remind me of the Brazilians, those wonderful people did whatever they could to make us feel safe and comfortable and the further we strayed from the tourist traps the more we felt the warm embrace of the country.

We travelled back in time to a world where old men and women worked in the fields, and young children played simple games with stones and sticks. Little villages surrounded by agriculture and rustic homes offered daily bread and supplies, maybe fuel. The town of Sariveliler clings to the side of a mountain, and we filled the fuel tank while marvelling at the contrast of ancient village and new apartment buildings. The wind blew cold as Luisa searched the navigation apps for some mountain trails, which she found and directed us too. Just off the D340, a track had been carved into the side of a mountain, and I piloted the Defender up into a world of grey rock and an undulating plateau where ancient caves still served as corrals for goats and sheep. The municipality had dammed a stream and the resulting pond teeming with a million tadpoles, the pond itself the only vestige of a once immense lake which had sculpted the landscape and dug the caves (You can watch the video Fethiye to Cappadocia on our YouTube channel A2AExpedition). Luisa, Jessica and I hiked around the area for a while and found an eroded outcrop which consisted of layer upon layer of shells, presumably seashells, though we would need a gifted geologist to explain how seashells were present a few thousand feet above sea level.

Back on the well-paved road, we headed towards Cappadocia, our navigator app doing the best it could to steer us in the wrong direction and often we would have to backtrack to where we had instead yanged. The weather was superb, the sky a deep blue and the air fresh and cool, perfect weather for mountain driving. Switchbacks led over mountains into valleys where we would find next to nothing or a large town equipped with multiple mosques - one on every other corner, or so it seemed. Young men would point and laugh as they saw us coming, joking with each other and laughing. Old men would stop in their tracks and watch us pass, almost all likely thinking the same thoughts. Turkey was the centre of the Ottoman empire which fell after WW1, and the country has since been excluded from Europe, a landmass which itself is politically defined, certainly not by geography. What could have been if Turkey had been the last state in wealthy Europe and why exactly were the Turks excluded? Politically it seems to us as if Turkey has drifted even further away from Europe, under the stern leadership of Erdogan, the antithesis of Ataturk. As mentioned before, Erdogan uses religion as a political tool, there can be no other reason why mosques are built with roads and the volume of the adhan is so loud that you have no choice but to stop what you are doing and participate, whether you are religious or not. Maybe those old men, who could only assume that we are European, either lamented what could have been in their lifetimes or resented our apparent wealth, a wealth which they could not share. But none made us feel anything but welcome and most returned a wave with a smile. Young ladies, many dressed in modern clothing, most wearing head shawls, would ignore us as we passed.

The mountains themselves were mostly covered with green grass and ground covering with variations of white stone - from gigantic boulders to fields of pebbles. Many of the houses were traditional and multi-level with an ancient bathroom balcony from where occupants would relieve themselves. Some houses seemed modern and inspired by Europe, with pitched roofs and well-maintained flower gardens, a low painted wall and a shiny sedan parked under a carport. It was at an intersection adjacent to one of these modern homes that our navigator told us to turn right, instead of left. A perfect paved road looped through a valley and up the side of a hill where nomadic families lived in large tents and tended their herds and rock walls, housed ancient caves. Returning to the correct road, we passed more modern houses and vast green fields. Turkey truly is a land of contrasts and I can almost guarantee that the modern homes were inhabited by the followers of Ataturk.

At the crest of a mountain, we discovered a change of rock, from white limestone to cream sandstone. An engineering feat had harnessed the power of a crystal blue river, a cement tunnel aqueduct snaked along the contours of the mountain slope, and at the bottom of the valley we found a large flat area, perfect for camping but which bore a sign reading, in English, French, German and Turkish, "This area is vulnerable to flash flooding, camping and parking forbidden". In four languages, in the middle of nowhere? The Turks are full of surprises. Reluctantly we continued to drive, looking for a place to camp, following the river knowing that we would eventually find a recreation area, of some sort. At a bend in the road, a small track sloped down to a field, bordered by trees and the river. I drove down as a few men on motorbikes were leaving. As expected there was a place to park and evidence of many small fires and evidence of our nemesis - the Gunubirlikciler. It took just under an hour to clean up all of the litter and the broken glass bottles, to prepare the Land Rover and collect wood for the campfire. We were parked on a sandy triangle with a small grove of trees and the blue river to the right and a fast-flowing stream to the left. Beyond the stream, a farmer toiled, preparing the earth with a hoe. I shouted a hello, not sure if I needed to ask permission to park for the night. The farmer stopped digging, walked to and opened a small gate in the logwood fence and walked down to the stream to wash his hands. Huseyin introduced himself and soon revealed that he had lived in Amsterdam for many years. I switched from pidgeon Turk to Afrikaans and together we shared a cold drink and spoke as if we were standing in a field in Holland or South Africa. He had a wife and children waiting in a home he built on the hill, they had chosen to live a simple life working the soil under the sun, rather than driving a taxi through endless rain. He had coarse hands, veined, strong arms and a face lined by the ravages of experience. As we spoke, the men on motorbikes returned, took selfies and photos of each other before swimming in the river, just beyond a sign which forbade swimming due to the risk of flash floods. Huseyin thanked us for the drink and returned to his work, Luisa prepared lamb and chicken for the grill, and I chopped the firewood with my axe and machete while keeping an eye on the men, one of whom was tall and overweight, with an open and friendly face. He stood by the bank of the river surrounded by sandstone boulders and spoke for an hour to his phone while the other men played in the water like boys. As the sunset the men rejoined and prepared to leave, and we answered the usual questions. They told us that we could catch fish in the river and that we did not have to worry about flash floods or people bothering us during the night. The largest of the three told the others to collect more firewood for us before sitting down beside me and continuing to ask questions about South Africa and the countries we had been to. When his friends returned with logs and kindling, they said goodbye and rode off, the large guy again deeply involved with his phone.

I lit the fire and cracked open bottles of cold Efes beer for Luisa and myself as the sunset, and a cool breeze began to blow through the valley. We grilled the meat seasoned with coarse salt and ate it together with a salad and a bottle of chilled rose wine. It was a calm and beautiful evening with the river and stream providing a soothing soundtrack.

We awoke late to a warm sun, and the Land Rover surrounded by new, sparkling cars. Old men stood and chatted, dressed in Sunday best while their wives prepared pots of food over small fires and young children played in the stream. We were camped in the middle of their weekend and packed quickly after a swim, Luisa providing much entertainment with her cold water antics and blue bikini. When Luisa swims, the water is always far too cold for her liking. With her arms clenched over her breasts, protecting her heart, she submerges one centimetre of body at a time, squealing as the water reaches her knees, her belly and eventually dropping up to her shoulders with a sigh of great agony and displeasure, shouting warnings, "If you splash me I will kill you!". She then bobs in the water and if the water is not glacial, she might drop her head under the surface for a moment. Jessica refuses to swim until she is thrown in the water and, once the tears are washed away, she will have the time of her life and refuse to leave the water. Keelan, who was away with our friends in Denizli, is always the first in the water and the last one out, his body covered in a cold rash.

Clean and refreshed we packed up, had a chat with the old folk and headed off towards Cappadocia, a two day drive away.

Jessica loves music, and when she sits in front of the Landy, she has two equally important tasks; navigator and DJ. The navigating task she will perform competently if not halfheartedly (at the age of nine she navigated us from Coquieral to Sao Paulo International Airport where we were to collect Luisa and Keelan as they returned from a month in South Africa). The DJ task she performs with great enthusiasm. And she does a sit down dance. After many years of driving around the world, she has learned to dance without legs. Her hands flip and gesture, a sign language translation of the lyrics. Her shoulders bounce and her head sways and cocks to one side, pouts, screams, whistles and sings. She listens to all the good pop music and will mix the most modern stuff with Arctic Monkeys and Abba. She headbangs while I drive, smiling, her arms in the air, fingers clicking, shoulders bouncing. It is an art and a pleasure to witness, though there is a downside - our Land Rover is right-hand drive, and many think that the passenger is driving. The look on a truckers face as we barrel towards him, a blonde ponytail rotating and fist rocking out the window is priceless. But, the look on a policeman's face may not be as entertaining, and I have to keep an eye out for the law and give Jess a smack on the thigh if I spot a copper. So far, we have not been "caught".

We drove up towards the central Turkish plateau, and Jessica was in fine form, full of energy and rocking along to Snap Out of It, by the Arctic Monkeys as we drove through a village and turned left past a field where young boys stopped playing football to watch us pass. The loud white and blue Defender rumbling along, music blaring, a beautiful blonde girl having a party in the front seat. I watched the boys as we passed, they froze as they stood, in a line, trying to understand what they were seeing. All froze, but for one little guy in blue jeans who started rocking hard, air guitar, swaying hips and his headbanging to the tune. He fell in love that day and will never forget us as we will never forget him.

The road took us north, past new dams and earthworks, ancient villages with flocks of long hair goats and herds of cows, up a mountain and down through a valley. Luisa asked me to stop the Landy so that she could take a few photos of a picturesque stone village built into the side of a large hill, small children joined us and posed shyly for the camera, two girls and a younger boy who was clearly in charge and who they obeyed. Too soon we crested the last mountain and joined the main road which crosses the great plateau, the road bordered by immense, functional houses and fields where workers would stop their hard work to wave us by. We reached a city and bought supplies, a defiant young woman greeting me with an intense look, "Take me with you". Outside the city, we filled up with diesel and enjoyed tea offered by the gas station attendants who looked at Luisa and Jessica with passionate eyes, looks which were not intentional but nonetheless unwelcome. We ate bread and cheese and connected to the internet, planning the route ahead. Before Cappadocia, there is a large city called Kayseri where we could possibly rent a small apartment and spend a week working, writing this book and articles, processing images and organising our finances. But, it was late in the day and it would be a waste to pay for a nights accommodation if we could not take advantage of every minute of check-in and out. Luisa pored over her maps and found a mountain range near the city, where we could perhaps find a free camp, she plotted the route, and we headed out along the long, perfectly flat, straight road.

The city approached, and we could see the tall, snow-capped Mount Erciyes in the distance at the northern edge of the plateau. Mount Erciyes is an active volcano, and at almost 4000m high it is the tallest mountain in Central Anatolia. We left the double lane highway and drove parallel to a large, dry field until the field met the hills. The road turned to dirt and led us through a few small agricultural villages before splitting into tracks with unknown destinations. We followed our noses, choosing to go deeper into the hills, away from villages or farmsteads, driving until we found a remote field surrounded by hills in the shadow of the distant mountain. Rock corrals dotted the landscape, and we waited until the sunset, no vehicles had passed before opening the top of the camper and preparing a simple dinner. It was not long after we had eaten and complete darkness enveloped us that we heard a repetitive yell. "Heeya. Heeeya!". A dog barked, deep and low. "Heeya. Heeeya!". Looking out from the camper, we saw a torch beam sweep across the rocky field, slowly and repetitively. Again a dog barked. I waited until the shouting man was ten metres from the Landy and stepped out to meet him only to be met by a massive lion, as I opened the rear door. My heart stopped. There were three lions surrounding the rear of the camper, in an offensive/defensive triangle. Luisa clicked on the rear light, and I realised that the lions were not cats at all, they were large, golden dogs with heads as large as a tiger. A man approached from the shadows, short, wide and dressed for cold. A large wooden stick in one hand and a torch in the other, shining into my face. "Salaam Alaikum" I greeted, stepping forward with a hand outstretched. The man dropped the torch, looked at me sternly for a moment then saw the concerned girls seated behind me. "Alaikum salaam" he responded with a smile and shook my hand. He was a shepherd, and he had brought his flock up to graze for the night. The shepherd smiled at me, inquisitively, "Where are you from?", "Africa!?" After granting permission for us to camp, the shepherd moved on but the large dogs remained, settling down in a larger triangle around the Land Rover, keeping an eye on both us and the herd of scraggly sheep which were exactly the same colour as the Kangal dog (or they might have been Anatolian sheepdogs, I can't tell the difference). The Kangal is a fascinating breed who are excellent flock guardians and are known to care for a flock for up to a year without human contact, never eating from the flock but surviving on rodents and ground squirrels. Throughout the night the Kangal protected us as part of his flock, occasional barking if he spotted something in his territory. Safe from harm we slept as if in a fortress and woke to a clear blue sky. The dogs were both guard and warden, the priority was the flock, and they moved on to watch us from a distance after the sun rose. We ate a breakfast of yoghurt and strawberries, had a cup of coffee and prepared to leave, the Kangal trotted beside us, at a distance, as we left, guiding and escorting until we were far from their herd.

The following five days, essentially a dull work week, staying in a small, bright apartment, working and eating baked food (the apartment had an oven, and we bake when we can). Luisa was fighting against time and technology to produce a series of short documentaries, an extension of my handheld "on the road" videos which I had started as we crossed the USA and which I have to constantly remind myself to film. Those short videos are a fascinating glimpse into our lives and are a world apart from the

Facebook and Instagram posts which tend to highlight the more glamorous aspects of permanent overland travel.

Our books sales had dipped significantly since we left Greece, and it drove me to distraction, trying to figure out what had changed. Facebook had bought Instagram, our two main social media platforms, and had changed the algorithms, something which the company does with irritating regularity. Facebook needs to grow exponentially and the platform who for years bore the slogan "Facebook, It's Free and Always Will Be", had made the decision to charge for the boosting of posts. Essentially your posts are hidden from view until you pay in increments for the post to be made available to those who already follow you. Eventually, and after much research, I decided that we needed to play the game if it meant that we would continue to earn sales. The only problem is that a company with a client base of billions is never going to be able to provide a reliable service. We soon learned that paying Zuckerberg helps only him, and when posting a link or certain keywords, a post is flagged and buried requiring increments of continuous $20 payments for the post to be seen. Pay to play is similar to playing tennis alone, you hit the ball, and it never comes back. Well, as long as Zuckerberg is making good money, that's all I really care about.

Luisa has a skill - she always manages to find what countless others have not. Be it a butchery, a store, a visa loophole or an epic campsite, she has a tenacity which sets her apart. Our journey to Cappadocia proved again her immense resourcefulness. Cappadocia is world-famous for the incredible sandstone landscape of weathered spires, valleys and gulleys, for the subterranean churches and cave dwellings, some of which remain occupied to this day. We drove in on a blistering hot day, not knowing quite what to expect and surprised by the ramshackle layout of touristy villages which coexisted along with local businesses set up to serve the community who profit marginally from their geographic location. I can tell you who is making the big bucks - the air balloon tour operators. There are more air balloons in that small area than in all of Africa combined, and the legendary Albuquerque hot air balloon festival is mirrored in Turkey when the sun is shining and the wind still. We drove past endless tourist offices and curio stores, restaurants and Chinese girls falling off quad bikes until eventually, with Luisa's expert guidance we drove up a serious of steep switchbacks and emerged onto a plateau. "Go left here, now straight, past the school, now past the farm, there should be a track here, another 100 meters. OK here, no not this one, the next one. Yes, I am sure. Keep going, take this track to the left, a bit further. No, wrong track, back up. All clear. Take that track to the right, keep going, I think it is this one, no, keep going. Turn left. Yes, I am bloody sure. Keep going. OK slow, Graeme, look out for that cliff!". In the industrialised world, we are accustomed to signs and barriers to keep us from plummeting to our deaths. In the developing world, you need to employ common sense. What Luisa had found was a level area to park on a small bluff surrounded by steep cliffs and overlooking Cappadocia and the surrounding villages. To the east, a mountain loomed and in its shadow, tourists enjoyed horseback tours, within sight but out of reach. Jessica and I laced on our boots and set off to explore the area, carefully hiking down a steep sandy slope to find abandoned caves and pottery and no other footsteps. I tried to negotiate a sandy gulley a meter wide by placing my feet on either side of a natural drainage trough. I slipped and miraculously landed squatting on my feet sliding 30 meters straight down accompanied by Jessica's laughter; there is nothing she loves more than a good wipeout. An hour later we managed to slip climb our way back up to the Landy to find that Luisa had set up camp and prepared for the evening. As the sunset, we lit our small BBQ and watched as the night came to life. The Adhan call reached us across the valley as city lights sparkled in the distance and a full moon rose. As before in Pamukkale, we were rendered speechless by the sheer beauty of the scene before us, and it was reluctantly that we went to bed after grilling dinner and enjoying a glass of chilled Rose. These are the experiences which make all the hard work, sleepless nights and hard travel worth every ounce of effort, and these experiences are unique to overlanding, no high priced tour can give you such an experience of absolute freedom, satisfaction and bliss.

I must have had too much wine before bed, doubly intoxicated by the unworldly beauty. In the early morning purple, I heard a loud whoosh and another then silence. Forcing my eyes to open I looked up from my bed through one of the two large windows. The sky was dark blue, the sun only beginning to rise. Whooosh! I sat up and watched, as in a dream, as a hot air balloon glided past my window, twenty eyes looking back at me through the camper window. "Shit, Luisa, wake up, the balloons!". Luisa stirred and rolled onto her side. "Luisa!". Without Keelan in the camper, the floor (where Luisa usually makes her bed) was clear. I swung out of bed and threw open the large rear door - fifty balloons filled the sky framed by the open door. "Luisa, get the camera!". Luisa does not do early mornings, Luisa will sleep until ten every day if she can, a habit we learned while living in a roof tent which needed time to dry before we could pack and hit the road. "Keep your pants on, dammit". Jessica, whose superpower is the ability to sleep anywhere enthusiastically, also resisted my unwelcome interruption to her dreams. The balloons do not fly every day if the conditions are determined by the authorities to be unsafe, then the balloons are grounded, and the tourists refunded. We and the tourists were lucky - the sky was clear, and only a gentle breeze blew as the sun rose, blowing the balloons on course. Some balloons rose high, and others stayed low, some were piloted by experts, men who could steer the unsteerable with great precision, not unlike driving a battleship around a racecourse. A balloon approached our Landy, too low, much too low, the basket only a few feet off the ground and seemingly on a collision course with our home perched on the edge of a cliff. The pilot grinned at me and blasted a flame. The Asian occupants squealed with excitement as the balloon drifted inches above the camper. Wanker. "Hey, the roof needs a clean!". Cameras clicked a chorus, capturing our relief. Another balloon floated next to us, so close that we could talk to the occupants in bedroom voices. "Good morning. Coffee?". The pilot dropped the balloon down into the gully, her passengers reaching out to touch the sandstone cliff walls. The pilot stalled the balloon and floated it back up, following the contours of the crags, against the breeze, defying the laws of nature. For two hours the balloons continued to surround us. We made tea and sat quietly marvelling at the ingenuity of man in a surreal environment. We watched as the balloons floated and hovered, bounced off each other, listening to the squeals of delight and shouts of joy, we witnessed the scene with such intensity that the experience left us silent and quiet, exhilarated and drained.

By 10 am the show was over, the sky empty and the sun hot. Jessica and I went for a walk while Luisa packed the Landy. After setting up camp the night before we had watched bemused as a large white camper struggled to find level camping on the slopes of an adjacent green hill. For two hours, the camper manouvered - stopped, moved, reversed, moved forwards, up and over the terrain, never finding satisfaction. For two hours we watched as they struggled without a Luisa to guide them to the perfect site and we know they saw us alone on our perfect perch, smugly enjoying their suffering which we knew too well. Eventually, the camper found a site on a large clearing which led to our camp, the clearing used by balloon operators to launch. Jessica and walked over to say hello and found an elegant Swiss couple and their son, who drove a 4x4 van while they drove a Bremach T Rex. An imposing vehicle of great value which offered not much more living space than our Landy but did so with impressive proportions. The Bremach is smaller than a truck but much larger than even a large 4x4, but its weight is low enough than it can be legally driven with a European car drivers license.

The Swiss family had just returned from Iran, and we would soon learn that they had been travelling the world overland since they were in their twenties. They had explored Africa by motorcycle before their son was born and had built and used every type of overland vehicle imaginable on almost every continent. They declared the Bremach to be the perfect overland vehicle. And their experienced showed. She appeared as fresh as a recently watered daisy, dressed in white linen and smelling lovely, as if she had just emerged from an air-conditioned spa. Their son had the confidence of a well-loved and educated only child and the father had the composure of a man who had seen all you can and had done so with mild curiosity and Swiss indifference. I returned to the Landy and drove her back to where the Swiss parked to continue our typical overlander discussion. Iran had been wonderful, but they lamented how the country had modernised, when they first travelled there in the '80s the country had been more rustic, charming and inviting, they felt a world away from their Swiss utopia and had loved the old world charm of a people unencumbered by modern needs and amenities. Iran had changed, they said, the people were still as amazing as ever, but you needed to travel much further off the beaten path to find that authentic experience. This was definitely not the first time that we had heard elderly overlanders complain about modernisation, and I always have mixed feelings. I can appreciate that modernisation can often be detrimental as ancient culture is replaced by TV culture, a progressive dismissive of ancient, learned culture and a desire for all things western. But, it can't be fair to deny people the advances you enjoy for the sake of "casual" experience. Electricity and reliable vehicles, health-care, satellite television, the internet, clean water and modern appliances all make life easier and more convenient, these things lead to the progress of communities, cultures, science and experience and, inevitably, that which elevated Western society should eventually become accessible to everyone. We have witnessed how modernisation can bring a degree of misery as necessary values are recklessly and ignorantly replaced by the shallowness of a world which worships wealth and "success" above all else, where respect is confused with fear and idolization and outer beauty valued above the superior inner beauty. The West evolved eventually into the culture it enjoys today, and we are better equipped to understand the nuances of that culture while those exposed to it through the lens of discovery might struggle to draw the line between fantasy and reality. But what is good enough for us is surely good enough for them?

Our Swiss friends explained that Turkey too had changed and while Iran is an Islamic Republic, Turkey has institutionalised Islam as a political force. In Iran, the Adhan is called gently, but in Turkey, it is called at high volume, mosques are built with roads and on every other city block, conversation is drowned at least five times a day by an insistent reminder. The volume creates the impression that belief is total, that the religion is omnipotent and everywhere, as sound can intrude through locked doors and over high walls. We found that Turkey consists of two worlds, and it is those who are faithful to Ataturk to whom the Adhan wails the loudest for they are enlightened by knowledge, not scripture.

We said goodbye to Daniel, Brigitte and young Etienne and drove down into the sculpted valley to meet Abu and Dorothy and their little dream bus. We had to wait for them for a while and chose to explore the area, find shade and have lunch. Again we were able to experience Cappadocia, unlike all the multitudes of tourists by finding a quiet clearing where locals went about their business, where ancient caves are still casually employed as storage or a workshop. We ate fresh bread and cream cheese while enjoying a breeze in the shade of an Acer Cappadocicum (Cappadocia tree). A flock of ducks heard Jessica was in town and came over to meet her, ducklings in tow. Jessica squealed for half an hour as she fed the dirty ducks chunks of bread. Luisa made a phone call to Keelan. He was happy. For a while now Keelan had been struggling with teenage angst and he had discovered that he had the power to force his frustration on us all, I battled to remain patient with him though I understood his need to be free and tried to explain to him that if he just did what he was supposed to (schooling instead of gaming!) he could go out into the world and be his own man whenever he chose. All he needed to achieve was the high school certificate, which with his intelligence, experience and book knowledge he would not struggle. He just needed to finish the final book work, and we could schedule the exams. But, he chose to be a gamer, to misappropriate our trust and to sit in a corner and watch YouTube videos and play games while insisting that he was doing his schooling. My goal has always been to teach the children life long self-education, to not only study books but to study life itself, and for that, they need curiosity and the ability to self motivate and practice self-control. Keelan had chosen to waste the dedicated time which he had been given and now was frustrated that he did not have the freedom which the hard work would have delivered. His frustration boiled over, and he had become increasingly hostile and passive-aggressive. At 18 years old he needed to be out with people his age, meeting girls, having fun but he was stuck with his family, living in a car and often having to deal with long days of discomfort and all the challenges which the road can force you to suffer. He would be happy with love and attention but became sullen and withdrawn if we reprimanded him. Instead of simply doing what he needed to do he would create hostility, arguing with Jessica and disrespecting Luisa, a sure path to massive conflict. A home of 2m x 3.3m is much too small for a massive teenage attitude, and I found that I was losing patience with him. It is my role to keep the family together, happy and satisfied. I have to please everyone, and I have to ensure peace, it is a role which I play with patience because I realise that while the children did not choose this lifestyle, it is the very best life they could live. Yes, they have lost out on a "normal" childhood, but how many of you would swop your childhood for theirs? I would. They have had the privilege to experience what very few ever will, in fact, they represent a minuscule fraction of humanity. They are one in a billion, they call the planet their home, and they have been raised with love and compassion. They sometimes forget this.

Keelan was happy with Ergun and Asla, he had become part of their family, and he enjoyed the normality of their lives. He rose to breakfast and laughs, he went to work with Ergun and learned new things every day, he was meeting new people and having unique experiences, he was in the world alone, but he was safe and comfortable in a family environment. That meant the world to us, and it meant the same to him.

Jessica is calm and relaxed. She is still young and yet to go through the worst of teenage growth, but we will deal with that when it happens. She calms Luisa and I and in the absence of a rowdy son the camper became calm, we missed Keelan, and we knew he missed us but the month he spent with his new Turkish family was exactly what we all needed, the time gave us the luxury of space and reminded us all of why we loved and cherished each other so dearly. Luisa had cried most of the day when Keelan had left on the bus, and those tears were necessary and valuable because they were tears of love, not frustration or regret.

With the ducks fed, we drove to the village and bought groceries and connected to the internet. A caravan of quad bikes driven by young Chinese tourists zig-zagged down the road and towards the spires. Two girls struggled to control their bike and accelerated in panic, their Turkish minder racing after them on a scooter. They narrowly missed a concrete traffic circle and veered onto a dirt road heading for a brick wall like fashionably attired moths to a flame. The minder caught up with them seconds before they hit the wall and grabbed the handlebars and the brakes while piloting his own bike with his knees. In a cloud of dust, he brought the disaster to a halt. Perhaps the other girl might be a better driver. She was not. We later witnessed the caravan again as we parked amongst the spires waiting for Abu to arrive. The harassed Turkish minders took the time to teach their clients how to ride their battered rental quad bikes. Abu arrived and led us past the "no vehicles beyond this point" signs and through a maze of tracks to a hidden level area where they had camped almost every year for the last two decades. No-one knows Cappadocia as well as they do and the signs are for others to obey, they have earned the right to break the rules. The camp area was surrounded by tall rounded cathedrals of sandstone, ancient natural pyramids into which generations bore homes and storage and churches and pens. We hiked along a path through tunnels bored by time and past vineyards and ploughed fields surrounded by walls of surreal stone. We found Christian churches with elaborate carved ceilings and painted murals of saints who had all had their eyes gouged out of the stone by the spiritually insecure. Cappadocia had long been a Christian haven where subterranean cities had been carved by the hands of those seeking shelter from persecution. Ruled from centuries BC by the Persians, Assyrians, Alexander the Great, the Romans and other regional players. Each had left their mark, and the modern inhabitants of the area live and breathe a living history, absentmindedly.

We hiked until late in the afternoon but not once were we harassed by other tourists, Abu knew exactly where to take us so that we too could experience the unique and untrodden Cappadocia which he and Dorothy loved so dearly. The sunset and we made a small campfire, drank sweet homemade wine (not too sweet, just perfect) and spoke about travel and life and Turkey. Abu is a precocious man, full of nuance and easily distracted by an imperfect world which does not follow the rules which he considers to be universal. If it does not fit, he will make it fit or argue and complain until eventually, he realises that it is faulty, badly designed or ridiculous - which exempts whatever is challenging him and which he can then, eventually, ignore. Dorothy loves him dearly. She dreams but is not a dreamer, she accepts what Abu cannot and quietly endures his whims while awaiting his brilliance. She lives for their annual trips to Cappadocia and Greece, where they have found a slice of paradise which few know about. There they live amongst the gods they do not believe in for two months and return to their beautiful home surrounded by the stubbornly faithful where Abu struggles to speak with a subdued voice while that which does not fit rages around him.

It was in Cappadocia that we finally accepted that our dream of driving across Asia would not be fulfilled, this time. The Carnet de Passage which we needed for Iran and India was simply too expensive and with summer coming to an end we could not realistically cross Russia (for which South Africans are visa-free) not only because of the treacherous cold but also because we would have nowhere to go once we reached Vladivostok - every destination required either shipping or an expensive ferry (to South Korea) and while we have the self-belief, we could not convince ourselves that we would not find ourselves on the other side of Russia without the finances to leave! I am sure that if we had taken the gamble, we would find a way, we always do, but the winter, distance and budget all suggested we try something different. Staying in Europe was an option, of course, but that meant we would have to give up the overlanding lifestyle and settle down. While settling down may be a good idea it is not something which we want to do, even Luisa who often confides that she sometimes wants a normal life, admits that she does not ever want to stop living the life we do. And we love chasing the sun. I do not remember who made the suggestion, it was probably Luisa who fears ice and snow more than bankruptcy, who planted the seed of a route across Africa. We could head back "home" to South Africa and see our family and friends, we could enjoy the African sun and wildlife, camps, beaches and food, we could embrace and reconnect with Mother Africa, write a few more books and then take on Russia, ship back to the Americas and head back down to South America. It sounded like a brilliant idea. We had been in the Northern Hemisphere for way too long and it was time that we had a real adventure again, the African journey would provide excellent footage for our documentary series, and we all missed Mama Africa. We shook on it. We were heading back to Africa!

(Perhaps it would be prudent to remind you that we reserve the right to change our minds. If we announce that we will attempt a route, we will do everything in our power to achieve it, but if the journey becomes logistically or otherwise impossible, we have to consider and accept a new route which is possible. It is the reality of the life we have chosen and work endlessly to achieve).

Having made the decision to head back to Africa, we dismissed the idea of heading to the Stans and instead set a course back to Europe via the Black Sea. It took a couple of days driving north with a headwind which sucked every cent out of my pocket. The cities and town we drove through varied significantly - some seemed vibrant and colourful with students on the street and people going about their business with energy. Other towns seemed populated entirely by old people who had never left the town, who watched us pass with slack jaws. We slept that night next to a lake, on the verge of a dirt road. Some girls came to meet us shyly, left quickly and returned with a plate of grilled chicken and vegetables. A small boy and his larger, less courageous brother approached us and offered a bags of plums as a welcome gift, an old man offered us a cold bottle of Coca Cola and showed us where we could fill the water tanks. Turkish hospitality is legendary for a reason, and we often tried to reciprocate with gifts of wooden bead bangles or fruit.

The next night we chose to sleep next to a lake besieged by day visitors. Hundreds of vehicles filled the forest and the roads surrounding the forest which hugged one-third of the lake and suffered quietly. We chose to continue driving the circumference and seek an area without litter, music and the frantic chaos of people trying to relax. A herd of cows greeted us as we rounded a corner and drove onto a man-made bank, the lake was, in fact, a dam. I drove down a steep bank, past the herd and found a small beach which only needed an hour to clean. We were alone while a horde jostled for blades of grass a few hundred meters away. We were alone, but I was not sure if that was an entirely good thing as my two female passengers were my responsibility and a great attraction. As dark clouds rolled between the sun and earth, a family joined us to repopulate the beach with plastic, a few fishermen followed, and another family followed them. We sat quietly in the camper, Jessica hidden from sight, enjoyed lunch and read books, waiting patiently for the night to fall. But it was not night fall which removed our neighbours, that job was performed suddenly and effectively by the clouds which blackened and attacked, a ferocious wind accompanied by thunder, lightning and an impressive deluge of rain. Luisa is petrified of storms - each clap of thunder and crack of lightning produced a scream and a face frozen in terror, eyes to the sky, anticipating death from above while cringing in a corner. Jessica and I reacted the opposite of how nice people might think we should. We teased Luisa rather than consoling her (if we are smiling and joking she feels silly and relaxes and laughs at herself while promising to murder us after the storm, if we show fear she will be unconsolable). And yes, it is naughty fun to see a woman who the Norwegians call Shieldmaiden (and who can strike fear into my soul with one mean glance) cower like a small child from a faraway beast in the sky. The Landy hardly shook as the trees which surrounded us bent and seizured by the wind which eventually calmed after an hour but continued to drive rain throughout the night. We slept soundly listening to the rainfall on the roof, sure that no-one would venture out into the storm to disturb us.

That last afternoon of driving to the Black Sea offered excellent roads but yet more headwind which did not subside until we drove high up into the western edge of the Pontic mountain range and descended to a city called Samsun and into a world which was not the Turkey which we had grown to love. It was a world populated by people who did not look like Turks, who were often tall, thin, weathered and faintly Slav or Russian in appearance. And that would make sense as the Black Sea also washes onto the shores of Georgia, Russia, Ukraine, Romania, Moldova and Bulgaria. The sky was grey and the land deep green, some cities were industrial, and others entertained tourists, some seemed to have the blackened heart of an alcoholic coal miner, and others were bright and colourful, dotted with expensive campsites, restaurants, hotels, fun fares and beautiful, miserable Russian girls. Luisa guided us west of a town called Sinop where a large, lawned campsite called Akliman Mesire Ve Piknik Alani (Akliman Recreation and Picnic Area) hugged a picturesque bay where colourful fishing boats bumped against each other upon crystal clear water. The campsite asked a ridiculous fee, and we left reluctantly, driving past seafood restaurants bordered by rubbish skips overflowing with garbage, old tyres and construction rubble. The colourful boats bumping upon the clear water were surrounded by plastic bags and beer cans and hundreds of plastic bottles. Geographically the bay reminded us of the spectacular Oregon coastline, but Americans don't litter for sport. The Gunyebilikchler Turks do (remember the Goonies from earlier?). A beautiful quiet beach seemed like the perfect place to park for the night, but as we drove closer, we saw that the beach was covered in litter dropped, not washed in from the sea. On the navigator app, Luisa could see a small trail which led to a pier, and we drove on the muddy track with branches scratching the windows, hoping that the bad road would deter the day camper Goonies who had nothing but obvious contempt for a spectacular coastline. We emerged from the trees onto rolling lawn. We were at the northern end of the bay with the expensive campsite directly across the water roughly 400m away, the fishing boats to our right, a pier protecting the bay and connecting the land to a small island ahead of us, a grassy hill behind us. It was possible to drive down onto and perhaps park on the pier, but we would be trapped there should someone assault us in the night as the pier was only wide enough for one car and you would have to reverse to leave. We chose to drive up the grassy hill to a level area where old campfires assured us that we could park for the night. A spotted dog emerged from the treeline and followed us as we walked around the hill trying to understand what kind of person dumps all their trash before leaving after a pleasant evening of burning tyres, drinking heavily and smoking profusely. Well, they were the type of person who had babies which crapped a lot and witnessed their parents dumping their nappies into the campfire, a good habit to be learned for the future. They were the type of people who brought toilet seats and old Tupperware to dump in the trees, and they were the type of people who relieved themselves where others might want to grill a dinner. It was as if the local municipality had chosen to repurpose a botanical garden as a rubbish dump. I had rubbish bags, but it would take at least two hours to clean just the area where we intended to camp and another hour to collect all the bottle caps and cigarette butts. We cleaned for a while, filling two large bags, threw those on the bonnet of the Landy and headed back to the filthy beach we had passed earlier (the beach bordered by a forest and four large, empty recycling bins) and parked on the beach. I cleaned the beach while Luisa set up camp before helping me and within an hour we had "our" section of narrow beach looking beautiful. I set up the little BBQ, and Luisa passed me a cold drink, a reward for my efforts. Sitting quietly with the sun setting behind grey clouds, the bay revealed her true, unmolested beauty of green land, gently lapping clear water, a few lights twinkling from the fishing boats huddled together against their memories of the sea and the spotted dog at our feet, sniffing the BBQ with anticipation. The evening was perfect. And then a fleet of Goonies arrived, parked their crap little poor boy racers on a patch of lawn and cranked the music up to 11. Beer bottles were soon being tossed while raucous laughter urinated on our evening. I could not hear Luisa complain, even though she was sitting a foot away from me. Usually, we have no choice but to let the locals do their thing, we are visitors and have few rights, particularly when free camping. I walked up to the Goonies, introduced myself politely, told them where we were from and asked them if they could turn the music down. They said sure, no problem (problem yok). They changed the music to Spanish guitars and turned it down. It stayed that way. An hour later, they tossed a bag of trash on the lawn and left, big grins and waves.

Peace returned to the beach, we fed the spotted dog bones and sat quietly, enjoying the full moon and land lights sparkling on the water which broke like a lake, gently on the beach. I walked to the water's edge and threw a stone into a puddle of moonlight. A thousand multi-coloured effervescent lights erupted just under the surface and slowly extinguished. Phytoplankton! I called Luisa and Jessica, and together we marvelled as stones entered the blue-black water and created a dazzling light show, an aquatic fireworks display. Moments later we were swimming amongst the plankton, stars above and below us, adrift in a salty universe, enchanted by the lit little creatures who tried to lure us out to sea. The Black Sea is called that for good reason. A layer of fresh water fed by surrounding rivers lies above a layer of saltwater supplied by the Mediterranean, and the sea is respected and feared by all those who survive on her shores. It is believed that the name Black Sea came about because sailors who drop clean anchors retrieve black anchors stained by the ancient rot which lies deep beneath the surface. It is rumoured that bodies do not decompose and the victims of shipwrecks are doomed to languish weightlessly in the black depths for an eternity. The lights wanted us for their own, they longed for us to become them and we had to break their spell before they succeeded.

The Turkish Black Sea coast from Samsun towards Istanbul is dominated by the Kure and Pontic mountain ranges which we had traversed in part en-route from Cappadocia. New roads are being built along the coast but most of the day's driving is spent on endless switchbacks which deliver you again and again to the shoreline. The weather was cool and wet, the sky grey, the atmosphere depressing. We made the decision that if the weather did not improve, or if the roads deteriorated further that we would head inland and drive to Istanbul via the straight inland paved highway which enjoyed sunshine and bright cities. After a day of endless up and down, we chose to camp on a harbour wall which we had spotted from the road. The wall itself was thick, level and wide enough to park a hundred cars. Inside the small harbour and across the little bay, sat fishermen cottages, made of wood and all identical except for the one in the centre which had a higher roof bearing three old, grey speakers. The fishermen watched us curiously as we opened the camper roof and sparked a fire in our little BBQ. Yes, we braai as often as possible. Some weeks we will braai almost every day, and we grill whatever is locally available, usually accompanied by a parcel of vegetables or sweet potato, pumpkin or garlic bread. If we ate like our European friends (who mostly survive on pasta, tuna and salads while travelling), we would spend half of what we do on food. But, and this is a big BUT, our one luxury is food. We do not have air conditioning, or ten pairs of shoes each, or regular manicures, spa days, date nights, movie nights or restaurant food. We live on a shoestring and Luisa would probably leave me, kids in tow, if I ever tried to force her to eat pasta, tuna and salad every night. Man, I might even leave myself. Turkey boasts great supermarkets, and every town worth its salt will have a branch of Migros, the Swiss supermarket chain. Luisa will visit each one as we drive, she adores modern supermarkets. We used to let the kids go into the supermarkets with us, but they would just lose their shit (if you will pardon the expression) and go giddy with excitement, sneaking treats into the cart and standing in front of me jabbering on about the electronics section while I am trying to choose a mustard. No, now they are banished to the Land Rover where they guard our home and play on their phones (if there is free, open wifi they would refuse to leave the Landy anyway, the internet tops everything else) leaving Luisa and me to enjoy the air-conditioned fruit and vegetables, the butchery, bakery and sweet aisle.

We grilled fish that night while watching the fishermen go about their business. Every couple of hours, the tallest cottage would emit a piercing call to prayer, and one fisherman would leave his duties to fulfil the obligation. After dark, many of the men congregated in one cottage to play a game of cards or some kind of board game, I could not tell which from our relatively distant vantage point. They did not seem to mind us, but we did not feel entirely welcome, I suppose it was not often that a foreign family camped on their harbour wall. We slept to the sounds of the sea and the gently banging of boats. At 5 am Luisa woke me up to flashing blue lights. "The police!". They knocked on the back door and ordered me to open up. I fumbled with the rear window and opened it clumsily, blinded by torchlight.

"Something in Turkish"

"Sorry, English, South African"

"What are you doing here?"

"Oh, we are sleeping"

"Why?"

"Because we were tired. I hope it is not a problem. We will leave when the sun rises"

"Yes, but why are you sleeping here?"

"It seemed like a good place. Safe"

"I do not understand"

"My family and I are exploring Turkey, it is very beautiful. We are on the way to Istanbul and decided to stop here for the night"

"OK, welcome to Turkey"

"Thank you very much"

"You will leave soon?"

"Yes, sir".

The policeman flashed his torch on Luisa and then Jessica, who was fast asleep in the upper bunk. They muttered to each other and left. A minute later, the call to prayer erupted, perhaps the Muezzin was distracted by the drama on the harbour wall. This was the first time the police had ever knocked on the camper door.

We slept an hour longer and left, heading back over the mountain to the sunshine and perfect highway. It was the tail end of winter, the Black Sea coast did not seem to offer the attractions of the interior and the endless coastal switchbacks, heavy forest and grey skies had done little to welcome and hold us. The D765 road to the interior was approaching, and if we decided to continue along the coastline we would have to drive almost all the way to Istanbul, it was decided that we would take the D765 and head back to the interior and the Turkey which we loved.

I received a message on Instagram from a student who lived in the small mountain city of Gerede on the slopes of the Bolu mountain. He invited us to visit him and promised to show us a forest at the summit above the city. We arrived late and waited at a gas station forecourt for our new friend to arrive. A green Land Rover Defender arrived, and Hassan, a well built and European featured young man emerged with a tall, thin friend. Hassan and Huseyin were students at the local university. An hour later we sat in a traditional log coffee house shrouded in mist and surrounded by sturdy wooden benches roughly hewn, "wild" hogs and their piglets (Turkey has an abundance of hogs as pork is not eaten by the majority Muslim population) and a forest which reached up into the clouds. We had to drive up switchback passes to reach the restaurant and were waited on with antediluvian service by the staff. The coffee shop was built as a winter refuge, and the heat of the fire soon drove us to remove layers of winter clothing. It had not been cold since we had left Burhaniye on the west coast, but there had been a chill in the air since we had arrived near the Black Sea and now we were at altitude. Hassan offered to organise any Land Rover parts that we may need, and we realised that his intentions were at least in part commercial. After coffee, we drove up into the mountains, the sun setting. Muddy tracks led us upwards, and we emerged from the pine forest in a clearing populated by a collection of homes, some well maintained, perhaps a hunter's weekend retreat, and others ramshackle and guarded by large ferocious dogs. We drove for an hour through the forest, past a small dam and a few more smallholdings. We stopped near the summit, and Hassan explained that there were bears in the area but he had only seen them on rare occasions, he came here as often as he could with the local 4x4 club and they explored the lesser-known tracks, it was his getaway from student life and he knew the mountain well. We were tired after a long day on the road and asked Hassan if we could camp in the mountains, he did not think it was a good idea but did not explain why, he said that we could instead camp outside the restaurant or we could camp outside his apartment block if we needed a shower. We did need a shower, it had been ten days since we had left the small, bright apartment in Kayseri to head to Cappadocia and we had been free camping ever since. We probably smelt worse than the oldest, dirtiest mountain bear. With headlights on, we headed back down, out of the forest and returned to the coffee shop area where a large tree shimmered with strings of multi-coloured lights. The tree lit the area with a soft glow, shrouded in thin mist and was completely enchanting, the broad tree itself unlike any other we had seen on the mountain.

I followed Hassan through narrow streets and evening traffic and arrived eventually at a pair of unloved apartment blocks, without balconies or living areas for the occupants, the type of accommodation affordable for students and labourers, though a new black BMW stood quietly outside. Inside the musky apartment, we were introduced to five of Hassan's roommates, all students, all friendly and welcoming. I became slightly paranoid - my girls were about to shower in this apartment, no-one knew where we were, and I was outnumbered 7 - 1. But, of course, the students were gentlemen. They explained that they were all studying business administration, though of the seven only one intended to work in a bank. The others were either going to be policeman or engineers. They explained that it was impossible for a young person to start a career in Turkey unless they had a degree, that those without university degrees were doomed to be the working class labourers or mechanics or builders. It did not matter which degree you held to enter the corporate world, and we were told that a B.Comm was the most affordable degree and the university in this city was the most affordable. They had all travelled there from around the country to study and once they had graduated they would then move on to pursue either a career or further education in their chosen field. In a country of great wealth and ancient poverty, it stands to reason that the dividing line would exist, and the opportunity to elevate existed for those who were willing to work hard enough. It reminded me of why family values are essential but had I been a Turk, I may have been relegated to the life of a mechanic or a builder, I never had the option to study which is perhaps why I have chosen to study life.

The students chatted with us as and we felt more human and comfortable after a hot shower and once dressed in clean, fresh clothing. Hassan lived elsewhere we discovered, and he walked us down to the Land Rover where we prepared a quick meal before bed. It had been a long and interesting day, we had covered a large distance across the central Anatolian plateau and then explored a wet, dark mountain, we had made new friends and had once again been completely surprised by what the day had offered. This surprise, the originality of the experience is what keeps us going, the motivation to suffer through hardship and hard work which represents many of our days - there are very few people who have been able to achieve the degree of independence which we have, and we do what we do for very good reason. One life live it can be either a casual dream, a logo plastered on a vehicle driven for fun every other weekend, or it can be a way of life. We have one life lived well. I believe.

After an evening exploring a forest near Istanbul, we drove towards Yalov, where we had been invited to stay at the workshop of Emre, the owner of Anatolian Overland. Emre is a tall handsome man with dark, brooding eyes. He kindly allowed us to use his workshop to fix a couple of problems we had been experiencing with the Defender - a heavy oil leak and a persistent pull to the left on the steering. I suspected that the front left swivel bearings needed replacing and the oil leak was mysterious. So we started out fixing the obvious bearing problem while Luisa worked on the campers water system, which was leaking, and the solar system, which also appeared to have developed a leak. As with all relatively minor jobs, all it takes is one sheared nut for an hour-long task to become a late night. The ball joint thread had become damaged when I put too much pressure on it to remove the nut. Without a replacement ball joint, I spent hours cutting through the damaged section with a hacksaw blade (the blade broke, and I had to do all the cutting by hand with a fragment). Emre had left, and though we had keys to the workshop I did not see any hacksaws and did not want to dig through his tools. Eventually, I managed to convince the thread to accept the castle nut and reassemble the front hub after replacing the top swivel bearing. It was a frustrating day.

The following day we were joined by Robin and his wife, Kim and Dave and his wife, Angela who were touring Turkey in their Defenders. Robin and Kim were heading east across the Stans and Russia to Mongolia before shipping to the USA, and Dave and Angela were following a similar route, though not shipping across the Pacific (Angela fell horribly ill in Russia but recovered thanks to excellent medical treatment). With the two British Defenders and South African 130 parked outside the workshop, we had a typical overlander evening, grilling meat, drinking various beverages and swapping tales of the road. Overlanders can camp almost everywhere, and an industrial area suits us perfectly, there is usually security, and there are stores which provide the tools and parts we always need. Robin and Dave had some bags made by a hasty tailor and then helped me diagnose my oil leak. It seemed to be coming from below the oil cooler and with that side of the engine stripped of exhaust, oil filters and turbo we were able to get to the oil cooler which did indeed have a broken oil gasket. Robin did most of the work while four bearded men looked on, I then prepared the oil cooler for a temporary (which became permanent) silicone smeared gasket, and we re-assembled the various part and tested for a leak. Solved! The leak had pestered us for a while, and it was a relief that we had finally found the cause and solved the problem. That night we all drove to Emre's apartment near the sea and parked in a parking area outside a restaurant. Luisa grilled a meal for fifteen people on two small BBQ's, and we solved the world's problems until late in the evening. A battleship cruised past us in the morning, and a few military helicopters flew overhead, across the water lay Istanbul.

In convoy, the three foreign Defenders drove to the coast where Luisa found a quiet beach where we could park in a laager. We all cleaned the beach of plastic and bottles and collected driftwood for the campfire, Angela gave me a haircut, and we enjoyed a swim in the sea. It was an idyllic camp and good to have friends, the kind of people who understood us and shared similar dreams. Robin and Kim had spent some time with us in Portugal where they had visited us in Figueira da Foz and had stayed at the excellent municipal campgrounds. Robin, who refuses to dance and can't be made to do so (Luisa tried to extricate him from his seat but could not budge him, nicknamed him Strong Like Bull), is an ex-Navy Chief and he seems fearless. Dave is also ex-military and told incredible stories from his maritime career. Both men had lived lives which made international overlanding seem like a gentle pursuit. Ex-military men tend to make great overlanders, they understand risk, are able to take care of themselves and are accustomed to dangerous places and heavy machinery. Both Robin and Dave's Defenders were examples of minimalism - sleek, functional and made for purpose. Those near-standard Defenders made my camper look like a fat-bottomed girl in a blue dress. I would not swop my girl, I love her big butt. Robin and Dave were heading east, and we were headed back to Europe, after breakfast and a swim we said our goodbyes and promised to meet on the road again one. It is just a matter of time.

There are two airports near Istanbul, and after a full month of being separated from our firstborn, we were due to collect him at the smaller of the two airports in a district called Sanayi. We arrived the night before his plane was due to land and negotiated a complex system of roads to find the one road which led to the airport and did not require a massive detour around the city. This and Oliver Tambo International Airport in Johannesburg shared a road network and signage system designed to ensure that arrivals are lost as soon as they leave the airport and even the most conscientious self-driven traveller will stand an excellent chance of missing their flight as GPS systems shut down in confusion and inconsistent signage ensures that the lane which was previously marked Arrivals eventually terminates in the airport service area. We were determined to greet Keelan as he stepped off the plane and spent the night at a large gas station en-route to the airport. We parked in an empty lot close to a food court and enjoyed a hamburger before the gas station security boss shouted at us to move because the rear door of the camper opened over a walkway which no-one used.

That morning we discovered that despite our careful preparations to be on the correct road we were in fact on the incorrect road and needed to do a half an hour detour to reach Arrivals. Luisa and Jessica ran into the airport while I waited in the drop and go lane, avoiding eye contact with airport security. Half an hour passed and I spotted a Keelan draped in mother and sister heading towards the Landy. He shone with happiness, and we hugged for a minute before loading the family into the vehicle and heading towards Istanbul.

Keelan had a wonderful time in Denizli, he had settled into a routine and had become part of the family. It was the routine which he enjoyed the most - he knew when and where he would awake and go to sleep, he knew he had an hour for breakfast, an hour for lunch and an evening for dinner. The work he did was challenging as Ergun sought to teach him how to rebuild an engine and insisted that Keelan know exactly what he was doing and not just spinning wrenches. He had met a local celebrity called the Watermelon man who drove a VW bus decorated with watermelons and who was an actor or a singer or both. He had worked almost every day with Ergun, rebuilding a VW Beetle and learning to speak Turkish while Asli did her best to keep him fed and happy. She did a good job. He returned to us re-motivated, happier and full of stories; he returned to us the Keelan who we loved so dearly.

Cities do not hold much attraction for us - they drain our resources and immerse us in a world of concrete which is unfamiliar to us. If we do explore a city, we should do so as part-time residents, renting an apartment and living as the locals do. The idea of shuttling from market to mosque to monument to museum does not appeal to us now. It might when we are older and wealthier and calmer. It was good enough for us to drive through and cross the Bosphorous, the tail end of a gigantic circle which we had drawn around the country. Crossing from Asian soil back onto European was significant for us, but saddening as we had not been able to achieve our goal of continuing to drive across Asia. The skies over Istanbul were clear and fresh, it was early June 2018 and we knew that a glorious European summer lay ahead of us as we drove north accompanied by an endless convoy of trucks delivering to massive infrastructure projects, such as the new airport, slated to be one of the largest in the world once complete.

An hour before the border, I felt the Landy pulling hard left as we were driving along the freeway and stopped in a small town to have a look at the problem. Most Turkish gas stations are happy to let you do quick roadside repairs, but we had pulled into the one gas station whose owner was on-site and not happy. The top swivel bearings were crushed, and shards of metal had threatened to damage the CV joint (a complex shaft with a rotating head consisting of a brace and large ball bearings, it is the CV joint which allows you to steer while receiving drive to the front wheels). Keelan and I worked together and stripped the front hub down, removed and cleaned the CV (which was not damaged) and replaced the main seals and all swivel bearings including the swivel pin, luckily I carried a full set of spares. It took an hour to complete, and we filled up with fuel to appease the gas station owners, bought cool drinks and ice creams for the kids and headed to Bulgaria.

Turkey had been a revelation for us. It was the first time that we had spent any significant amount of time in a majority Muslim country. We had found the people to be compassionate, kind, generous and honest, the country itself to be spectacular, safe and immensely rewarding. It is the kind of country where a person could live their lives and never want; where communities are families and where every drop of water is beautiful blue. We love you, Turkey!

Atop the Smugglers Route, Andorra

Picos de Europa

Exploring France

Boondocking at the beach

Northern Spain

The Pyrenees, Spain

166

Galicia

The Guardian, A Coruna

Galicia, the only waterfall to fall into the ocean

Bremach T Rex

Che Guevara, Galicia

The Best Beer

Bossons Glacier

German toddler with French bulldog

Mex, Switzerland and a new toy

With Eva and Lukas, Germany

Keelan leaving for the commune

Overland Truck, Abenteuer & Allrad, Bad Kissingen

Keelan hiking Bossons Glacier, Chamonix

With Markus, Rebecca and Louis, Germany

Jessica

The Wolf, Germany

Servicing the Landy

Keelan

Corne, Silver Island

Lissa, Silver Island

Alone together, the Aegean

Silver Island, Greece

Oreoi Dock, Greece

Glifa ferry, Greece

Greece

A Tauras Mountain Village

Above the balloons, Cappadocia

Asli, Go! Go! Go!

Cappadocia

Kos, Turkey

Lake Salda sand

Children of the Taurus Mountains

Jessica hiking Cappadocia

Luisa, Graeme and Jessica

The wind was too strong for flight

Sunset

Bolu mountain tree, Turkey

A new friend, Central Turkey

Boondocking with friends, Cappadocia

Turkish man

The best day, Cappadocia hot air balloons

Checking Leigh's chassis, Czech Republic

With the Grisby's and Spinks', east of Istanbul

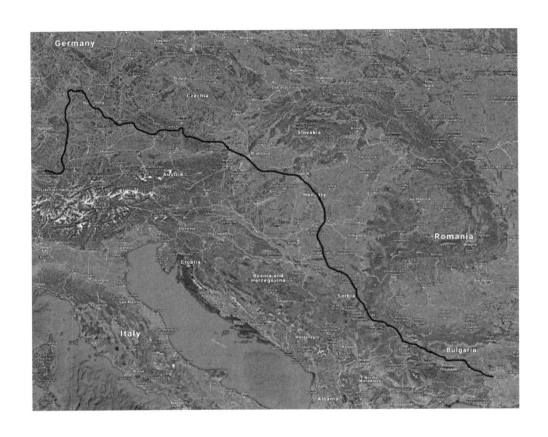

13

Bulgaria
Strange Englishmen and bad jazz

The route we were following to Germany to attend the Abenteuer and Allrad overland event, followed the same route which the thousands of Syrian refugees endured to reach Northern Europe. Evidence of this was clear at the Bulgarian border where razor wire surrounded temporary internment camps which had still not been removed three years after the crisis. We were nervous that we might have a problem re-entering Europe with the Land Rover as it, apparently, was only allowed to be in the EU for six months of the year and we had not been out for a full six months. If we were stopped before we reached EU proper, we would have to turn back but then where could we go? Georgia? East? The Bulgarians, who boasted an EU flag at the border, did not seem too interested in the Land Rover as much as they were interested in her contents.

"Drugs?"
"No, sir"
"Guns?"
"No, sir"
"This is a weapon"
"No sir, it is a tool, a machete, I use it to chop wood for fires".

The customs agent removed the machete from its leather sheath and inspected the blade which was scarred and blackened from hard and regular work.

"You are right, it is a tool. Welcome to Bulgaria".

Southern Bulgaria is hot and green and dilapidated, a thin sliver of tarmac serving the border to Harmanli where Luisa had heard rumour of a Lidl supermarket. The town stopped developing in 1987 as if it was preserved in a bubble where new cars, fashions, hairdos, music and art were forbidden. The woman wore tight colourful leggings, thick gloss belts and billowing white blouses, provocatively unbuttoned and held aloft by shoulder pads shrouded by tall perms of black or blonde. The men wore patchwork leather jackets, brown slacks and combed their hair back slick. The cars were Russian, and Ford parked outside Soviet-era apartments surrounded by green lawn and restaurants serving food in plastic or on plastic with plastic.

The Lidl was cheap, very cheap and Luisa celebrated by buying the entire store and serving it for dinner. The nearest campsite was run by a tall Englishman. He had once had a career on TV as the ugly guy in Men Behaving Badly, and now he was just the ugly guy in the campsite which advertised a swimming pool but forgot to install one. His father, who the ugly guy from Men Behaving Badly feared more than an angry, sober God, was all things back in the day and Ugly had driven or owned every Land Rover ever built and had been a pioneer of the Land Rover Experience, in fact, Ugly had been in charge of training all the Land Rover drivers for the blah, blah, blah. Ugly liked to talk non-stop and play Playstation all day and watch like a hawk when you went to the toilet. One morning the tinsel toilet seat broke. Ugly was not amused. "Is there something you would like to tell me about the toilet seat!" he bellowed across the campsite. Why yes Ugly, it is far stronger than it looks! It took four jumps to break it. Tough!

Despite the 50-year-old teenager, we decided to stay two nights in the camp which was pleasantly enough situated on green lawn beside a farm and an elevated railway line where occasionally a train from 1982 would rumble by at the speed of a slow rumble. A friendly shepherd passed the camp twice a day with his herd of goats, and we fed old bread to a frantic flock of chicken trapped in the 17th century. The only other inhabitants of the camp were an English couple who had moved to Bulgaria seeking to stretch their retirement pounds. Ugly had made all sorts of promises, and they were deeply reliant on him for both their residence and the construction of their home. They told us that there would be a festival in the nearby village that night. Ugly's parents came to visit the camp before heading into the village, they drove a new Land Cruiser, and I did not wonder why Ugly feared his dad, who had the countenance of a dangerous man.

The village was a short walk away along a road bordered by crumbling old homes. A band sat on the steps of the town hall and tuned their instruments vigorously while shoulder pads wailed to clear her throat. The speaker system worked perfectly and was cranked all the way to distortion. The villagers stood in a large circle and watched as a dance circle formed before them, tattooed bikers drank litre bottles of beer and women dressed as peasants sold mounds of sweets and plastic toys. To the left of the town, hall tables had been arranged in long parallel lines, and Ugly waved to us gleefully like long lost friends. Luisa and I bought beer for the three of us and a bottle of lemonade for Jessica. We could not hear our own thoughts and the music was too loud for food to bear flavour.
Manababababababababudabudabudababababababababababudabudabudabababab abababababudabudabudababababababababababudabudabudababababamana! The drummer suffered a stroke but soldiered on, the singer wailed louder and louder, the trumpeters both lost control of their fingers, but not their lungs and all had the greatest stamina. All the while Ugly jabbered and laughed and clutched at a blonde woman who, while young, had eyes so distant that you did not want to imagine what killed her soul, her dark-haired friend had a similar look but still smiled with her eyes.

We had to escape. The awful jazz chased us back up the road as the village shot fireworks at the sky. We could hear the jazz inside the camper until late that night when Ugly returned to the camp with the blonde to play with her Playstation while the brunette sat on a bench and smoked cigarettes.

The next morning we fled to the capital, Sofia, where we met an English couple who were on their way to experience the darkest depths of a Russian winter. There is a national park above Sofia, which seems to be an up and coming metropolis. Areas of the city reminded me of Cape Town particularly as the city is built onto the side of a mountain. The ominous swastikas sprayed onto innocent trees gave the forest an air of menace, and we chose to free camp beside an incomplete hotel which was fun to explore during the daylight but as creepy as hell at night. Either zombies or skinheads threatened our imagination, I am not sure which is worse, but I would probably rather have dinner with a zombie. Guy had built his Defender from scratch, and it was a thing of beauty. It always amazes me that our camper is only 20cm wider than a standard Defender, but it seems like we could park a Series Land Rover in the back, it is cavernous by comparison and this space was achieved by design. From the outside, the camper does not look too large, but people are always amazed at the volume within, "it is huge!". We achieved the space by installing four large windows and a large rear door as well as not having any storage above the counter height. Too often a camper is crammed with crap, space is the greatest luxury, that and a cold or hot beverage. Guy had a small space to work with and used that space very well, the vehicle looks as tough as a tank (and as grey as a tank too).

Keelan helped me collect firewood, and we made a bonfire to keep the zombie/skinheads away, the night was long and still, we were not eaten or beaten.

Luisa guided us out of Bulgaria, and we spent the next few days driving through Serbia and Slovenia. Both countries had excellent roads, relatively painless borders and endless fields of green, parts of Slovenia reminded me of Mississippi. In Serbia, we stopped at a gas station and discovered that the Landy had developed a fuel leak where the Turkish "mechanics" had ripped out the fuel lines. I tried to fix the leak and managed only to reduce the drip with the spare tubing and hose clamps I carried. We were at the gas station long enough to realise that all Serbian women are supermodels who do not smile and that the country is abuzz with businessmen and woman going places and closing deals, the gas station restaurant resembled a convention centre.

Hungary reminded me of the West Rand of South Africa in the 80's - agricultural and peaceful. Had we driven a Mercedes Benz or BMW we might have stopped at either of those automotive giants colossal factories where they maximised profits by paying the Hungarians less. The Hungarian Tesco is half as expensive as the British equivalent and for identical products, in case you were wondering. It always amazes me that you can find imported products cheaper than in the home country, which proves the thickness of margins and the impact of tax. We heard British accents in the pie aisle, and the check-out lady lived in London for a few years. She said that a lot of Hungarians had gone to live in the UK but were starting to return as the standard of living improved in Hungary and Brexit threatened to choke migration. Those weren't her exact words, of course, but the message was the same. From what we saw, Hungary looks like a decent place to live, much wealthier and better organised than poor Bulgaria and almost Germanic in culture, and I am reminded that Hungary was one half of the Austro-Hungarian empire. That was until defeat after four years of the completely senseless First World War, a war where technological advancements, pig-headed European monarchies and paper-thin agreements ripped millions of good men to shreds, for what? No-one really knows. Hungary seems to have weathered Soviet occupation well.

That night we parked at a gas station in the middle of a rural village which oozed old world charm - Wentworth Park in Krugersdorp circa 1972 (minus the fields), the store was open but unattended for an hour, the attendant had gone home for dinner and did not bother to lock the door before he left. A small pile of cash was left on the counter where patrons had helped themselves to a cold drink, a packet of pretzels or some motor oil. We camped quietly and watched the world go by - farmers returning their tractors from a day in the field, women jogging along the exercise path, teenagers staring at phones in skinny jeans, a man with a trailer full of racing pigeons having a chat to a farmer at the pump. A small dog emerged from a thick green field and joined us for dinner - spaghetti bolognaise - and a chat.

Hungary is the last physical border on that southern route into the European Union. The Austrian border guard waved us through, and we were back! The year before we had toured Europe with virgin eyes, now that we were returning and we knew what to expect and felt at home even though we were still very much from another planet. Yes, we are European by ancestry but African by birth. We were raised and educated quite differently from our northern brethren, and we see the same world but through completely different eyes. The wealth and organisation of the northern European countries are astounding, and we chose to camp next to a train station in a neighbourhood where Porsche is a standard second car, and American size houses are the norm. Luisa and I took a walk through the neighbourhood to find some drinks and fresh bread, we both walked quietly past the large houses and expensive cars, the swimming pools and perfect gardens, flower beds and summertime BBQs. Our standard of living in South Africa had been higher than that of these fortunate Austrians - the house we lived in had five bedrooms, 180-degree sea views, a swimming pool, double garage, tennis courts and the most comfortable bed in the world. Walking past the houses on a beautiful warm afternoon we were reminded of what we had left behind, we had given up a life of comfort and ease, of luxury and routine. We had had more than these people have, but we chose a life on the road, we chose a study of life rather than the accumulation of material wealth. Do we miss the old life? Oh yes. Luisa and I miss having a healthy bank account, we miss our friends and family, the weekend braais and rugby matches, we miss going to a restaurant twice a week and the Saturday market. We miss the comfort of that perfect bed and the speed and efficiency of the shiny new Volvo, the kids miss the swimming pool and their bedrooms and a chocolate milkshake every day after school. I miss walking into a store and buying whatever I wanted. We do not miss the 16-hour workdays and living for our client's satisfaction while dealing with a broken and corrupt system, the nagging disingenuous schools, the weeks and years which flew by, heavy drinking, overeating, living with no clear purpose. As I write this, I am sitting on the large patio of a house in Benin, often pausing to look at the milky blue equatorial Atlantic for inspiration. Nigeria is waiting, Cameroon is at war, the Democratic Republic of Congo visa might be fake, the wet season is coming, the roads in Gabon are either great or terrible, and there is a constant threat of malaria. But we are very much alive, and our purpose is crystal clear.

But I fear that I may be addicted to this lifestyle. If we are in a house for more than two days, I develop an insatiable craving which dissipates as soon as we are on the road. I try and satisfy the craving, but that only makes me put on weight. I am bored in the evenings, listless in the morning and grumpy all day like an old man imprisoned in a nursing home. I bicker with Luisa who tries to stop me from eating all day, the kids know that some cantankerous alien has possessed their happy, loving father, they leave me to work and know that the alien will leave when we eventually get back on the road. This craving is powerful, so powerful in fact that I am convinced that the years of exhilarating overlanding have created a chemical imbalance in my brain and body. Let me not understate this - travelling the world as we have has been the single most demanding and difficult endeavour I have ever undertaken, and I bear sole responsibility for our failure but share responsibility for our success which is the way it should be. I would not disrespect a soldier by suggesting that I share the emotions of a soldier returning from combat, a soldier who misses the simplicity and reward of war, but I feel that there are similarities. We have been in so many situations where the outcome could result in a massive failure, we have suffered incredible lows which have threatened to rip the family apart, and we never know what will be around the next corner, where we may sleep each night and where we will be in a week. This mixed with the uncertainty and difficulty of trying to earn money to pay for the journey results in great satisfaction when all the tiny battles fought result in a great success. And each day is independently rewarding especially in countries and on continents where the greatest perils exist. West Africa or the Amazon are the kinds of places where the tough can be swallowed whole and spat out limp and are therefore the most rewarding to explore. Perhaps when the kids move on and I am only responsible for Luisa and myself will I begin to relax, but I suspect that it is then that we will start to venture to places where few others dare. Time will tell, but for now, the addiction consumes us completely, for while the children may be immune Luisa is most definitely a fellow junkie.

In the Czech town of Cesky' Krumlov, I piloted my Defender 130 down a cobbled village road, heading towards the Vltava river. There, parked on the lawn next to a gigantic teepee, stood a spectacular Land Rover Defender 130. Leigh, a tattooed, muscular and energetic Australian mountaineer and oil rigger stood beside the Landy with his wife Stephanie, French, a climber and the trio's photographer and filmmaker. Leigh and Stephanie had been touring Portugal early in 2017 when a speeding truck destroyed their first Defender 130 (luckily the couple were wearing seat belts, and the Defender's large bull bar absorbed most of the impact) and they had used the opportunity to build a new, spectacular, vehicle. (By the way - Grizzly is the model of the camper and Bear is the Defenders nickname (named after Bear Grylls), hence the name GrizzlyNbear). Our time with them was short but entertaining, we had just missed each other in southern France the year before, and Leigh had sent me a few messages asking questions about the 130 which I had gladly answered. His vehicle is the perfect set up for a couple, particularly an adventurous couple who carry a lot of climbing gear and the camper can be removed and the vehicle utilised for other duties. Leigh works a month on and a month off which allows them the time and resources to travel without breaking the bank or having to resort to other means of income. They are smart, I am not.

We left the Czech and headed in convoy towards Germany. Leigh had told me that he drives at 80kph and we cruised slowly along the motorway all day, stopped for lunch at a Lidl and continued a long, slow drive. We stopped at a rest area late in the afternoon as they were about to split off in another direction and we were headed back to Nurenburg to visit our friend Marcus. I asked Leigh why he drove so slowly, he then said that he forgot to tell me earlier that he only drives 80 kph on secondary roads, he can drive 120 kph on the autobahn! At least we saved a lot of fuel. The amount of truck traffic on the autobahn is ridiculous and a very good sign for the health of Germany's economy. We had weaved in and out between massive convoys of trucks all day as they snaked between cities. I often wonder what the effect of a driverless truck and automation, in general, will have on Europe and the answer is most likely a universal basic income. We split from the Dearle's with promises to meet at the Allrad and a short while later we were driving in convoy with Marcus and Katherin, heading to her sister's farm in the countryside. As we left the autobahn I felt the Land Rover misfire and five minutes later, as we turned off onto a small farm road the vehicle began to buck, and the smell of diesel filled the cabin. The fuel line had burst! The Turkish "mechanics" had repaired the fuel line which they had cut and removed with pieces of ancient rubber which had finally failed but thankfully had not failed on the autobahn, smearing the road surface with gallons of slippery diesel, which could have caused a fatal accident at worst and at least brought us to the attention of the police as we sat on the hard shoulder trying to fix the Landy. The rubber had failed in the best possible place, actually. Markus made a phone call, and a few minutes later a large, friendly man arrived on the back wheel of a dirt bike. He had a look at us sitting in a pond of diesel on a side road, made a few calls and left, again with the front knobbly of the KTM high in the air. Markus and I worked on the fuel line but could not get a tight enough seal with a hose clamp. Otto returned after ten minutes at a much slower pace, sitting atop a new, large tractor. In his hand he held a thin copper tube, a few lengths of rubber piping and a couple hose clamps, the tractor carried a large pile of sawdust and a broom. With the vehicle jacked up and the rear tyre removed, Markus and I eventually managed to link the cut fuel hose with the copper piping and seal with the new hose clamps. While I tidied up, Otto spread the sawdust over the spilt diesel and cleaned up the slick, ensuring that no motorist would slip on the corner. Grateful for the help we followed Markus' Defender to a field where we camped between to large square reservoirs, had a swim and grilled a massive rack of pork ribs. Katherine taught us how to do the swish dance, there was some schnapps involved, someone fell asleep, and we all woke up wishing that we were not parked in a hot field.

Returning to the Abenteuer & Allrad, we drove through the pristine German countryside, past castles, beautiful villages and endless fields of green. We have described the Allrad to you before but, in case you need more info, the following is a short article which I wrote for Expedition Portal in June 2018.

"Europeans are famously prolific travellers, and it is no surprise then that the largest overland show on the planet is to be found in the town of Bad Kissingen, located in beautiful central Germany. We have had the good fortune of attending the Abenteuer & Allrad (Adventure and All Wheel Drive) in 2017 and again in 2018 and were astounded by the location, professional organisation and array of overland vehicles on show and, more importantly, in the massive campsites surrounding the village.

The event itself is held between the 31st March and 3rd of June every year for the last twenty years and attracts thousands of visitors from across the globe, but mostly from Europe. This year attendance was at approximately 24 000 event visitors on the first day alone, and there were a few thousand overland vehicles of every shape and size. Travellers begin arriving in the village a week before the event, and some leave only a week after and it is the overlanders themselves which make this event simply incredible.

This year the organisers rallied the Land Rover owners of Europe and further afield to attempt, and ultimately break, the Guinness World record for most vehicles in convoy with 632 vehicles (we attended the attempt in South Africa which had over 1000 vehicles but did not fulfil the minimum clearance between vehicles. Unfortunately, we were not part of the German attempt as our Defender decided to burst a fuel line en-route).

From the car park or campsite, buses shuttle attendees and the worlds motoring press up to the event which boasts hundreds of stands, a food court, a Land Rover Experience driving area, halls and massive tents full of gizmos and gear as well as presentations by some of Germany's most prolific adventurers. It takes more than a day to explore the event, and when you simply cannot walk anymore, you can rest with a cold glass of excellent German beer and local dishes. The staff and security are well trained and professional, the event information is clearly and readily available, and even the weather seems to be on its best behaviour for the event.

The world's premier adventure and outdoor brands are represented at the event, and you are sure to find the kit, gear, gizmo or vehicle which you are looking for. Depending on your budget you could walk away with a set of D shackles or a new 6x6 MAN truck complete with fold-out deck, accommodation for six, a granite kitchen, satellite TV and a BMW 1200 GS for popping down to the shop.

But, it is the campsite itself where the real action takes place. There the tribe is separated into its various clans. The Land Rovers tend to flock together but can also be found parked on stumps in the forest, the Unimogs form a lager, and the large overland trucks demand the most real estate. Some overlanders have yet to leave Europe, and others have travelled the globe, you can tell which ones have been whereby the wear and tear of both vehicle and owner. At night fire pits are deployed, and the smoke and smell of grilled meat floats over the campsite. Beers are shared, and circles are formed, stories are told, old friends are reunited, and new friendships are made. There is a sense of community among the campers, it really does not matter whether you drive a VW bus, a DAF truck, a Mercedes station wagon or a Land Cruiser – they are all united by a common passion for overlanding.

If you can, we highly recommended visiting the Abenteuer and Allrad show...".

We parked with our friends Lukas and Eva (who had played a huge role in distributing many of our books internationally since 2017) and their group of Vanlifers. A tall man bun was not at all happy that we had parked our Defender in the middle of his Vanlife congregation and we did not know that we were crashing the party. Our friends Thomas and Sabine were at the show to do a presentation, they were leaving on the second day to travel to another event, but they were going to be taking someone special with them - Keelan. We had arranged before the event that Keelan could volunteer at the community known as Gemeinschaft Sulzbrun in the shadow of the Bavarian Alps, the same community which we had visited the year before. He was under strict instructions not to upset the gentlefolk with his unrefined internet personality, and we promised to visit him after the Allrad. Luisa made Thomas promise not to speed on the Autobahn, and wicked Sabine assured her that 200 kph was the maximum for their van. Again there were tears as the firstborn happily packed a backpack and headed off to a world of vegetarians, skinny dipping in a lake, meditation and poop heated showers. Mama, who usually gives the boy the most headaches, clung to him like he was going off to war and he smiled patiently and hugged her tight. Jessica cried, and I felt The Sadness of a lonely man losing his best friend.

Without the pressure of presentations, the girls and I took the time to fully explore the camp area and the event itself. We had press passes and were well taken care of by the organisers who had a dedicated press tent set up at the entrance where we could access wifi and event information and enjoy a snack. The organisers realise the importance of the press, and they had a PR minded elderly man attend to the press diligently, unlike other events we have attended where the organisers behaved as if they were doing the press a favour. With all the video and photography taken care of, a few small productive business meetings concluded, and an extensive scour of the goods and services on offer, we retired at the end of each scorching day to hang out with friends at the camp. It is impossible to name them all, particularly for fear of forgetting to name someone. We shared a few American beers (in Germany!) with Mike Woodier and Micheal Beltrami, who I nicknamed Tactical Spice as he had a very well kitted Defender including an indestructible carbon fibre spice bag. We had missed the opportunity to hang out with Mike the year before because we were rushing around like headless chickens. Mike has been an online friend for many years, and he has always been there for us when we needed some mechanical advice or a laugh. We were both saddened by the sudden passing of our friend Torsten Deventhal who was one of the people I had most enjoyed meeting the year before and the one person who I regret not spending more time with. Life is short, live it. We met Borre Bratvold from Arctic Trucks and gave him a tour of our Defender. I was a bit nervous showing my vehicle to men who make a living building highly modified vehicles for the world's wealthiest adventurers, but Borre seemed more interested in our way of life than the Defenders horrible, scratched paint job and messy silicone seals.

Johnny and Debbie Boma gave me a tour of their tipper green Defender camper which they had built to explore North America. The vehicle was equipped as a tipper for landscape gardening, and Johnny simply built the camper on top of the tipper mechanism, perfect for levelling the camper and checking on the hand brake. They sat in the sun and drank beer while my blood turned to gloop and I had to go have a lie down after two litres of cold water. We made a few new friends who followed us on social media (it is always strange to be recognised and congratulated by people you have never met), hung out with people whose vehicles interested us and shared a beer with Andrew from the UK and his Land Rover obsessed daughter. We hung out with Gerfried Swoboda who we had met in Chile and who was now setting off to tour the world in a 6x6 monstrosity, we had a chat with Ulrich Dolde and his lovely wife, sold shirts for Melvill and Moon while talking Africa with Johan (who made us promise to visit his farm in Namibia), met another couple of Aussies in a Nissan Patrol (more about them later), hung out with Landy Bean and friends from Belgium who brought us powerful beers, had a long pow-wow with Mike, the editor of Overland Journal Europe, and swapped stories with a steady flow of travellers who sat by our fire for a while until the wind grew too strong and blew us over.

If I have forgotten to mention anyone, please forgive me, the weekend was long, hot and blurry. Lukas and Eva said goodbye as they had to return to work. There is a sadness which ex long-term overlanders carry with them once they return to the normal world. It is The Sadness of time lost, a regret and nostalgia for what had once been and it is an emotion deep and permanent. The only cure for this depression is overland travel somewhere remote and beautiful. I could see Lukas staring into the fire after the stories had been told and memories shared. He and Eva had enjoyed a long journey across South America, and they longed for that freedom every day, and work hard to achieve it once again. They understand what we have achieved, and I will do my very best to help them liberate themselves when the time is right. They have a solution to the work/travel dilemma, and that is the combination of their passion for overlanding and Stand Up Paddleboarding. They have a project called Into The Blue, and by guiding and teaching others with the same passion, they will be able to liberate themselves. I wish them all the success in the world!

We awoke the last morning to find the entire camp area empty and clean except for a few dusty long-term overlanders. Sabine and her husband Ollie, who holds the record for owning the most vehicles in Germany (who also hails from Paderborn and has never, to his eternal shame, owned a Land Rover) were camped near to our Defender. There is a video on the internet of me teaching Jessica to drive the Landy. She never stalled even once while pulling off on the thick grass and drove perfectly, if not a bit too fast for my liking. She drove the Defender from the grassy camp to the dirt road, through a few muddy ditches then turned the vehicle around and headed back to where we had been parked. She asked me if she could loop around and return to where Mama stood watching nervously, and I said yes, but go slow. She steered the Landy in a perfect arc and then drove, at speed straight at a Mercedes Benz SUV, afraid to drive over some towels drying on the grass. "Slow down, turn, slow down, turn, SLOW DOWN AND TURN NOW!" She narrowly missed the Mercedes, sped up past Sabine (who can be seen in the background with her hands over her mouth in fear) and made a beeline for a field, laughing nervously. "SLOW DOWN!" I grabbed the steering wheel and piloted the Defender away from the field, straight towards Luisa. "Push in the clutch and brake, now". Poor Jessica. She stopped the Landy perfectly, put the vehicle into first, engaged the hand brake and laughed her evil laugh. She will be an excellent driver one day, but I may teach her to drive in a smaller vehicle.

The Aussies in the Nissan Patrol were called Kyle and Lou, and they travelled with a Staffordshire Terrier called Quinn. If I had to travel with a dog it would be a Staffie - they are intelligent, powerful, friendly, loyal and short-haired (if you like Staffies I suggest you read the book Jock of the Bushveld, classic South African literature about a loyal and brave Staffie). There was no doubting that Quinn was an alpha male, he was bestowed with the gifts of a Death Valley donkey, but Lou called him Queen, which puzzled me. "C'mere Queen, hoosa beeg boy than, yes yoo ah Queeny boy".

We left the event with the Aussies and found a free camping spot up amongst vineyards where, surprise surprise, we made a braai. The next day we headed further south and camped in a quiet lawned campsite near the town Würzburg. Luisa and I borrowed bicycles from the friendly camp owners (who had given Kyle a really hard time for putting his feet on the rest area table) and cycled along a river where large riverboats floated by delivering goods and housing families who lived in apartments built at the rear of the boats. The supermarket was supposed to be only a short ride away, but the navigator app had been incorrect, and we had to do an 8km cycle to buy Luisa's orange juice, red wine, baguette and tea bags. I had still not lost my American blubber, and a good cycle certainly would not do me any harm. Back at the camp we sat on the grass in the shade and played with Quinn and chatted to Kyle and Lou. Having had a few days together we had realised that not only did Lou call Quinn "Queen" but she also called Kyle "Quail". Quail and Queen. I asked Lou if she realised that she called them those names, she did not and refused to believe that she did until she said their names out loud. Lou looked horrified. "Quail, do ah caw yoo Quail?" Kyle nodded. "Wha didntja tell mee?" For almost a decade Lou had been calling Kyle "Quail", and he had never corrected her. Of course, I am teasing, Lou speaks perfect Australian just like any other Australian. Quail had built his camper by hand, and it was very well thought out, compact and airy with a focus on minimalism, air and space rather than storage. Unfortunately, they had to cut their travels short to return to the United Kingdom to save money for the summer travels as Collecting Bliss.

We said goodbye and unfortunately did not reunite as planned, they headed for Switzerland, and we made a beeline for the Gemeinschaft Sulzbrun where we could visit and check on Keelan. He was doing great, of course. The community had him housed in a simple but charming trailer next to a field, and he proudly showed us his living area which was not electrified, but he did not mind. During the day he worked in the garden, and he proudly showed us his work area where he cleared a large area of weeds and had rearranged the greenhouses to be more efficient in their use of water and light. He showed us the beds which he had prepared for planting and the small mountain of stones which he had cleared from the growing area. I was proud. The years on the road, working together on the farm in Baja, Mexico and the island in Greece had taught him how to work hard and smart. If anything he might have been working too hard, which made the Peace-ies (which is what he called the community members) slightly uncomfortable - perhaps his energy made them tired. We worried that he was not getting enough protein, but he assured us that he was eating enough and drinking a lot of water, that Thomas and Sabine were treating him like family and that they had made Spaghetti the other night, with beef! We camped with him for a day and then left, happy in the knowledge that he was surrounded by good people who treated him well, who had not shaved his head or had forced him to sit and meditate for four hours a day. There was one, young, shaven head and charismatic dress wearing man who I suspected of a messiah complex and advised Keelan to befriend cautiously. We did not have to worry about Keelan being easily influenced, he had spent his youth travelling the world and had met every shape, colour and creed of human, his casual knowledge of the world is far beyond what many will ever achieve.

Close to the city of Salzburg, where the commune is located, is the lake called Bodensee which is shared by Germany, Switzerland and Austria. While exploring the Abenteuer & Allrad camp, a young man had called to me from his white VW camper. Markus had been following our journey for years and introduced us to his wife Rebecca and his baby son Louis. Markus lived in a town called Uhldingen-Muhlhofen on the shore of the Bodensee, and he had invited us to visit them when we headed to Switzerland. We struggled to find their home (we really need to invest in a proper GPS) because it is hidden between an apartment block and a warehouse. The home was more of a compound, two large buildings divided into apartments and large garages.

Markus and British Rebecca shared the same sadness which plagued Lukas and Eva as they had lived and worked in Australia before driving their Toyota Land Cruiser across Asia and back to Germany. This is a warning to you, dear reader - once you become an international overlander there is no going back, your entire life will become dedicated to a single cause and no other experience can fill the void left by absolute freedom and grand adventure. Markus worked for a construction company and worked long hard days, he also was studying for a heavy-goods driver's license and did all that he did to one day be able to hit the road again. He was up before the sun and returned home after dark while Rebecca took care of the home and little Louis. In their spare time, they worked together to refurbish the interior of the Land Cruiser in anticipation of that day when all the hard work paid off. The apartment block belonged to the family but only had one other couple living there, as well as Markus' dad who quietly lived in a house attached to and behind their own. Rebecca showed us to a small apartment which we were welcome to use for as long as we wanted. I suspect that my German grandmother had decorated the apartment, which is a very, very good thing indeed. We could have stayed there forever. Lying in bed, you could look out the shaded widow at the bougainvillea which framed the window and a view of a large, leafy tree. The patterns on the ceiling, the paintings on the wall and the dark wooden furniture transported me to another time, a time when life was simpler, easier, better. It was 1979, and I was a toddler playing with my cousins while my gran chatted in German to her cousin visiting from Paderborn before a dinner of Eisbein (pork thigh) crispy roasted potatoes, cabbage and chocolate pudding served with a thick skin.

During the day, I worked on articles and processing images while Luisa caught up with the book orders, arranged tax, planned a route and a million other Luisa tasks. At night we sat with Markus and Rebecca and spoke about travel, shared ideas for earning money while on the road, agreed that Land Rovers are far superior to Land Cruisers and shared meals. I think Rebecca was a bit shocked by how easily we made ourselves at home and that is an occupational hazard of being a scroungy overlander - we have spent many nights in other people's homes and long ago forgot that we can't just open all the cupboards in the kitchen if looking for a glass, or take over the washing of dishes and cooking of meals. We were there for three or four nights and one day I walked around to our apartment and found the door open, entered the kitchen and noticed that the bathroom door was also open and there stood Luisa having a shower like any blissful German girl, so safe and secure that the thought of someone entering the apartment with bad ideas never crossed her mind. I made sure to teach her a lesson she won't soon forget. Boo!

Earlier in the week, resourceful Markus had asked me what was missing from the Landy, and I said a pair of sand ladders might be useful. The day before we left, he took me to the workshop of a company called Entreq, who designed and manufactured Defender accessories of the very highest quality. The owner gave me a tour of his workshop and offered me a set of sand ladders, stainless steel and mounted on fold down brackets to double as a table. He even installed the unit for us! Luisa has used the table almost every day since but we have never been able to test the sand ladders for recovery, I am sure that day will come soon, but we do drive a Defender, and we drive it well!

While staying at Markus' home, we received a message from a Swiss doctor who we had met in Tanzania back in 2010. Helene and her husband Jacques were leaving for a month in Australia and offered to let us stay at their house for a month while they were gone. They lived on the side of a mountain near St. Maurice very close to Mont Blanc and it took only a minute for us to accept their offer. We said see you later to Markus, Rebecca and a lucky little man and headed off to take the ferry across to Switzerland, the Land Rovers fridge packed with German meat and French cheese. We felt sad leaving the little family behind, we had grown very close, and I can imagine we will be life-long friends, we hardly ever convoy with other overlanders, but if we were to travel long distances with someone, it is them that we would want to travel with.

14

The Overland Addiction

Recently I wrote a short letter to my friend, Dr Rosselli seeking help. Dr Rosselli is a world-famous Colombian neurologist and himself an overlander who primarily travels unknown and dangerous corners of South America in an old Land Rover Series 3. We had met years before in Bogota, and I knew if anyone could understand my "condition", Diego was the man for the job. The letter read as follows:

"Hello old friend, I hope you are well.

I am busy writing my fourth book and need to consult you to flesh out an idea that I have and perhaps find some peace of mind.

I am wondering if the following behaviour is psychological or neurological (i.e. a chemical imbalance) and perhaps you may have some personal experience.

My problem is that when we are on the road in our Land Rover, I am satisfied, no matter how difficult the road may be. But, when we stop for a few days or more in a normal home and settle into a routine, I experience an insatiable craving (for lack of a better word) which nothing can satisfy - not food or drink, or any other stimulant can permanently quench the craving.

When we pack the Land Rover to continue our journey, I initially experience a degree of anxiety, but by the end of the day both the anxiety and craving are gone completely, and I am satisfied.

Could this be caused by the release of a chemical in the brain, or is the satisfaction, psychological?

I fear that I may be "addicted" to overland travel. There are worse things to be addicted to.

Thank you so much".

Diego recruited his mother, a fellow esteemed neurologist and they asked questions primarily, "Would I get your consent to publish your case in a psychiatric journal?". Not really the answer I was expecting. Mrs Rosselli then asked if I have nomadic ancestors as the Rosselli's do, and I suspect they understand my "condition" on a personal level.

I imagine the case study would read something like the following:

The Overland Addiction

The addiction is typified by the following behaviour:

1. Euphoria

Like a surfer in a barrel, on the road, with the wind blowing through their hair and plans for a campfire and cold drink in the near future, the addict will exhibit gleeful behaviour - singing, joking and laughing often. Even when the vehicle breaks down and they are covered in oil and grease the addict will continue to smile, saying things like "rather broken down beside the road than stuck in an office", and "it could be worse, we could be having dinner with your family". The "subject" may often slip into long periods of content silence, staring at the road ahead, saying nothing but smiling like a simpleton.

2. The Sadness

To loosely quote Laird Hamilton's wife in Riding Giants, "without giant waves to surf he is like a dragon slayer with no dragons to slay". The Sadness is not depression but rather a permanent longing. The greatest sufferers of The Sadness are former long-term international overlanders who are now forced by the real world to once again become wage slaves. You will recognise The Sadness when you see it (or feel it yourself), and all one needs to do is attend an overland gathering to witness it first-hand. Usually, a couple suffering from The Sadness will tell stories around the campfire all night and the next day mope together around their perfectly restored/prepared/rebuilt rig, counting the seconds until they can drive it further than the nearest border. The only known treatment for The Sadness is a six-month, long-distance overland journey, and even then the treatment only treats the symptoms, not the cause. The Sadness has also known to infect those who do not ever see the opportunity to travel the planet overland but desire nothing else (rest assured, there is always a way!).

3. Irritability, mood swings and irrational behaviour

An addict, deprived of the distraction and satisfaction which overlanding affords will be almost impossible to live with. One second high (thinking about the road), next second low (thinking about not being on the road), the addict is not bipolar or schizophrenic, they are simply not in their natural environment, "caged like a beast of the wild" might be a phrase which they mutter often. For the sake of a marriage or relationship partners are advised to seek immediate opportunities for relief (i.e. a weekend in the mountains).

4. Alcohol abuse and pyromania

The addict may seek to alleviate the symptoms of addiction by making campfires on a Tuesday night while drinking a six-pack and insisting that he or she will be cooking in the garden from now on. This is perfectly normal behaviour for a sufferer in the advanced stages of addiction.

5. Improper behaviour "online" (note, not all addicts exhibit this
    behaviour)

Before overlanding the addict was meek and mild and a pleasure to follow and interact with. After that international overland journey they become "experts" online obsessed with, but not limited to, the following subjects;

- Tire sizes
- Free camping vs wild camping
- Strategies for saving money while on the road
- Calling out wannabes and begging to be made a moderator
- Shipping routes - RORO vs container
- mocking vehicle modifications of any sort other than those which the addict implemented on his vehicle
- 2x4 vs 4x4
- The "perfect" overland rig.

In addition to the above, the sufferer will scour the internet constantly seeking overlanders to follow or hate, bargain overland vehicles, tools and a set of Michelin XZL's.

6. Financial parsimony (stinginess)

The addict might once had been generous. They paid for dinners at restaurants, had hobbies and occasionally took beach holidays (in an actual hotel) and bought their partners lovely, useless, romantic gifts for their birthday and Christmas. Now that person spends money on nothing at all unless that something is overland related. Their house has slowly but surely emptied of furniture and electronics, the flat screen has been traded for a Panasonic Toughbook, the lounge suite for a raised suspension, the dining room set and silver for a plug and play solar system with split charger and lithium battery. On a partner's birthday they receive a new set of tires and for Christmas are blessed by a khaki-clad Santa with a Snomaster fridge. When the in-laws visit they sit on camping chairs in the lounge while the addict is burning meat in the garden and informing them of plans to "downsize" from the double story house to a "cute little shipping container".

7. Questionable Personal Hygiene

They shower twice a week, brush their teeth outside, wear flip flops when they do shower and only change their clothing once a week - a quick armpit sniff is followed by the innocuous but troubling statement "yeah, I'm good for another two days". Fingernails are kept extremely short but toenails ignored, hair is either grown to flow or shaved short weekly, deodorant is reserved for special occasions and previously clean-shaven, respectable men now wear un-brushed beards. Women who once wore only the latest fashions now wear khaki and Crocs and Sackwear T-shirts.

Treatment Strategies

While there is no known cure for the overland addiction, the available treatment is relatively inexpensive (or incredibly expensive) and effective. It is worth mentioning that a sufferer will not suffer any physical deterioration as a direct result of their addiction, in fact, they will be healthier than most non-sufferers as they breath more fresh air, are more physically active than most and suffer lower levels of stress as they pursue a minimalist lifestyle.

We recommend the following;

- Bi-monthly overland camping trips. They do not have to travel far, they just need to travel.

- Subscribe to Overland Journal and Expedition Portal and read my books.

- Relocate to Utah or Arizona (or Spain if you are European)

- Fly and drive. Drive the rig to somewhere awesome, leave it there, fly home, source cash and return to the rig to continue when possible. You *can* travel the planet overland!

- Save every cent, sell everything and hit the road!

15

Switzerland, again

The Bodensee is a European paradise in the summer. The beaches are packed with people sun tanning and eating ice creams while moms of all shape and size change out of their bikinis where they sit. I remember a French overlander tanning topless at the campsite pool near our old home in Cape Town. What a scandal! Old fashioned young women made their children close their eyes and husbands were slapped for looking at the scandalous European airing her dirty pillows. Some people even packed up their picnics and left the pool area. I prefer the German way.

The ferry was quick and efficient and not too expensive, we sailed past sailboats and yachts and dinghies and arrived in Switzerland, horrible, poverty-stricken and terribly disorganised Switzerland and stopped at a corrupt border post to buy the Swiss motorway vignette which costs about 40 Swiss Francs and which allows you to use the motorway. We then drove straight to Wil and our friends Ursi and Michel's new home. There we met not only them but reunited with Erica, one-half of the creators of iOverlander who we had met in Arizona. Erica and her boyfriend Alex, an overlander who travels by motorbike, were in Germany for a few weeks and came down to visit. Ursi and Michel too have The Sadness, but they are not too far away from the cure - Michel is building a new V8 powered camper and they often escape to distant shores to practice their world-class photography and Spanish. Ursi and Luisa bond like long-separated sisters and Michel is always good company. We were all well behaved, and there were no trips down to the river to grill large slabs of meat and swim in the fast-moving tide. Instead, we drank wine and devoured platters of fine cheese brought by Erica. Ursi and Michel had to work the next morning and had to leave early, we were handed the keys to the house and kissed goodnight. The Sadness of leaving great friends is sometimes overwhelming, and it is very tempting to suggest that we should settle down in Europe, the centre of it all, and be closer to the people who have changed our lives. We are truly blessed to have so many amazing people in our lives, back in South Africa we had a few very good friends who I could count on one hand. I now need all the families fingers and toes to count the friends which we have made, friends who will be part of our lives no matter how distant they may be geographically. That, I suppose, is the one saving grace of social media, we are able to stay connected with the people who have made an impact on our lives as are you. I have hovered my finger over the delete button on my social media accounts more than a few times, but I knew that I would be losing direct contact and regular interaction with the people who make life worth living despite having to endure those who make life difficult.

The next morning we tidied up from the nights' festivities and drove to the house of the Swiss family we had met in Cappadocia. Their son Etienne took Jessica for a five-hour ride on his motorbike, and she returned glowing, he then wanted to take her to a party at midnight. She is 14 amigo, now way Jose, ain't gonna happen, nein, verboten! We had a meal of raclette, similar to fondue but not quite. You melt cheese and fry bacon on a hot plate and keep eating until your heart explodes. I asked about the rumour that almost every Swiss house is home to an assault rifle and Etienne left the table for a minute and returned with a pale green killing machine. He explained that he had no bullets, but in a time of war, they would be issued with ammunition and would report for duty. Believe me, Switzerland is the place to be if you fear the imminent collapse of the civilisation. Future generations post-apocalypse will speak Swiss German, eat raclette and live to the tune of very loud ringing bells. We went for a walk after lunch and visited a farm which was unfenced and open for locals to cross as they went about the daily exercise. A woman with two small daughters dressed in matching white frocks and carrying miniature guitars on their backs skipped past us towards the rolling green hills which overlooked Bern. The sky a perfect blue and snow-capped mountains framed the horizon.

Etienne was the European Scale Electric champion and waited patiently while Luisa and I played cops and robbers and raced little race cars which cost as much as my Land Rover controlled by handsets designed by MIT and built by a small introvert with nimble fingers in a subterranean Japanese workshop. I won, of course, and Luisa accused me of cheating because I had found the best strategy to be a constant speed while she tried to master the controls and often flew her little racer off the racecourse which was linked to a computer program which measured lap times and calculates precise analytical data which allowed the racer to find their flaws and improve their skills. Luisa's problem was the same as when she drove the Defender, too much power! She hates losing, and I let her win a few races to ensure the peace, a gift which infuriated her more than losing fairly. I won the battle but lost the war.

That evening we arrived at Helene's home perched on the side of a mountain above a picturesque village called Epinassey, where pure glacial water ran into a bath in the town square, waiting to refresh the traveller or fill large bottles for domestic consumption. Helene works as a doctor in the nearby city, and her husband is the local fire chief. They are both obsessed with Africa and their home overflows with African sculpture and art, they are a Tanzanian sculptors dream come true. Their home was an apartment built on the top floor of a well-converted barn, and the neighbour/landlord came to say hello and offered fruit and vegetables from his garden and cheese from the herd which swatted flies and donged bells across the road. The home sat at the base of a mountain above which the picturesque village of Mex (awkwardly pronounced Meh) overlooked the valley cut by the Rhone river. Jacques had a surprise for me - parked outside under a cover sat a well-loved 1000cc Honda Varadero in silver and blue livery. He handed me the keys and the insurance document and told me that I could ride the bike whenever I wanted. I told him I would ride it across the planet, he thought that may be a bit far. They left early in the morning and shortly after I dressed in jeans, a thick jacket and stepped outside to ride the bike. I was nervous. The last time I had ridden such a large bike I had wrapped my right leg around a concrete lampost which hardly seemed to notice the damage it had done to me. The leg suffered eight fractures between knee and ankle, and I spent a couple of months in hospital and another four months recovering at home watching every single match of the 1995 Rugby World Cup on a black and white television screen. That experience solidified my loner lifestyle and nearly drove me mad. Or perhaps it succeeded. Luisa would kill me if I killed myself playing silly buggers on a motorbike so I took it easy. Plotting a route with minimum traffic and corners, in Switzerland. I pulled out the choke, started the engine and sat quietly for a moment letting the engine warm before engaging first, gently releasing the clutch and heading down the mountain to a road which led straight to the large nearby town of Martigny. I was a tense as fat girl jeans and had to force myself to relax. There was a large parking area near a factory (which had a yard full of old Series Land Rovers and Defenders including a Defender 130) where I could practice low speed turns, accelerating and emergency braking as well as getting used to the signals, lights and hooter. I was 23 years rusty, but the skills which I used to possess in abundance soon returned. Other than great sex there can be no better feeling than riding a motorcycle well down a beautiful road. That afternoon I set out again, more relaxed with fresh muscle memory. I constantly reminded myself not to get cocky. By the third day of gentle riding, I was ready to take on a mountain pass. The road up to Mex was quite early in the mornings, and I set off up the Swiss mountain. The road zig-zagged with very few straights and many blind corners, three quarters up the road hair-pinned beneath a concrete tunnel, through two narrow tunnels, wide enough for only one vehicle at a time - I was pushing my skills to the limit. Exiting the second tunnel the world disappeared, and the thin sliver of tarmac veered to the right hugging the side of a cliff face, a distant glacier before me a sheer drop beneath me, meters away and Mont Blanc in the distance. I did not pay attention to the mountains or glacier, all I could see was an abyss and all that stood between me and a five-minute fall was a barrier dented and bent by bodies, bikes and vehicles. I imagined a rider exiting the tunnel to quickly, swerving to miss a Volvo or Subaru coming the other way, losing control, hitting the barrier and somersaulting to his death. I imagined that rider to be me. Two last steep and tight hairpins stood between me and Mex, a car heading down entered the hairpin at the same time as I entered heading up, gravel-covered the inside lane, I had to go in tight and accelerate, keep my feet off the ground, not lose balance. The car cruised by nonchalantly, and I made the corner, entered Mex and sat quietly for five minutes, enjoying the vast beauty of the mountains and the valley below. Yes, I was having an adventure! The ride down was much easier, and

I concentrated on my gearing, memorising which gear I was in (the Varadero had no gear indicator or fuel level) and making sure that I used both front and rear brakes. I swooped down carefully and returned to Luisa grinning from ear to ear. That night I sat and studied the map of the area, looking for roads to explore. Across the valley, there was a road climbing up to a place called Cabane Sex Carro (which in Spanish translates possibly as "Cabin Expensive Sex" or "Cabin Sex Car" in Portuguese), but that road was far too narrow and busy with traffic, I had a few close calls with hairpins and rushing old women and decided never to ride that road again. The next morning I rode the straight valley road to Martigny and road up the mountain pass which led to France and Chamonix. I felt confident to open the bike up on the longer straights and was soon making myself feel nervous, a great feeling.

The town of Martigny is located on the Rhone elbow (where the Rhone river makes a 90 degree turn northwards towards Lake Geneva) and is the hub of the pass routes, Great St. Bernard (to Italy) and col de la Forclaz (to France, the pass which I had ridden in the previous chapter). This strategic geographic location was, naturally, incredibly important to the Celts and the Romans and the Battle of Octodurus was fought there, the Romans won, of course. Luisa is a quarter Italian, and my people are Germanic/Celts/Britons, we are from this soil and, my, what beautiful soil it is. The Rhone valley is walled by Alpine peaks which are ravaged by glaciers which feed the ancient river. The valley is fertile, green and pastoral, grapes grow on the slopes, fat cows (€ 90 a kg!) wander fields enjoying the summer sun on their backs. The air is crisp and clean, the forests preserved and open for exploration.

Because I had the bike to ride I suffered less the terrible cravings which afflict me when we are in a home. If Luisa needed a loaf of bread, I was dressed in my riding gear in a flash and ready to take the long road to the furthest shop. Jessica rode with me one afternoon to Martigny where we needed to buy a can of beans and an earbud. The ride to the town was easy and smooth, but once we left the shop and crossed the main road, the bike died and would not start. Poor Jessica knew the drill, sit in the shade and wait while dad figures out which Land Rover part had been installed on the Honda. I had a phone, but no wifi and a confused gas station attendant allowed me to log onto Facebook and message Luisa to come and fetch us with Helene's Mitsubishi Pajero. There was a bike shop down the road, and I pushed the heavy bike the kilometre to the shop, and the mechanic told me to leave it and he will let me know what was wrong. I had just filled the tank, perhaps I had put in the wrong fuel. He had a sniff and looked at my gas station receipt, "No, that's the correct fuel". I felt terrible, I had broken Jaques bike! Luisa fetched us with a thunderstorm brewing between her ears. "I told you that you would break it, dumbass!". Well, at least I had her can of beans and earbud, ungrateful woman.

A week later, I was told to fetch the bike. The fuel pump had failed and a replacement cost €800 installed. Luckily Jacques had no problem paying for the repair, the fault was not caused by the user. Jessica refused to ride with me anymore. Etienne was more reliable and better looking, she could spend five hours hanging on to him, but fat old dad was boring, she made up some excuse about the seat hurting her legs. I rode twice a day, every day for a month and spent every Saturday washing and cleaning the bike and the Defender. If I could have hit pause and lived the rest of my life in that perfect Swiss summer I would have, but life must go on, and there is no way on this blue planet that we can afford that lifestyle in Switzerland, especially when a steak costs $80 a kilogram. I would rather eat the bike.

Four days before we were to leave Switzerland, Keelan returned to us by train from Germany. We drove into Montreux rushed to the impeccable train station to collect him, we had arrived at the exact time that his train was due. We could not find him and Luisa began to spin, worst-case scenarios bubbling over in overactive imagination. I went to the lower level to look for him and could not find him. Well, there was that one young guy with the blonde hair but… It was Keelan, and he looked incredible. I jogged over to him and gave him a bear hug. "Man, your mom is going to faint when she sees you". She nearly did. Keelan and I had put on a massive amount of weight in the USA. He went from a size 34 to a size 44 (UK size) in six months, and we could not figure out why he put on so much weight, it is still a bit of a mystery, but the basic answer is carbs - sugar and bread and sweets and fruit juice. I had managed to lose much of the weight, but Keelan had struggled. He must have been close to 140 kgs by the time we left the USA. He returned to us slim. Six weeks of hard work, a vegetarian diet, plenty of exercise and copious amounts of water had drastically reduced his weight - he looked amazing. Back at the house he was full of energy and rode bikes and hiked with me every day and the weight has fallen off, he is now a tall and sleek young man. He told me a story of how one day at the commune he had left without breakfast to ride an ancient bike twenty kilometres and hiked to a cafe on top of a mountain and then did it all again in reverse. He believes that is the day that his metabolism kicked into a new gear and the fat began to disappear. He lived on a diet of pasta and salad and water and hippy happiness. I am forever grateful to the Peace-ies for returning my beloved boy in a better condition than when they received him.

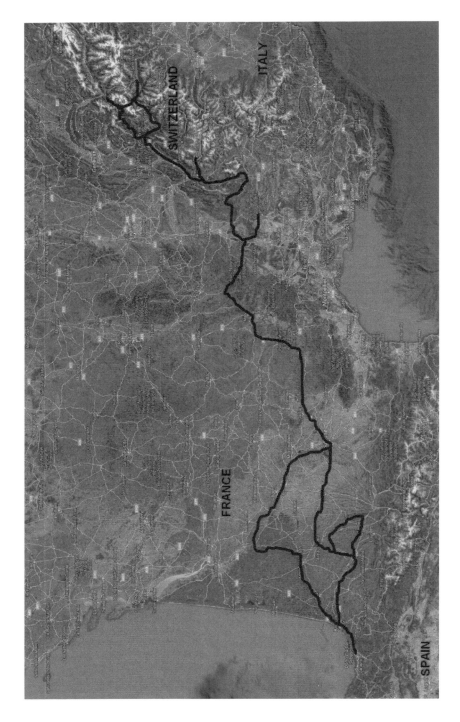

16

France - Part Deux

Between Switzerland and France, there is a small village called Trient, which is nestled deep within a valley and receives little sunshine in summer and even less in winter. The location is stunning though and we found a public camp area next to the road to the border. The camp had toilets, a large and very well-built wooden shelter area, BBQ's, electricity and a playground. When we arrived, there was not a person in sight except for the traffic which occasionally zoomed past. We camped for the night and came up with an idea to do thirty hikes in thirty days - we were inspired by Keelan's transformation and wanted to emulate his success and make sure he did not regain the weight. The camp was one of the most beautiful we had experienced with a view of mountains and glaciers next to a glacial blue raging river which sign warned was too dangerous to swim in. That morning a lady approached the vehicle and asked us to pay €10 for the camp and we happily agreed, we had in the distant past paid four times as much to park in a horrible parking lot when no other options had been available and particularly when we still travelled with a rooftop tent. The new hard side camper gave us the freedom to camp anywhere and,= even though she is not as popular as the old 130 on social media, she is a hundred times more practical for long-term overland travel.

As I handed the lovely lady the single note, I complimented her on the beauty and build of the camp. "Of course it is beautiful", she said, "this is Switzerland".

There seemed to be a few hikes in the area but not much sun, we drove up along a winding road and past a few ancient villages. The border infrastructure was intact with immigration and customs booths, but the booms were open, and there was not a soul in sight. We drove slowly through the border and back into France and almost immediately entered a tourist village in the shadow of Mont Blanc. Luisa was searching for a Carrefour Supermarket, not just any Carrefour, she wanted a very large and ridiculously inexpensive Carrefour. She did not find one, but she did find a Lidl where unhappy people with old cars shopped.

Now you might think that our story could end here. We had already driven through France and Spain and Portugal, surely that story has been told? Well, not quite. We discovered that there are two France's and Spain has hidden secrets. Read on, and I will explain.

Near Chamonix, we left the valley road and drove under a bridge and up the side of Mont Blanc to a parking area at the head of a trail. Actually, the parking was at the halfway point of the trail which began at the valley floor, but luckily Luisa did not tell us that until after the hike. Keelan and I used to climb Table Mountain every other weekend. We would climb up Skeleton Gorge, and the hike to the Bossons Glacier was remarkably similar to that faraway African knee killer. Keelan hiked wearing an Expedition Portal T-shirt, billowing hippy "Aladdin" pants, a pith helmet and no shoes. His energy and fitness were incredible, and he basically ran up sections of the mountain and then waited for me to catch up before sprinting off again. Jessica hates the first half of a hike and rushes the second, she just wants the misery to end. Do not forget though, Jess climbed Torres del Paine when she was eight years old and nailed it, beating fit adults to the top. It is not that she can't hike, she just does not enjoy it, I think she is spoiled, she has seen the most beautiful sights that this planet has to offer, hiking up a mountain to look at a small receding glacier is an almost pointless exercise when you have slept beneath a glacier in Alaska or watched massive chunks of ice calve from Perito Moreno Glacier in Argentina or have filled your water bottle from a pristine glacial river on the Carretera Austral in Chile. But a hike is good for the body, soul and brain and this hike was also educational. At the summit, we came to a restaurant where the cable car came to an end and where people who earn Euros or Dollars or who had saved all year were able to eat a cheese platter and drink cold bubbly stuff. We walked past. Two Air India aeroplanes have crashed into Mont Blanc - the first, Air India Flight 245 in 1950 and the second, Air India Flight 101 met it's end in almost exactly the same spot in 1966. Both were en-route to Geneva and miscalculated the flight path over the 4,750m high Mont Blanc massif. Wreckage from that crash is displayed along the path to the glacier viewing point just after the restaurant - a life raft, an engine, part of the fuselage. The glacier itself, which as it recedes reveals ever more frozen relics of those disastrous accidents, is a mere shadow of its former self. In the 1800s the glacier had encroached on the La Fouly village in the Chamonix Valley where it slowly ploughed homes, barns and fields. The villagers called on the clergy to exorcise the demons from the glacier, of course, and in 1815 the community erected a cross at the snout of the glacier and that cross is now the measure of the glaciers dramatic retreat. I guess the crucifix did its job then, perhaps it is time to remove it.

Over the next week, we explored rural France staying at free overnight camp areas (called aires) in villages and towns with names like Albertville, Grenoble, Valence and Pussy. Many of the aires had basic toilet facilities and running water, some were basic and unloved, and others were beautifully situated next to a lake or beneath an ancient castle or in a forest. We hiked each morning, despite the heat and Jessica's protests, and drove a few hours every afternoon. The best of France we discovered was on the border with Spain. In a small village, which was a way off the beaten track Luisa found an aire which was perfect, in every way except (and maybe because) there was no mobile signal. The aire sat opposite a small town hall and next to a river, a large green and shady lawn between the river and parking area. There were clean toilets, a BBQ area, a playground, free electricity and a waste area. Upstream, the river flowed beneath an ancient bridge and flowed crystal clear and ice-cold through a forest and over perfect boulders where freshwater shrimp fed. Downstream the river joined another river, deep and murky where a father taught his small sons to row and fish. A beautiful young woman with deep red hair and a slim, teenage body arrived on an ancient moped. Her name was Juliette, and the bikes name was Vicky. Juliette was a carpenter exploring southern France searching for a location where she could build her home. She needed to find somewhere affordable and beautiful with an abundance of straight, old pine trees and a view of the mountains. She would build the house herself with the help of her brothers. Keelan and I were tempted to volunteer. I built a campfire and listened to Luisa and Juliette chat the evening away after taking a walk up the quiet, twisting road where large, airy homes stood quietly enjoying the summer on their own large plot of land, each with private access to the river. Many of the houses were professionally converted barns and there were signs of an afternoon and evening well enjoyed - a beach towel hanging beside a hammock between two tall elm trees, an empty bottle of wine and a book half-read alone together on a garden table, a gentle laugh and warm light through a large door half open. I hope Juliette finds something similar, I am sure she will.

The next morning a man arrived on a large tractor, he trimmed the hedges and brought us a few cold bottles of fruit juice when he took his break. His name was Paul, and he lived in a treehouse which he had built not too far away. Juliette packed her tent and loaded her belongings onto Vicky. Vicky was petrol and pedal-powered, and she needed a bit of motivation to get going. With her flaming red hair spilling out from under her retro helmet Juliette pedalled Vicky in large circles and asked her sweetly to start. We had already said our goodbyes. Eventually, on the third lap, Vicky spluttered and came to life, Juliette rode off onto the road, her fingers in a V for victory crying "Vicky!".

This was the France we had come to see.

We stayed one more night, but our peace was disturbed by a large, white camper dinosaur which, despite having a 50m x 50m parking area to choose from, chose to park so close to the Landy that I had to walk sideways between the two vehicles. "Hi there pal, can you move over a bit. No. Why not? Then get a longer extension cable, or park over there. Here you can use my extension. No? Fine, I will move". The fat man and his poodle seemed offended that we did not want to park in the shadow of his apartment block and listen to him grunt on the loo while we ate our pasta dinner.

Our next camp was a free community camp in the mountains. Unfortunately, we had to put our thirty hikes in thirty days plan on hold as a heatwave hit northern Spain and southern France. The camp was built on a hill overlooking a valley, carved logs served as loungers, there was a compost toilet inhabited by wasps, a brick and mortar BBQ and a very large tree which offered shade. The sun did not set until 9.30 pm, and we suffered in the heat, trying to remain cool. Keelan and I explored and found another pristine stream in the shadow of a forest where we could lie in the shallows and relax until the worst heat had passed. A man with a sweet daughter and a belligerent pony walked by, a family came down to the river for a swim and the afternoon passed slowly by. The next day we returned to the river for a quick swim before heading further along the border and up to the Pyrenees mountains, knowing with elevation comes cool air, the only good way to beat a heatwave is to head up into the hills. Some people head to the beach during a heatwave, but this makes no sense at all - you might as well head to the desert and take a puddle with you. Luisa had found a wine farm which offered free camper parking. After a wine tasting we bought a bottle of red and a bottle of white. The farmhouse and winery stood on top of a hill, the vintner was a bull of a man, macho and hairy and probably the star of the local rugby team. He had the humour and great confidence of a man who had never been beaten, and if he had, he had found revenge. He wore a thick necklace and a vest with black track pants and black boots, I had never seen anyone quite like him in the winemaking regions of South Africa where winemakers tend to be well-groomed and wear expensive watches, chinos and tucked in dress shirts. The wine was excellent. While we were there, camped near a covered dining area with a superb view and under the watchful eye of mama wine farm, a German couple arrived with an ancient camper and young children and a medical company delivered a care bed and oxygen bottles. A day later we camped next to a lake where white Tupperware campers played a game of Round Robin, jostling for lakeside campsites. We parked in town squares and in the shadows of castles, beside rivers and yet more lakes. Luisa borrowed corn from unfenced farms, we swam every day, we hiked when we could and enjoyed what would surely be our last European summer for a while.

We rolled into a small village south of Bordeaux; camped surrounded by a hundred white rolling boxes and made a beeline to the beach where we cooled in the Atlantic for most of the afternoon. The second tour of France had been a revelation, and we now understood why so many people loved the country dearly. Yes, we had struggled with the language but had enjoyed warm hospitality and kindness from a people famous for not welcoming foreigners. France, merci beaucoup!

17

Galicia - Where the Soul Finds Salvation

 While staying in Switzerland I had written an article from the heart and submitted it to Petrolicious, the following is that article:

"Blood, Sweat, Tears and Glory

A six-year intercontinental overland journey of self-discovery.

I sat in my Land Rover, stuck in Cape Town traffic. Another torrid day in the office under my skin, trapped in a sea of metal built for mobility but going nowhere. I drove that same Land Rover from this port city to Dar es Salaam, my wife and children trusting me completely, by my side. For six months I had been liberated, I had been the man I was born to be. The sunset over a horizon I longed to chase while exhaust fumes filled my nose. I remembered the freedom of the open road, the daily, tangible, difficult reality of Africa, I remembered the Mozambican virus which had wracked my body, I remembered my children swimming blissfully in Lake Malawi, and I remembered the ice-cold beer I had shared with new friends in the Zambian bush. We had returned from that journey cloaked in dust and a film of joy, all too soon washed clean from our skins by the arduous monotonous demands of civilised life. Fuck it, Luisa. Let's go. Go where? There, South America lets go there.

It took almost two years to extract ourselves from the real world, to remove the straightjacket which we had once willingly worn and worked to wear. We sold all the crap, the business, the cars, everything except that with which Luisa could not part. We removed the children from school, cancelled the debit orders and prepared the Defender for the journey across the Atlantic. In November 2012 we escaped on a jet plane and arrived in The New World.

The Defender joined us in Uruguay, and over the next two and a half years we circumnavigated South America, gasping in the beauty of the tips of the Andes, soaking the moisture of the Amazon jungle and shivering through the gales of Patagonia. The vehicle broke, we ran out of money, we faced down government thugs in Venezuela and fell deeply, madly in love with a continent which we would call home tomorrow - if there were not entire continents still to explore.

Slowly, day by day, we transformed as if from a cocoon, we grew and broke and were reborn under a blue sky. We were reinvented, I as a writer, my wife as a photographer and our children as free spirits. We were no longer South African or rich or poor - we were stateless, free agents of the universe, limited only by our imagination. And the fuel in the tank.

Our first book paid our way through Central America to Alaska and back down to Mexico. We needed a break. The road teaches but also takes, living in a tent loses its lustre after four years, you need to stop, think, re-evaluate, plan. In Mexico's San Pedro de Martir mountains, we again changed - from travellers to professionals, eager to learn and teach and grow and achieve the impossible. Six months after working day and night on new projects we emerged from our seclusion ready for the next stage. With our own hands, we converted the Land Rover into a globe roaming super camper, capable of providing shelter and protection and the ability to travel to even the most remote corners of the planet. We have never before worked as hard.

We again crossed the Atlantic and soon found ourselves on the shores of the Mediterranean, the snow falling while I wrote my third book, cosy in the camper, Luisa working tirelessly to deliver our story to a new market, becoming a filmmaker while the children prepared themselves for the world.

Crossing into Asia our son chose to become a man, choosing that it was now time to meet the world on his own terms, he is ready to make his own mark, and we are delighted that we have filled him with courage and curiosity which cannot be contained. He will now go off into the world while we continue to discover our own until he returns, understanding us better than he could have before.

The future is our own, and we will write the story. A bird set free. We Will Be Free. "

A few days later I was contacted by a tour company who had read our story, they offered to send us to a hotel in Galicia and arrange for us to have a private guide, all expenses paid. All they asked for was a video of our tour and a write up about our experiences.

The following is that report:

"Those of you who enjoy a good, long and tortuous hike would have heard of the Camino de Santiago pilgrimage. Essentially all roads in Spain once lead to Santiago de Compostela. Originally the pagan Celts made the pilgrimage to Galicia, seeking to travel to "the end of the world" and the Fisterra peninsula, the Milky Way guiding the pilgrims to the coast where the sun terminated taking the souls of the dead with it before reanimating in the east the following day. Galicia eventually became a Christian stronghold even as the Moors established the Caliphate of Cordoba on the Iberian Peninsula. Apparently, it rains too often in the mountainous north-west, and the Moors preferred the warmth of the sun.

Recently I had been listening to a podcast titled The Celtic Genocide (Hardcore Histories 60 - Dan Carlin). At the time I did not realise that we were heading to a significant Celtic location, in the next week we were to learn not only of Julius Ceasers exploits in Europe in his quest to decimate and control the Celts, Franks, Gauls and Germans but also how later the Roman Catholic Church was to expropriate a pilgrimage and a small ancient city.

It is when the Catholic Church became interested in the region that the story really starts to spice up. I am a cynical person, particularly where superstition is involved, and I like to look past the obvious, to find the story behind the story, so please forgive me for not sticking to the traditional narrative. (It must be noted that for a few days in Galicia we had a private guide, Marian, who was born and educated in Santiago de Compostela and who had a huge breadth of knowledge which was illuminating, breathing life into the ancient marble and statues. Marian provided the background, and I came to my own conclusions).

The story goes that the beheaded remains of Saint James (Santiago) of the Field of Stars (de Compostela) were found by a hermit who was guided by mysterious lights. The local bishop, Theodemar of Iria, declared the remains to be those of the saint. Cue the construction of a legend and a city which not only held the remains of the saint but offered something far more valuable and enticing - the city eventually became a portal to heaven, and you could earn your place in Catholic nirvana either by the sweat of pilgrimage or a lifetime of service as either a priest or a nun or with cold hard cash. Yes, in Santiago you can buy your way into heaven. As a pilgrim, you had to walk a minimum of 100 kilometres to the city where you would light a candle and confess your sins to a beleaguered priest. The wealthy needed only to be buried within the Cathedral de Santiago to earn a spot in heaven and they could achieve that by either purchasing an apartment in the Pazo de Raxoi (built in the 1800s and now the town hall), by undertaking the expense of maintaining one of the various chapels within the cathedral or by offering extravagant gifts or offerings to the church. The gifts of the wealthy provided the cathedral with exquisite works of art and the finances to rebuild and modify the cathedral through the centuries, a task which was performed with much care for the renovation but with little concern for the history of the cathedral - much of the former art, statues and masonry were simply discarded or used as construction aggregate! Interestingly, despite the cities importance to the Catholic Church, only two Popes have ever visited the city in an official capacity - Pope John Paul and Pope Benedict.

Our tour of the historic city centre took six short hours and we retreated to the San Francisco Monumento Hotel for a much-needed dinner after listening to a very loud punk rock band sonic-ally assault mysterious, almond cake selling nuns (almonds were traditionally used as legal tender by the pilgrims as no almonds grew in the area). The hotel itself was originally a monastery and has been tastefully renovated as a modern, contemporary hotel which is located a stone's throw from the historic cathedral and which serves an excellent breakfast to fuel a day of exploring. We planned to wake early but, for some reason, we slept so well in the hotel that we overslept every morning. A pity, I wanted to lie there among the crisp white sheets and ponder the expertly crafted wooden ceiling while listening to the city come to life before wolfing down two cups of excellent coffee, a bacon and egg sandwich and a sweet fruit salad. (*Note, we had toured Santiago de Compostela the year before, and we had walked past this very hotel. I had promised Luisa that one day we would return and stay in the hotel, almost exactly a year later we did exactly that!*).

Instead of a long slow morning, we bundled Marian into the Land Rover, and she directed us west, up over a mountain towards the Costa de Morte, the end of the earth and the villages of Muro and Fisterra. We learned that there are three things specific to Galicia, which were particularly significant - the stone crosses (cruzeiros), granaries (horreos) and manor houses (pazos).

The stone crosses can be found at crossroads, churches and cemeteries and are built to obtain forgiveness for sins, protect travellers and would protect Galicians and pilgrims from the procession of the dead - the bedtime story which scared the wits out of little Galician kids. The grain stores are synonymous with the agricultural heritage of the region, and the stone manor houses were the refuge of Galician nobility. All three of these structures are built of stone, and you will be hard-pressed to find any structure which is not built of stone. Along with the scallop shell (which is symbolic because of its structural perfection and role in the story of Saint James) it is these structures which you will eventually associate Galicia. Tireless Marian regaled us with tales of ancient Galicia intermingled with stories of her family linking ancient and modern, helping us to realise that, unlike much of historical Europe, Galician culture a is living, breathing continuation of its incredible past. The fisherman fish, the churches serve, the pilgrims keep on coming, and the river Xallas ends its own pilgrimage west as the only European waterfall directly into the sea.

The entire region is dominated by an invasive alien; a tree which was gifted to the Iberian peninsula by the fascinating Catholic monk Rosendo Salvado. Thanks to him, an entire industry was formed around the exploitation of the Australian Eucalyptus tree, and Portugal burns to the ground every summer. The eucalyptus is an excellent agricultural plant, with many uses and great value, Salvado was gifted a bag of seeds by his Australian brothers, and he returned to Galicia with a gift which promised economic growth but hid a few dangerous secrets. The eucalyptus is so flammable the seeds are propagated by fire (the Australians call them fire sticks), and the trees have an insatiable thirst for water; hence they have often been used to dry out swamps. Luckily Galicia is far damper than Portugal to the south.

Our day tour ended at the lighthouse where countless pilgrims ended their journeys and where they would burn a memento, a private sacrifice which accompanied the setting sun and terminated their quest for salvation and forgiveness. At least for modern pilgrims, the journey may end there, but for ancient pilgrims, this point was where only the first half of the pilgrimage terminated - unlike modern pilgrims, the ancients could not catch a taxi, then a bus and an aeroplane, no they still had to travel back to their homes, usually by foot and usually very, very far away.

Driving back to the hotel, we discussed the following day's activities with Marian. The itinerary suggested we would drive a 400 kilometre round trip to Ribeira Sacra where we would visit a winery or two, monasteries and explore the region. I had been reading about the city of A Coruna and suggested to Marian that perhaps we could visit that city instead. I suppose that maybe one of the greatest benefits of having a private guide - not only should they be of the highest calibre but they are also flexible and will accommodate the client as opposed to having to accommodate a group. It was decided that we would visit the city (where Marian lived with her family) and would get a glimpse of modern and ancient Galicia existing side by side.

The day started and ended at the Torres de Hercules (the Tower of Hercules) which is the oldest operational Roman lighthouse in Europe and was constructed in the 2nd century before being renovated in 1792. It looks like it was built in 1952, so well has the stone withstood the elements. Again Marian was strapped into the front seat of the Land Rover and guided us around the city. By now she had become part of the family and knew that we enjoyed a tasty picnic much more than a sit-down lunch and had brought Galician bread, cheese and meat for us to enjoy while we sat on a warm rock surrounded by immaculate lawn and views of the city from the vantage of the Punta Mexillosa hill. The old city itself is built on a thin sliver of land with beaches facing the ocean and a port within the bay. Picasso attended school here, and it seemed to me that this was a city which truly valued its children as schools occupied the very best coastal real estate. It was a public holiday, and the beach (which, in winter, is converted into a wall of sand to protect the city from storms and massive waves) was littered with the bronzed bodies of sun worshipers. I felt like I was walking the Dizengoff promenade in Tel Aviv, the sun beating down. Having a local as a guide guarantees that you will visit not only the most significant buildings, plazas, monuments and statues but you will also find the best ice cream or street food in town and the vendor will treat you like family because your friend's family have been loyal customers for the last few decades. And if it is shopping you are after your guide can take you to the best stores in the district, you know, those stores which cater to the local population and charge local prices.

Marian guided us towards Santa Cruz, across the bay from A Coruna and one of the wealthiest areas by GDP in Spain. Imagine our surprise to see an eight-meter high statue of Che Guevara standing guard over the entrance to the district. The story goes that mayor Angel Garcia Seonae of Oleiros de Santa Cruz was once a friend of Fidel Castro (who was himself Galician) and had secretly built the statue under wraps, at night using $170 000 of public funds. When local politicians and residents protested, the mayor responded tersely, "If it were a statue of Christ or the Virgin Mary there would not be a single protest round here. God damn them".

Standing later studying a statue of women facing the sea awaiting their menfolk to return from working in South America, Marian sang the beautiful song by Rosalia de Castro, (Adios Rios, Adios Fontes) which stirred our emotions. Once again Marian had brought the past into the present, and we felt an affinity for the people of A Coruna, the people of Galicia and for the city in which we stood. Galicia has a soul, and I believed we had glimpsed why this land had promised salvation to so many for so many years. Yes, Galicia has a soul.

Before we hugged Marian and said truly heartfelt goodbyes we were surprised to be invited to Marians home district where we were treated to local paella, excellent crumbed calamari rings and a large, ice-cold draught of Estrella Galicia - a beer so delicious, fresh and smooth that we returned to the Tower of Hercules feeling refreshed, relaxed, enlightened and ready for a good nights sleep in our Land Rover camper."

Just before we left the crowded bar, Luisa had gone to the toilet. Two hours later, as we dozed, there was a knock on the window, it was Marian's husband.

"Is this your phone?".

Yes, it was! Luisa had taken her best friend Samsung to the loo and had left it there. Someone had found it, took it to the bar owner who searched for the owner. Marian recognised the screen saver image of the Defender and her husband returned the phone to us!

We enjoyed that tour experience, but if we had to do it again, we would ask for a rest day and a briefer itinerary. We were absolutely knackered after the three days and needed a break, but it was a fantastic opportunity, I hope to do it again soon.

From A Coruna we headed to the beach to camp and rest. Luisa found a surfers spot where we could free camp, and we arrived in the evening and set up camp at the top of a rocky hill overlooking the ocean. Vans and 4x4's decorated with surfboards dotted the hill and not long after we set up, an Irish Defender Pulse camper arrived and set up camp. The view of the ocean and the rolling waves were what we needed to recharge, and we spent the next couple of weeks exploring the coastline and enjoying inexpensive green lawn camps perched on the edge of cliffs.

Northwestern Spain and Galicia, in particular, is a very well-kept secret. While it seems that most of Europe like to relax on the Mediterranean beaches of southern Portugal and southern Spain, we found the north-west to be heaven in the dry summer months. I say dry but that only means that it does not rain every day. The vegetation itself is thick and green, the mountains moist and cool, there are blue flag beaches and an endless coastline to explore. While in the South; campervans crowd each other and police patrol (not a bad thing when they are after criminals, not a great thing when they are chasing campers), beaches are packed, prices are doubled, kids are wailing, you need the loo but the hotel or camp is 500m away and a fat man just made a mess of the public loo, and he is now washing his butt at the outdoor shower. Of course, if you have the money you can pay for privacy and professional service, the best beaches and great food. Disposable income is a myth, for us at least. When we first became infected

236

with the travel bug (I blame Top Gear, The Long Way Round and the Travel Channel) Luisa and I sat and planned a holiday, somewhere beautiful with white sand and palm trees like those which hung above our bed 1m x 1m framed. We had spent some time in Mauritius when we had sensed that South Africa was in a downward spiral and was looking at options for a new home. Mauritius is small, overpopulated, polluted and expensive and the only decent beaches are occupied by hotels. We thought about flying to the Seychelles on a full board package deal but soon realised that a two-week holiday cost almost as much as a second hand Land Rover Defender. "Hey, here is an idea. Let's take that holiday money and buy a newish Landy (we had two old Landy's, but neither was suitable for long-distance overlanding), let's drive to Kenya, then fly to South East Asia for a backpacking holiday then return to Kenya and drive back to South Africa". We still travel in that Land Rover to this day.   An annual beach holiday for a family of four is, in most cases, money badly spent and the commute and expense often scrub the few hours of relaxation from your skin. This is why overlanding is so appealing. The vehicle can usually be sold for a percentage of the cost of purchase, sometimes more than what you paid, and that vehicle can carry you and accommodate your family in beautiful places where few others go. You are able to bond as a family and enjoy the beach or mountains or desert, spend a fraction of what your neighbours spend on a holiday and you can head out to explore whenever you have a few days off work, a month-long holiday or you can just head out for the weekend. There was nothing we enjoyed more than packing the Landy on a Thursday night and then fetching the kids from school on Friday (we were self-employed and could leave our assistant to man the office) and heading out to explore. Luckily we lived in Cape Town and a three-hour drive would either find us on a remote beach, in the mountains or in the desert. Sunday afternoon, we would return home, grab a bite to eat and enjoy a lazy evening, ready for work the next day, but dreaming of the open road. Beware, overlanding is addictive.

Europe holds similar opportunities. For a month of overlanding, a ferry from the UK can deliver you in hours from Portsmouth to Santander in Northern Spain from where you can be in Morocco in two days, from Germany a two-day blast on the motorway will get you to Spain, and it takes three days of driving to get from Zurich to Istanbul, or you can take a ferry from Italy to Morocco. But, you do not have to travel to Morocco or Turkey to have a great overlanding experience. Scotland and Ireland offer wild opportunities for the British and Europeans need look no further than Northern Spain for an authentic experience. I think I have made this point before. The Pico de Europa and Pyrenees mountains are as worthy of exploring as any destination a day's drive from Cape Town, and we truly fell in love with Galicia. So, stop wasting your money on brochure holidays and horrible commutes, invest in an overland vehicle and get out there - you will not regret it!

Our Landy delivered us to the border with Portugal where we enjoyed a few last days on the topless beach, swimming between buoys, as tanned thin people sipped orange juice and ate melon on the deck of their yachts, fishermen brought in their fresh catch and families relaxed on a quiet beach - not a restaurant or tourist tout or overpriced souvenir shop in sight. Those in the know, know that Northwestern Spain is the place to go in summer while the hordes head south.

18

Back to Portugal to Prepare for Africa!

We returned to Portugal and felt a sense of home. The Portuguese people had always welcomed us warmly, and we knew what to expect as we rolled into the North of the country, invited to spend a few days at the hostel of our overlanding friend Hugo. Casa do Sardao is a beautiful and tastefully renovated and re-purposed old farmhouse built on a hill along the Camino hiking route. Hugo opened the gates to the parking area where we could leave the Landy (don't let the horses out when you open the gate, ok?) and showed us to a loft where we were welcome to stay as long as we wanted. Beautiful, sweaty Europeans floated in until evening, showered, ordered a beer and massaged their blistered feet. As witnessed in hostels around the world, a lone man sought romance and spent a wasted hour pretending to be interested in a dull Scandinavian beauty's simple world view before moving through the herd and sniffing out an older female who, though not as beautiful as the simple blonde girl with sculpted breasts, was less chatty and more likely to need bedding. We found that many young travellers liked to ask us complex questions which they do not always enjoy the answer to and we avoided conversation with a blonde head of piercings and instead chatted to a Swiss couple who we had met camping with their parent's camper van down by the beach. They had a flat tyre but did not know how to change it, and we helped them before telling them that we would be at Hugo's hostel that night. I used to enjoy hostels when I was young and dumb and full of rum (I spent a year living in hostels in Israel), but there are only really two types of people who stay in hostels - young people exploring the world and old people exploring themselves. The young tend to be naive but full of the certainty of youth, looking for a good time, finding their way in the ever-changing group dynamic, way too interested in recreational stimulants (not that we witnessed any of that at Casa do Sardao) and being rock stars. The old either want to relive their youth or they keep to themselves, to the latter, well done, to the former, stop it, you are making a fool of yourself! Our kids don't socialise with the young hostel dwellers as they have had enough conversations about the same thing. Our kids would rather enjoy a quiet corner to read or use the internet. Jessica is still young and not interested in temporary relationships with people she has nothing in common with and Keelan is intelligent and mildly conservative. He would rather research the design and engineering of tanks and aeroplanes and hang out with his gamer friends online, he has no time for silly young people and much prefers the company of us silly older people if he is going to relax and enjoy an evening.

After saying goodbye to Hugo and his exceptional hostel (we would likely meet Hugo again in North Africa), we headed to Porto and a Land Rover meeting where we did a small presentation and were reunited with friends we had not seen since Brazil four years earlier. Rafael and Isabella (known as DayTrippers) had arranged for us to stay on their parent's farm in Coqueiral in 2014 and we had only spent a week with them before they set off with their Land Rover to drive around the world. Isa is tall, slim and beautiful, a true lady with a huge heart and Rafa is a bit of a rogue, very successful in his industry and both are longing to be on the road again. They too have The Sadness, but they live great lives in Brazil and, of course, Brazil is relatively close to Argentina, Bolivia, the Amazon or the Andes. A couple of months overlanding every year should be enough to keep The Sadness at bay until they can make more long-term plans. She has built a business selling natural cosmetics which are exceptional in quality and a good business model for us to emulate if we ever do settle down. They are famous in Portugal, as are all published Brazilian overlanders and the book which they produced after their journey is second to none in terms of quality, design and photography. Being reunited with the people who were the first overlanders we had met, the first weekend of our first week overlanding South America was very special for us, and it was astonishing how much we had all grown and changed over the last seven years.

We were also reunited with many friends we had made the year before at the Portuguese Land Rover meeting, and we left the event dehydrated, very hot and ready for a shower.

We returned to the apartment which we had rented the first time we were in Portugal and reunited with our friend Ruben. Rafa and Isa came to visit, and we did our very best to dehydrate again before they left.

Figueira do Foz is a quiet city, but the neighbourhood where we stayed was not quiet. Most of the apartments are the apartment blocks which surrounded ours and were holiday apartments, and in the off-season months, hardly anyone lived there. There are two houses surrounded by all the apartment blocks, and the residents were a throwback to a past Portugal where people raised chickens and grew their own vegetables and, unfortunately, chained dogs about the property to protect their crop. These dogs barked constantly and drove us mad as we tried to work, sleep or watch a movie.

The apartment itself was lovely, three large bedrooms, a good size kitchen, two bathrooms and a large lounge area. Despite the barking dogs, which I believe are common in Portugal, we were very fond of the apartment which had a slim patio from where you could watch the sunset every evening, our friend Rubens restaurant visible at the summit of the large hill to the right. My routine was to be asleep by 10 pm and to be awake early, have a cup of coffee and get to work writing and taking care of the various aspects of our income for which I am responsible. I had always dreamed of becoming a writer, and I am now a professional writer as almost all our income comes from the articles I write and the sale of our books. With headphones on and Erik Satie's Gymnopedie 3 playing to cancel out the constant barks, I could make the most of the morning when my writing tends to be more creative and then wake the family with tea and breakfast before taking one of the kids for a morning walk, down the steep hill to the beach where a few residents did their morning exercise, and the kids and I could talk about the things they wanted to talk about without the distractions of screens and mother. Most mornings I would walk with Keelan and talk about robotics, engineering, mechanics, conspiracy theories, capitalism vs communism, girls, motorbikes, travel, life in general and video games. Almost every morning the sun shone bright, and a perfect surfing wave broke over hard rock, hardly anyone surfed there. At high tide, elderly people in rubber boots scoured the exposed reef for crustaceans, mussels and octopus while a few camper vans would park on a strip of land across from the beach. A new restaurant had been built on the promenade, which I took to be a good sign for the local economy and often Keelan would admire the motorcycles parked outside while the riders enjoyed a morning coffee. It was not a long walk to the nearest supermarket, about two kilometres, but the walk gave us plenty of time to get in each other's heads. Keelan was making plans for moving on, and I encouraged him to finish his schooling so that he could do just that. His latest mechanical obsession was self-built gaming computers and motorbikes, and he wanted to study at a university in Portugal, have a girlfriend, ride a bike around the country in his free time and make a supercomputer out of parts sourced from around the world. He spent every spare second researching how to make the ultimate water-cooled gaming PC, he knew exactly where to source the parts and how to assemble them while squeezing out each atom of performance, the screen would be X, and the hard drive would be Y and the motherboard Z.

We walked and talked every morning and most afternoons as we have done for years and it is that hour with him almost every day which I treasure the most. At the supermarket, we would fill a basket with yoghurt, fruit, baguette, butter, maybe some eggs and always orange juice for Luisa. Keelan would carry the heavier bags, and together we would slog up the steep hill to the apartment to shower and begin our day's work. That time in the apartment was the closest we had been to normal life in years, but I felt incredibly pressured and suffered from anxiety. The West African route played heavily on my mind not least because I needed to generate the finances to afford it - not only the day to day expenses and the many expensive visas but also to have an "egg" fund available for emergencies. I was concerned that the Defender had been in Europe for too long and that some snoopy policeman might take an interest in it, so we never drove it around the city as the vehicle would be confiscated if deemed to have been in Europe too long. I worried about the children's schooling and our future, about book sales, social media presence, my life in general.

Sitting at the kitchen table one afternoon, writing this book, I became disoriented - I couldn't remember the name of the town I was writing about and my thoughts seemed to bounce around the muggy waters of a fish tank. I stood in the kitchen wondering where I was, I couldn't remember which country we were in, I felt dizzy and went looking for Luisa. I did not need to say a word for Luisa to know that something was wrong. I stood staring at her for a while. "Where are we?" I asked. Luisa does not handle these situations very well, and I vaguely remember trying to calm her, to assure her that I was fine, just a bit confused. But I was not fine. My mind swam in a sea of quiet, I could not hear very well, and my sight was not blurry but not entirely in focus. I felt weak, I struggled to lift my arms and swayed as I stood. Luisa called Keelan, and together they led me to the bedroom where I lay and asked questions I cannot remember. The world was very bright, I watched the curtains sway in the breeze, I faintly heard Luisa ask if she should call an ambulance, I felt suddenly and simultaneously like a very old man and a young child occupying a single mind and body. Jessica fetched a glass of water, and slowly I began to feel normal, I could stand and walk. Luisa ran me a bath, and I lay in the warm water and floated, my mind floating with me but slowly, very slowly, my thoughts came together, my arms regained their strength, and I was able to dry myself and get back to the room under the families watchful eye. Luisa told me later that I was very confused that I "lost time" and that she was afraid that I was going to pass out.

That experience scared me. I do not think I had suffered a stroke, it is far more likely that I had suffered an anxiety attack, something that I have never experienced before, but Luisa had. Luisa and I had been carrying the weight of the world on shoulders for years, and eventually, the totality of the burden had caught up with me. There is a reason why people do not live the way we do and that reason is that it is incredibly difficult to raise a family while earning enough money while exploring continents and dealing with impossible situations as daily routine. It is the constant weathering of a powerful wind which erodes and wears a man's mind, I have to remind myself that this lifestyle is a choice and the suffering we endure is worth the effort considering the reward. Believe me, it is far easier to live a "normal" life with a predictable routine than it is to do what we do. Overlanding is addictive, and like all addictions, it is possible to overdose, and we are extreme. I had to remind myself to take it easy, to breathe and relax, to be humble and realistic, to not always attempt to achieve the impossible.

A day later, a hurricane struck Portugal and hit our city the hardest, I have said it before, wherever we go extreme things happen, climate change and all form of terrorism dominating the negative experiences. Luckily no-one was killed, but the wind lifted roofs, flattened telephone poles, moved cars, destroyed balconies and covered the city in broken glass. We had been ignorant to the coming storm - being too caught up in our own world to keep an eye on the weather forecast, and the hurricane took us by surprise, with winds of 190 km an hour ripping around us. Most apartments in Portugal have aluminium blinds which close on the outside of the building with protection from storms or even criminals, of which Portugal has very few, with the blinds closed and power off we sat in the darkness listening to the storm. I worried about the Land Rover while Luisa worried about the roof falling on us. It was a very long night, but eventually, the storm passed before dawn, and the city came out of hiding to count the cost. The ubiquitous Portuguese clay roof tile covered the ground accompanied by various debris, glass, plants, rubbish bins, pot plants and litter. The Land Rover stood perfectly unscathed! I had worried that the wind would lift the roof and once that flew off the interior would be destroyed. The vehicles surrounding the Landy all bore the scars of a long, horrible night, broken windscreens, dented roofs, broken tail lights. The Defender did not have a scratch on her, and only the puddles of water in the footwells indicated that there had been a huge deluge of rain.

We had a few more visitors while we were there - Hector came to visit us from the Canary Islands with his girlfriend and old Toyota, and we were able to reunite with our friend Charles who we had last seen in Ushuaia, Patagonia. Charles is the lead mechanic for an international classic car rally, the kind of rally where millionaires drive million-dollar vehicles to remote parts of the world. Those of you legends who have read We Will Be Free will remember how Charles, with an introduction from David Priddis, had been kind enough to sell us his spare wheel and tyre from the backup Defender which he was about to load in a container bound for the United Kingdom. Charles could have made a quick buck but instead sold us the wheel at the UK replacement price, a very reasonable price compared to what we would be charged locally. Charles and his wife came to visit, and Luisa spoiled them with baked camembert, and homemade pastries, we enjoyed an afternoon together before they had to leave for Porto and head up to Santander in Spain to catch the ferry. Charles is one of the people who are always there for us, quietly behind the scenes, when we have a mechanical problem he is quick to message us with intelligent solutions and has often helped us to get moving again when the Defender has had enough.

A distraction arrived in Portugal in October, a chaotic ball of energy which would spin around within our little world and cause all kinds of mayhem. Laila is the daughter of our friend Marcelo, and she had arrived in Portugal looking to study and trying to convince her family to move there from Brazil. We had met Marcelo and his family while camping in Florianopolis, south of Sao Paulo in 2013. Laila is a teenage boys dream - voluptuous but slim, pretty, blonde and effervescent. She sent us a message saying that she was heading to Portugal and we invited her to visit us, she arrived by train one rainy Friday afternoon. Back at the apartment, we caught up for a while before the kids peeled off to do their thing. They had known each other for years and were soon very comfortable in each others company. We left them to it, schooling was put on hold for the weekend as Keelan and Jessica took Laila on a tour of the Foz (as we call the city). Marcelo had sent me a hand-made knife which he had forged expertly in his home foundry, he is the kind of man who learned Mandarin for no particular reason and who commits himself to master new skills once he has achieved mastery of the last. The knife now sits between the Defenders seats and will one day be the property of an heir.

Keelan and Laila soon developed a relationship which had been born years ago on South American soil, we were happy for him but knew that the relationship would face challenges particularly as Laila had decided to stay with us for a few more weeks and possibly join us for the journey through Morocco. Unfortunately, Laila is not the kind of person who makes solid decisions - she had come to Portugal to study but had decided not to, she had decided to come with us to Morocco but "ran out of courage" according to father, breaking Keelan's heart. On the day we travelled to Lisbon to apply for our Moroccan visas we dropped Laila off at a hotel, her flight to Brazil leaving the next day. My heart broke for Keelan. He and Laila had made plans for him to travel to Brazil to be with her, but I needed him to stay with us a while longer, I did not want to travel West Africa without him, and he needed to at least earn his high school certificate before he left. The cold realities of adulthood began to dawn on the young man.

A year earlier, I had written an article predicting that Keelan falling in love would eventually separate us. I showed the article to him as he fell in love with Laila, and he offered his perspective:

"Love will tear us apart, again

The Father's Perspective

Our children have been travelling the world for so long now, they hardly remember a life before living in a Land Rover. They have explored much of Africa, Europe and every country in the Americas (except for El Salvador).

We have shared every day, every meal and almost every experience over the last seven years of full-time overlanding. We are affectionate, we joke, we argue, we live for each other. Love keeps us together but, as the children age, I know that it is most likely love which will separate us.

In late 2014, we were semi stranded in Salta, Northern Argentina, waiting for a replacement fuel pump to arrive from the United Kingdom. The breakdown kicked off a series of circumstances which led to the man child, then 15, losing his heart.

Within three weeks, the replacement pump arrived, and Luisa and I were able to install it. With Christmas approaching, we decided to stay in Salta but would move to a more comfortable camp outside the city. Our home in Salta, the rough but charming Municipal Camping Xamena was hardly ever dull but had become a holiday playground for the rural proletariat who would burn baby's nappies after a rowdy BBQ.

The new camp, Los Alto, had a large, clean swimming pool, a soccer pitch, a view of the mountains and a lovely family running the show. Keelan made friends with the family, and the teenage children invited him to go to a party in the city three days before Christmas. We were reluctant at first, our number one rule is that we do not leave a safe camp at night. We were assured by the parents, whom we had befriended and trusted, that the kids would be fine. With our approval, the young man dressed in his finest, least stained clothing and set off into the unknown, his mother shed a tear. It was a long night in the lonely roof tent. By 2 am the firstborn had not yet returned - his curfew was 12 pm. A call to the parents reassured us, "don't worry, this happens all the time, maybe the taxi is late". At 7 am a Fiat Punto drove up the driveway and deposited an exhausted but happy teenager on our tent step. Mother was too relieved to deliver the diatribe she had planned and father was still fast asleep. That afternoon while I tried to fix our broken and hated Coleman stove Keelan joined me for a chat. He had met a girl at the party, her name was Micaela, and she was dreamy. She was going to visit him, and he wanted some girl advice. "Treat them mean and keep them keen" had been the advice from my absent father. My advice was more along the lines of "be cool, be a gentleman, let her do all the talking". The young lady was an absolute beauty, Selena Gomez meets Sophia Vergara, 14 years old and crazy about the blonde, blue-eyed Adonis.

Christmas was celebrated in accordance with our limited means. I received a wooden cutting board and a bar of chocolate, Luisa was lucky enough to receive a box of chocolates, and a bottle of wine and the children were absolutely spoiled with gifts of chocolate and basic but very expensive MP3 players. One each. After a slow Christmas day lunch, Luisa and I agreed to stay in Salta at least until after New Years. Our decision was made, mostly, with young Romeo in mind. He woke each morning with purpose and vigour, he was happier, healthier and less productive. We knew that we were delaying the inevitable but, if I am honest, we felt guilty. You only have one childhood, and while there are many benefits to taking your children out of school to travel the planet, the downside is they will undoubtedly miss out on a few important experiences. I remember falling in love when I was his age. I fell hard. Too hard. He is more level-headed than I was, but, we had already broken his precious heart once before.

Rewind to Bogota a year earlier - we were invited to stay in the home of Colombian Land Rover enthusiast Memo Botero. The Land Rover needed a complete overhaul of the brake system after months of hard slog in the never-ending Andes, and the Land Rover Legion club had taken us under their wings. Memo's large and lovely home was situated in a town west of Bogota, and he had three beautiful daughters who competed for Keelan's affections. He fell for the younger of the three, and she was a perfect match for him. Her name was Lucia, intelligent, sensitive and she, like Keelan, loved alternative music. He introduced her to Interpol, and The Cure and The Pixies and the two of them became inseparable. In total, it took three weeks for us to source and install the parts needed to stop the Land Rover. We drove out of Bogota on a cold, grey morning. Keelan sat quietly in the back seat and said nothing for a long while, he cried quietly, his mother began to cry, then little Jessica. My heart broke for him. Luisa and I had seen this coming and had even discussed maybe settling down in Colombia for a while to let the romance run its course. But, we had realised that we had neither the finances nor work opportunities and could not realistically put all our plans on hold for a teenage romance. I spent a lot of time with Keelan before we left Bogota, explaining to him that we would have to leave but, perhaps, we would return one day. He did not blame us, he was not angry, he accepted his reality with a maturity I have seen in him before and which I deeply respect.

The day before we were to eventually leave Salta, Argentina Keelan asked if we could take him into the city to say goodbye to Micaela. It was a substantial detour, but we agreed and the next morning delivered him to her apartment for the sad goodbye. We waited in the Landy. The minutes passed. "Ehm, Luisa, do they have a chaperone?" "What do you mean, I thought her parents were at home?" "I don't think they are". Luisa leaned hard on the hooter.

The road from Salta to Jujuy (pronounced hoohoowee) was winding and beautiful. Keelan did not say a word for two hours and would not be cheered, he did not make any sound at all, he just stared out of the window. Just as we entered Jujuy, he spoke.

"Dad, please stop here. I am going back"
"What do you mean!" Panic
"I am going back to Salta"
"How?"
"I will take one of the bikes and a bag of clothing"

"Where will you stay, what will you eat, how will you make money?"
"I don't know, I will figure it out". A hint of doubt in his voice.

Matter of factly we told him that he simply could not leave, that we were his parents and legal guardians until the age of 18 and he had to get our written permission to leave, or he would be committing a crime. Yes, I told him it was illegal to leave us, which is actually true. He went back to staring out of the window, and we began to breathe again.

Love will tear us apart, again. My son is becoming a man. In a few short months, he will be 20. What will happen next time his heart is stolen? Will he leave us to begin a new life? It is his right, and we will not be able to stop him if our logic does not trump his emotion. Only time will tell.

The Son's Response (written by Keelan in March 2019).

It is my time to say goodbye and set off headfirst into the sea of opportunities.

I am approaching my twentieth year of life, and you have taught me a lot, but I am still a boy. I need to do this to become my own man and grow in ways that I simply can't learn now and haven't learnt in the past. I am naive about many things in this world, and you have tried your very best to enlighten me, but I feel that leaving this family is the best thing for me to do. Otherwise, I might never grow up.

I hate to admit that I don't remember as much of these travels as I would like, but I do remember all the times that we've broken down or run out of the correct currency leaving us stranded at a toll gate or service station. The true hardships of our journey have shown me how great this family truly is when we breakdown we don't panic or get mad we come together and become a team with the sole focus on fixing the problem so that we can return to the road and explore more of this world. We nostalgically remember a time of financial stability which left us many years ago. We have good and bad times, but we get by, we are far from wealthy, but we choose happiness and freedom over wealth any day of the week. These experiences and life lessons will stay with me until my inevitable death.

There are many reasons why I have decided to leave but the main reason, despite what you may think, is not solely my love and longing for my amazing, talented and beautiful Brazilian girlfriend but also my eagerness to grow and experience the things that I simply can't experience in depth while with this amazing family. It is time for me to be my own man and chase down my own interests as I grow. I will never take for granted how I have grown thanks to these amazing travels over the course of the last seven years and doubt that I'll ever truly "Settle Down", this lifestyle that we have pursued has moulded me for the rest of my life whether it be a blessing or a curse. I will always be grateful to you both for showing me this truly phenomenal world that we co-inhabit. Thank you for everything you have done for me as I've grown up, I feel that you have given me all the tools I need to have an amazing life.

I feel like the point of me leaving for love would be the thing most likely to 'tear' us apart although I am a fan of Joy Division I don't think I would say 'tear' but would rather say I am jumping out of the cosy nest at my own free will without any pressure to leave besides pressure that I have put on myself. The only 'tear'-ing that would occur is when I give ma the final hug in the airport as I'm leaving. These travels, no matter how incredible they may seem to the outside world, have for me fallen into a mould of routine and normality, one of the reasons for travelling was to break the mould. So it is time for me to break the mould again".

It is impossible not to shed a few tears reading his response, but Keelan has been groomed for success, it is only natural that he would be eager to set out to start his own life.

(The long-distance relationship lasted four months but ended while we were in Senegal. Again Keelan accepted the situation with great maturity, but the writing is on the wall, the romance was a catalyst - I doubt that he will continue travelling with us when we leave South Africa. There will be tears, but the door is always open for him to return to us).

19

So, Can Overlanding Europe be an Adventure?

The question we had asked ourselves before heading over to Europe was simple - can overlanding Europe be an adventure? The answer is both yes and no. The subcontinent is not nearly as crowded and developed as you may be led to believe. We were certainly surprised to find more rolling green hills, majestic mountains and wide-open spaces than we had ever anticipated, Europe may be the birthplace of modern civilisation, but it remains a wild and natural place, you just need to go looking for it. We did not have the opportunity to discover far northern Europe, but I believe it is the extremes of north and south where the greatest adventures await but while Scandinavia is horrifyingly expensive Spain, Portugal, Greece and the Balkans are not and they offer mountains, deserts, wild forests and the Mediterranean. Yes, Europe is civilised and wealthy with hardly any internal borders to cross. But that does not make the experience dissatisfying. The fact is that you can find satisfaction overlanding in Europe simply because you can find almost whatever your heart desires. History buffs are spoilt for choice as Caeser, and his crowd left their mark from east to west, north to south, two world wars were fought there, and the ancient Greeks left much for us to marvel upon. Art, culture, nightlife, sex, music, hiking, climbing, skiing, kayaking - the best of everything exists in Europe. And, man, the food! Food culture in Europe is second to none and even a penny pincher family like ours can enjoy the best ingredients - every country contributes it's own to the great European feast. The Italians and French regard food with great reverence and refuse to eat anything less than the best and while the Greeks may be struggling to keep up with the rest of Europe the food grown on their soil is of the finest we have ever tasted (real, delicious, unsweetened Greek yoghurt at € 1 per litre, lamb, loukaniko sausage, excellent bread, tomatoes, oranges, onions and peppers - we need no more). You can travel from glaciers to desert, from boreal forest to white sand beaches, from the land of the Vikings to the gateway to Africa, Asia and the Middle East. Europeans are by far the most prolific international overland travellers. Germans and Swiss scour the planet seeking adventure and sunshine. Polish, French, Dutch, Spanish, Portuguese, British (Brexit notwithstanding), Scandinavians and the occasional Belgian or Italian can be found at the furthest reaches of the globe, enjoying a glass of wine and a salad. High salaries, protective labour laws and social systems allow the good people of Europe the opportunity to fulfil their dreams without having to compromise their future. And there would be many more families overlanding the globe if not for the restrictive European homeschooling laws - many young couples are choosing not to have children, they have dogs instead. All these globe trotters return to Europe and understand what a traveller needs, it is astounding how communities embrace you and provide all which you require in the hopes that you will contribute to their local economy. Avoid the cities, avoid the motorways, resist large urban centres and explore the back roads, mountain trails and follow the rivers. A European summer with a good vehicle and great friends is heaven on earth.

Over six years and extensive travel over four continents we have often shared a campfire with our European brethren, and we have learned a few things from and about them.

1. Travel when you can. The long, cold European winters have over centuries, moulded Europeans into the culture they enjoy today. We have cheese and sausage and jam and marmalade because the Europeans learned that they had to work hard in the summer months and preserve food for the winter, a strong work ethic and community bonds ensured survival. Modern overlanding Europeans do not need to survive the winters; instead, they follow the sun south from youth to old age enjoying glorious summers at home before returning to their overland rigs as autumn approaches. Students take advantage of the long summer holidays to travel as do bankers, engineers and the white-collared masses.

2. Multi linguisticity is an asset. It is rare to meet a European who does not speak at least two languages, and many speak English. The Swiss speak Swiss German, French, English and Italian, the Germans speak French and English, and the Scandinavians have run out of languages to learn. Not only does this allow them to immerse into foreign cultures, but it also allows them to communicate in other languages as they have an excellent base for understanding new dialects and nuance.

3. Do not fear the planet or her people. Europe suffered enough war and bloodshed to learn unity and compromise. Yes, there is a rivalry between the nationalities (and the French can be maddeningly, stubbornly French, which is not a bad thing, being French that is) but the subcontinent is small - modern vehicles and unfenced borders allow the flow of people and ideas. It is only natural that people who do not exist in a monoculture become great travellers as they explore the planet overland respectfully.

4. Don't fear the cold. European campers are almost always equipped with a Planar or Webasto heater, the younger dreadlocked overlanders may even install a wood-burning stove. And though they do not particularly enjoy colder climes, they will drive across Russia in winter if they must, some even do it for fun. We camped with a British couple in Bulgaria (they call themselves Trucked Off), and while we headed south to escape the winter they drove their self-built Defender into Siberia in December, and Dutch LandCruising Adventures beat a similar path through ice and snow. Where there are people, you will survive and the more hostile the environment, the more hospitable the locals are.

5. Be who you are and absorb what you can.

6. Eat your veggies and drink water. While us South Africans are grilling meat, potatoes and corn on a large campfire, our European camp neighbours are enjoying a balanced meal comprised mostly of grains, pasta, vegetables and fruit. And while it may seem like we are having a more enjoyable meal, they are eating the healthier, cheaper meal. Ten Euros will buy roughly two pounds of meat in Morocco while the same amount of cash will buy twenty pounds of vegetables! While we are swigging smuggled beer and burning through coal and wood, they are sipping on water and wine. Yes, we are far more interesting (and

significantly larger), but they are a hell of a lot smarter (must have something to do with all those nutrients). What we spend in four months on food and refreshments they spend in a year, and they are able to enjoy restaurant food occasionally while we simply cannot.

7. Everything in moderation. And I am not just talking about food and drink. Our northern cousins (remember, we are from the Southern Hemisphere) tend to walk the middle ground and have balanced, educated, and sensible opinions just left or right from a broad political centre. Of course, we are generalising, but it is incredibly rare to meet an extremist, they certainly do exist, but they are not travellers, they are staring at a screen somewhere dank, screaming. A good night drinking with friends ends with hugs and laughs, and everyone contributes equally to the festivities.

8. Modesty is admired. But man, the Swiss do not hold back when building an overland truck! And some Germans have vehicles which would make a Texan whistle. While their rigs may be OTT the (experienced overlander) inhabitants are usually friendly, curious, hospitable and sometimes quite charming. If anything, they are slightly embarrassed that they need so much muchness while treasuring ground clearance and indoor plumbing. And though the big riggers are without doubt well-heeled, they do not imagine themselves to be better than anyone else on an existential level - the population of Europe is majority middle class and therefore well equipped to relate to each other.

9. Never miss a chance to sit in the sunshine. In Africa we have a saying, "Only mad dogs and Englishman go out in the midday sun" and while us pale Africans are sweating in the shade the English, French, Swiss, Germans, Belgians, Dutch and Italians are eating lunch and drink aperitifs under a glaring sun. They seem to have the ability to absorb radiation and store it deep down inside, to be released as the mercury drops.

Europeans like to laugh, eat, drink and be merry, they live well, and they travel well.

*   *   *

It is just a pity the winters are so bloody awful. Hang on a second, what about Spain and Portugal? Sure you might get some rain and cooler days down in Southern Europe but no worse than a South African or an Argentine winter.

So, is there anything which we do not enjoy about Europe? Well, the European Union has been accused of being a Nanny state, and to a degree, I believe this to be true. While we never had any problems with the authorities, I always had this feeling, like we were being watched and we were. In the cities, towns and villages there are cameras are everywhere, and you have to trust that those doing the watching have good intentions. Countries like Switzerland (not EU) and Portugal are a stubborn bureaucrat's wet dream. France is different from the rest of the EU in many ways, and the cities are sometimes best avoided altogether (not that we had any real problems in any French city, but there is a crime problem on the motorways close to cities). We do not enjoy winter, and I enjoy being from a country which, like the USA, does not fine you a month's salary for bolting a bull bar onto your vehicle.

We truly loved Europe and highly recommend the subcontinent as an overland destination!

20

Africa Bound!

The preparation for the African journey had started as soon as we had arrived in Figueira do Foz and we had some time to prepare the vehicle, our finances and our minds. I was negotiating the supply of a new set of tyres from BF Goodrich, and they very kindly offered me a set of mud terrains, the only catch was that I needed to fetch them in South Africa. Billy, an American friend, had been trying to organise us a new set of General Grabber X3's and we had received a few months before the go-ahead to receive a set until the American distributor realised that we were in Europe! No, go. We really needed a new set of tyres as our Falken tyres had suffered uneven wear caused by the worn swivel pin bearing and the rushed drive from Turkey to Germany. I tried my best to secure the BF Goodrich tyres in Europe but ran into a brick wall - in the modern corporate world no response is a response. Billy, being a man of his word, sent me a message asking for our address, he would pay for the tyres out of his own pocket and have them delivered to us in Portugal from a European supplier. We gratefully declined the offer, it is one thing to accept products from a corporation but another altogether to accept such a gift from a friend. I did my best to secure a set of tyres and Billy insisted that he would buy us the tyres - his favourite General Grabber X3 Mud Terrains. Eventually, I realised that I would not be able to secure a European sponsor on short notice and humbly and gratefully accepted Billy's offer. I am often blown away by the support and generosity which we receive from people a world away who have no vested interest but to see us succeed. It is humbling to be the recipient of such goodwill and a reminder that we should do more to help our fellow man because sometimes we all need a nudge in the right direction. Sometimes a gesture of kindness and generosity means the world to someone, and if we all just did a bit more to encourage and help others who are working hard to achieve their dreams, then many more of us will be able to conquer the mountains which we all face. Thank you, Billy, I look forward to sharing a cold Marguerita with you one day.

We left Figueira after one last goodbye to our dear friend Ruben. Ruben had become a very close friend during our time in Portugal and had shown great hospitality to us and the travelling friends who had visited in Portugal over the two years that we were there periodically. He is an overlander, and he too suffers from The Sadness, we promised to meet again in Morocco and what a reunion that would be. Ruben is a man who understands the good in life, and he would be a fantastic travel companion, adventurous and knowledgeable, carefree and curious.

Our next destination was the surfing mecca of Ericeira where a new friend Sergio had offered the use of his home and garage for the final Africa preparation. And what a home it was! Almost empty because the house was on the market the Scandinavian log house was built by Sergio with the entire structure delivered as a "kit". We occupied the one room, the kitchen and the garage where we set up a workshop to rebuild the interior of our camper which had some flaws. The majority of the interior structure was sound, but the kitchen area had been built on a sandbag in the garden of the little Blue witch and was uneven and imperfect. The solar panels needed realignment, and the wiring improved, the shell needed additional chequer plate cladding, we had a fuel leak and a transfer box leak, the entire vehicle required a mechanical inspection and a major service, Bearmach had sent a box of goodies which needed to be installed (including a steering damper, wind deflectors, new 16 inch wheels and Billy's tyres, etc.) and there were a handful of other small projects which required attention before we could be confident enough to tackle Africa.

The West African overland route is, arguably, the last great overland route. Yes, there are routes which are more remote, wilder, more extreme in terms of terrain, climate and location. The Channing Stock Route in Australia is a good example of a great overland route which pales in comparison to the West Africa route simply due to the bureaucratic hurdles, deadly disease and opportunities for disaster which volatile crossing countries can present. We are experienced overlanders, and we have the advantage (or is it a disadvantage?) that we were born and raised in Africa. But, know this - South Africa is not "Africa", it certainly was not when we grew up under the fist of the apartheid regime. Many South Africans regard every country north of South Africa as real Africa ("Don't go there, you'll die!"). Yes, we had driven from Cape Town to Kilimanjaro in 2010, but the East Coast of Africa south of Ethiopia is considered a relatively gentle overland route.

With the threat of Islamic extremism, malaria, banditry and civil war at the forefront of our minds, we drove from Portugal to Spain and drove onto the ferry to Morocco.

Farewell Europe. We will return!

About the Author

Graeme Bell is a full-time overlander and author. He was born in Johannesburg, South Africa. He is currently travelling the planet with his wife, Luisa and two children, Keelan and Jessica, in a Land Rover Defender 130, affectionately known as Mafuta.

Connect with us

Did you enjoy this book? If so, help others enjoy it too.

Please recommend to friends and leave a review if possible.
Stay up to date with the Bell Family by visiting our website

www.a2aexpedition.com

Alternatively, visit our Facebook page a2a.expedition

MORE TITLES BY GRAEME BELL
We Will Be Free
Travel The Planet Overland
Overlanding the Americas "La Lucha"

Printed in Great Britain
by Amazon

66220780R00156